# THE ANTIQUES CLINIC

# THE ANTIQUES CLINIC

James Fielden, Richard Garnier, Paul Davidson, Bruce Luckhurst, Susan Duffield, Deirdre O'Day, Jill Barnard & Gilly Cameron Cooper

CONSULTANTS: Plowden & Smith and Ksynia Marko (Textiles)

Silverdale Books

A QUANTUM BOOK

This edition published by Silverdale Books,
an imprint of Bookmart Ltd., in 2005
Blaby Road
Wigston
Leicester
LE18 4SE

Copyright ©MCMXCVIII
Quarto Publishing plc

This edition printed 2005

ISBN 1-84509-223-6

QUMATC

This book is produced by
Quantum Publishing Ltd
6 Blundell Street
London N7 9BH

Printed in Singapore by
Star Standard Industries (Pte) Ltd

# CONTENTS

# LIVING WITH ANTIQUES

**A**T ONE TIME PEOPLE AUTOMATICALLY WENT TO THE DOCTOR WHEN THEY WERE ILL. TODAY, THE IMPORTANCE OF REGULAR HEALTH CHECKS, BOTH TO PREVENT AND TO HELP CURE ILLNESS IS RECOGNIZED, PARTICULARLY IN IDENTIFYING THE SYMPTOMS BEFORE AN ILLNESS TAKES HOLD. THE PRUDENT COLLECTOR OF ANTIQUES SHOULD FOLLOW THE SAME ROUTE FOR HIS OR HER COLLECTION.

Even if your treasured objects appear to be in good order, their condition should be regularly monitored, as should the environment in which they are kept. As human beings, we are constantly reviewing the effects of weather extremes, increased pollution levels, and everyday maintenance on our bodies. While antiques are inanimate objects, they too suffer from the effects of heat, light, pollution, irresponsible use, and abuse. They do, of course, also have a longer life—although this book covers 20th-century collectibles, an antique is officially more than 100 years old—and invariably show signs of frailty and age.

*To create a museum-like environment in your home is unrealistic, but it is important to be aware of the effects of sunlight, pollution, and air-conditioning, and to strike a balance.*

It is a great privilege to be able to buy, enjoy, and even use a beautifully crafted or historic artifact; to absorb a sense of the past from the materials, skills, and people involved in its making, and of the lives of its previous owners. It is also the responsibility of the owner of today to make sure his or her antiques endure for future generations to enjoy, use, and learn from.

## Awareness and care

Antiques encompass an enormous range of materials which react in different ways. Their very means of construction will have particular strengths and weaknesses, which this book will help you identify. Rarity, affordability, historical context, and compatibility are all important when buying, but an awareness of inherent weak spots, vulnerabilities in makeup or materials, and stresspoints that may have given way through use and possible abuse, will enable you to buy wisely, to gauge whether the damage is reparable, and what effect any repair might have on future value.

All artifacts have their weaknesses and are susceptible to some form of physical damage. Porcelain and glass are among the most fragile materials and should be handled with appropriate delicacy. As an appraiser and auctioneer, I have been astounded by the way in which some experienced collectors cram display cabinets full of delicate and valuable pieces from which it is impossible to remove a cup or saucer without displacing and threatening several others. Others display ceramic plates on their walls using a wire frame attached to the back so tightly that it scars the glaze or even the surface material. I regularly visit clients who have owned objects for the last 30 or 40 years, often having inherited rather than bought them, and have a tendency to take them for granted, or simply not to appreciate their value. Frequently, the condition of these pieces has deteriorated imperceptibly through wear, aging, or an unsuitable environment to an extent that is irreversible.

A typical example of this process is the accidental bleaching of walnut, rosewood, or mahogany furniture. One owner, faced with a move from England to Greece, wisely decided to leave a walnut veneer dressing table in the climate it was used to rather than subject it to the hot, dry, Mediterranean heat and light. Unfortunately, it was stored with a friend beside a south-facing window, and one veneered section bleached from a rich honey color to a dull gray-brown, resulting in a two-colored piece of furniture. It is difficult to restore the original color, and the results may not look convincing. In addition, the delicate wood veneer had dehydrated, shrunk, and was showing signs of cracking.

In the 19th and early 20th centuries, it was fashionable to collect Italian marble statuary to recreate the style of ancient Rome. Many of these were moved from the hot, dry, Mediterranean region to the colder and wetter climates of northern Europe and America. However, they were made of a more durable marble than the Carrara marble used in the 1800s and survived as long as the climate was not too extreme; some, though, were simply never intended for exterior display in intemperate weather and often became irredeemably eroded, finely carved features obliterated by wind, rain, and frost. Apart from the devastating loss of craftsmanship and beauty, the difference in value between a marble statue by a particular sculptor in its original state compared with a similar example that is intact but weathered can be as much as tenfold.

## Learning to look

The key to looking after any object is knowing what it is made of and how it is put together. For example, a painting in watercolor on paper is far more likely to fade if regularly exposed to sunlight than a painting in oils on canvas. The *General Health* section looks in depth at the range of materials, their various properties, and the environmental factors that affect them. Each chapter in the *Clinic* section focuses on a particular type of antique or collectible. The main feature pieces—whether a writing desk, a cut-glass decanter, a glazed earthenware dinner set, or a bisque doll—individually help you to learn to look and to identify areas of stress or possible restoration. Collectively, the chapters cover all the

*This 1920s dressing table (above) was spared a dramatic change of climate which would have caused its veneer to split and crack, but suffered instead from unwise storage.*

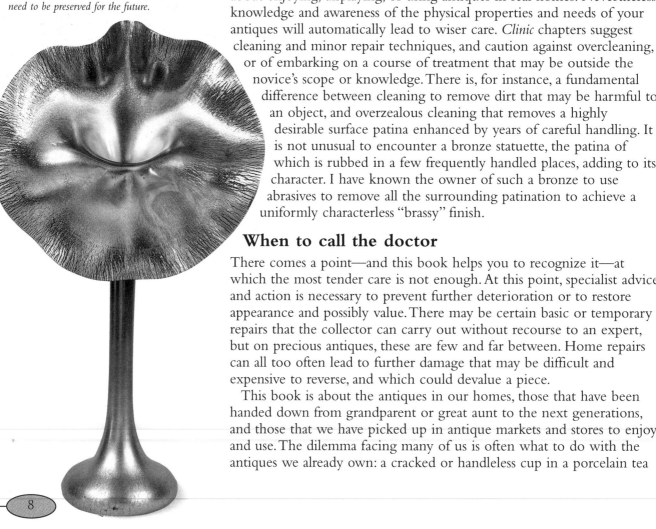

*The Dean's Rag Book Mickey Mouse of 1935 (right) may be tempting to play with but has become a serious collector's item. To retain his condition and value, he will have to be on display only, in a protected environment.*

*Strictly speaking, an antique is more than 100 years old, but 20th-century collectibles such as this Favrile glass vase from the Tiffany Studios need to be preserved for the future.*

materials you are likely to come across, from solid walnut or fine wood veneers, to ormolu, silver plate, and Bakelite. Each one of the chapters traces the materials and the methods of construction used throughout the development of a particular type of item—how the furniture woods and methods of joining changed through the centuries, for example, or the relative durability of one type of ceramic or painting medium compared with another. Equipped with such information, you will be better able to make wise buying decisions, to make an initial judgment on the need for restoration, and whether this is likely to devalue an object, and to care for your antiques well, with knowledge and confidence.

## General care

The ideal environment for a delicate, old, and precious item is in the purified, controlled atmosphere of a museum display case, where light is dim, and heat and temperature carefully regulated; but we are concerned about enjoying, displaying, or using antiques in real homes. Nevertheless, knowledge and awareness of the physical properties and needs of your antiques will automatically lead to wiser care. *Clinic* chapters suggest cleaning and minor repair techniques, and caution against overcleaning, or of embarking on a course of treatment that may be outside the novice's scope or knowledge. There is, for instance, a fundamental difference between cleaning to remove dirt that may be harmful to an object, and overzealous cleaning that removes a highly desirable surface patina enhanced by years of careful handling. It is not unusual to encounter a bronze statuette, the patina of which is rubbed in a few frequently handled places, adding to its character. I have known the owner of such a bronze to use abrasives to remove all the surrounding patination to achieve a uniformly characterless "brassy" finish.

## When to call the doctor

There comes a point—and this book helps you to recognize it—at which the most tender care is not enough. At this point, specialist advice and action is necessary to prevent further deterioration or to restore appearance and possibly value. There may be certain basic or temporary repairs that the collector can carry out without recourse to an expert, but on precious antiques, these are few and far between. Home repairs can all too often lead to further damage that may be difficult and expensive to reverse, and which could devalue a piece.

This book is about the antiques in our homes, those that have been handed down from grandparent or great aunt to the next generations, and those that we have picked up in antique markets and stores to enjoy and use. The dilemma facing many of us is often what to do with the antiques we already own: a cracked or handleless cup in a porcelain tea set, a 19th-century mantel clock that no longer works—if all or part of a clock movement is replaced, how does it affect value? If the cost of restoration vastly exceeds the value of an item—for restorers charge on the basis of time, irrespective of value—and yet in its damaged state, it is not only unusable but also disfigured, what do you do: throw it away? One of my clients had an Edwardian silver candlestick that had been irreparably damaged by heavy handling, overcleaning, and amateur attempts at repair. The thin plate silver had split and stretched, and the sconce had lifted from the stem. In such an extreme case, where the item is not of great value, but you still can't bring yourself to throw silver into the garbage, it is worth asking a restorer if there is a cheap and rudimentary repair that will just make the item usable. Ceramic household ware can be sensitively restored to maintain some intrinsic value, but never again be used except for display. Other antiques need to be left alone even if they are imperfect or stained, because they have acquired the patina of age and use which has become part of their working history, their charm, and their value.

## Buying tips

The book helps you to make an informed choice when buying antiques, to be aware of the effect on value that restoration may have, to distinguish between damage which is minor and that which will be expensive or difficult to put right. But do not be hesitant about taking professional advice when making an important buying decision, particularly if the object concerned has been shown to have weak points. Many collectors are prepared to overlook physical weaknesses in a piece because it will enhance their collection in other ways, but their presence may help the buyer knock down the price. If buying from a dealer, always obtain a descriptive invoice, and ask for a list of all known restorations and provenance. It is surprising how many collectors do not keep a record of the provenance of an object, both for the historical context that can add an extra dimension to its appeal, and for the documentation that can enhance its value.

When buying at a reputable auction house, the catalog description should be factual, but, if in doubt, most auctioneers will be prepared to provide a "warts and all" condition report. Some collectors engage the services of a reputable dealer with whom they have an established relationship to bid for them and advise on the suitability of an object for a relatively modest flat fee.

Finally, I have observed a strong correlation between the maintenance of a collection in good order and careful record-keeping, including photography. Not only will a photograph of a piece in its "as bought" condition provide valuable reference for the restorer in the event of subsequent breakage, but it also improves the chances of successful recovery in the event of theft. Collectors should make sure their works of art are fully insured against both theft and damage, at replacement values that have been properly assessed by a licensed appraiser.

*The value of the gilded, late 18th-century tallcase clock (above), would be greatly enhanced if details of its provenance, such as receipts and records from the original maker, and changes of ownership through the ages, were available.*

I F YOU HAVE JUST ACQUIRED A PRECIOUS OR
LONG-COVETED ANTIQUE, CONGRATULATIONS!
DO NOT CONSIDER THIS AN END IN ITSELF,
HOWEVER, SINCE ANY OBJECT THAT HAS SURVIVED
FOR, SAY A HUNDRED YEARS, WILL NEED CAREFUL
LOOKING AFTER IF IT IS TO SURVIVE IN GOOD
CONDITION FOR THE NEXT CENTURY.

# GENERAL *health*

# KNOWING YOUR PATIENT

THE POINT OF BUYING IS THE BEST TIME TO GIVE AN ANTIQUE A THOROUGH HEALTH CHECK. AS WITH ANY PATIENT, IF THE SYMPTOMS ARE SERIOUS, A SPECIALIST SHOULD BE CONSULTED. EVEN IF EVERYTHING APPEARS TO BE HEALTHY, PREVENTIVE MEASURES CAN AND SHOULD BE TAKEN AGAINST THE INEVITABLE EFFECTS OF OLD AGE.

Knowledge of the materials your antiques and collectibles are made of and their vulnerabilities is essential to an informed diagnosis of any problem areas, to general care, and before any repairs are carried out. First of all, it is important to establish whether the material is organic or inorganic, for this dictates how sensitive it is to the environmental conditions around it.

*Several different materials are represented in the photograph (right), each of which reacts in different ways to the passage of time and the environment it is in. The mahogany and inlaid materials of the 1790 drum table are organic and swell and shrink with changes in humidity, for example; the metal castors may tarnish and corrode; the silver of the tray is prone to tarnishing and wear from overcleaning. Glass is the most resistant to the ravages of time, but could be destroyed by a single knock or fall.*

## ORGANIC MATERIALS

Organic materials are formed of once living matter, such as wood, bone, shell, leather, natural textiles, wax, and paper. All are sensitive to environmental conditions. They expand and contract with fluctuations in temperature (which in turn lead to weakening and cracking), shrink, swell, and warp with changes in humidity, and fade and suffer breakdown of fiber structure on prolonged exposure to light.

A wooden object adapts to the conditions it is in, even if these are not ideal. Problems arise if the conditions suddenly change. If wood is suddenly moved from a cold, humid atmosphere where it has been for years to a dry, warm, air-conditioned room, dehydration and shrinkage will result in warping and cracking, and buckling and lifting of any surface veneers. It is often assumed that dense tropical hardwoods are more resistant to variations in temperature and humidity than softwoods, but in fact both will be equally affected if the environment is not stable and constant. But different woods do have specific vulnerabilities. A hardwood such as mahogany, when transposed to a temperate climate, proves more resistant to another environmental hazard—the woodworm beetle—than temperate woods such as pine or ash.

However, it is often the way in which the wood is cut, crafted, and combined with other woods, in a veneered or inlaid surface, for example, that has a greater effect on durability than whether it is hard or soft. It is important, therefore, to examine the construction of items of furniture to identify woods of different character, density, or cut (with or against the grain), and how they work in relation to each other. A veneered fruitwood surface may bubble and lift from a soft pine carcass if exposed to changes in atmosphere because the two materials react at different rates.

*The wood and construction of the tester bed (above) would have settled in cold, relatively damp conditions over three centuries. To move it suddenly into an air-conditioned, heated home would cause problems.*

### Vegetable matters

Paper is made up of a delicate web of vegetable fibers, and is the most insubstantial of organic materials. It is highly absorbent, or hygroscopic, and in damp conditions, will stretch and distort, while in a dry atmosphere, it dehydrates,

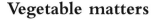

*Brown discoloration on works of art on paper (left) suggests low-quality woodpulp paper that has become increasingly acidic with age; the more acidic paper becomes, the more rapidly it deteriorates. In a humid environment spots of brownish mold known as foxing may develop.*

shrinks, and becomes brittle. Damp conditions also invite fungal attack. The quality of the paper has a vital bearing on its survival. A low-grade woodpulp paper, as opposed to one made from relatively pure linen rags, has built-in impurities, including chemicals used in the pulping process, that accelerate the breakdown of fibers in the finished paper, and increase the likelihoood of fungal attack. Such paper is said to be acidic and becomes increasingly so with age or if mounted on equally low-quality mounting materials.

Fungal growth may initially not be immediately visible, but in time may appear as brown spots known as foxing. Sometimes this brownish stain is on the surface and can be removed, but it may also penetrate and cause considerable problems. Unless it is coated, paper also absorbs dirt and pollutants from the atmosphere easily; they are literally sucked in with moisture and become trapped in the paper fibers; sulfur dioxide in the atmosphere converts to sulfuric acid on the receptive paper surface and accelerates acidification and breakdown.

Print and photographic images are more resistant to fungal attack and pollutants, because they form a protective coating on the paper, but are still susceptible to fading if exposed to light over any length of time. Both natural and artificial light have the effect of breaking down the delicate structure of fibers.

Textiles made from natural fibers are, like paper, highly absorbent and vulnerable to light, dampness, and pest and organic damage. Different textiles will clearly have different strengths and weaknesses, but the incorporation of other materials, such as metal threads or glass beads, cause most problems. Dyes and chemicals used in manufacture also have an effect on durability.

## Animal origins

Ivory and bone are particularly prone to cracking when subjected to variations in temperature and humidity. Ivory, unless it has been artificially bleached (a common practice in the second half of the 1800s), also tends to yellow with exposure to light. Ivory can be distinguished from bone by its discernible grain formed from the concentric rings of the tusk, similar in appearance to the grain of yew wood, whereas the surface marks on bone are normally limited to irregular black marks, formerly blood vessels. Ivory tends to be noticeably waxier than bone, which feels drier to the touch and is less dense. The absence of any grain or surface marks, together with a lack of provenance, should alert you to the possibility that the object is synthetic (plastic), and therefore with different susceptibilities.

Tortoiseshell and horn both fade and become brittle with

*It is important to be able to distinguish between bone, ivory, and plastic imitations, so that you can be aware of specific vulnerabilities. Ivory (below left) is slightly granular, unlike plastic lookalikes; it darkens naturally, but can also be artificially stained. Bone (below right) is more clearly marked with the dark traces of former blood vessels.*

regular exposure to light, and tortoiseshell is particularly prone to milky surface discoloration. They are both likely to crack under unsuitable conditions, although horn is generally stronger. Both are frequently worked in thin sheets, and horn is often stained to resemble tortoiseshell. Mother-of-pearl, shell, and natural pearls consist of a series of layers that were built up over time, and in dry conditions these are in danger of peeling away or flaking.

Leather has been widely used for both decorative and functional purposes throughout history, yet the fact that relatively few examples of leatherwork from before the 1800s have survived, bears testament to its vulnerability. It hardens and cracks in very dry conditions, and can be scuffed, worn, or torn by careless handling. Leather can also suffer from "red rot," whereby the fibers lose their structure and the surface layer disintegrates. This is thought to be caused by the dyes used in tanning, and by air pollution. As with paper, it absorbs sulfur dioxide which leads to weakened fiber structures. The more delicate a hide is, the more vulnerable it is to damage from acids or bacterial action caused by frequent handling.

Wax, as found in wax dolls, for example, is particularly sensitive to fluctuations in temperature, disintegrating with with exposure to heat, and shrinking and cracking in cold temperatures and humidity changes.

*Amber, as in these chess pieces, is the fossilized resin of an ancient pine tree; if kept in a dry atmosphere for a prolonged period it will dehydrate and become brittle, and is also prone to surface flaking.*

## MANUFACTURED ORGANICS

Chemically produced materials known as polymers, such as plastics, fall into the organic materials category, but are more complex. Polymers, especially early plastics made before the 1920s, have often been combined with additives that may degenerate over time, making the material unstable. Simulated tortoiseshell, for example, was made from celluloid, a polymer incorporating camphor as a plasticizer (softener) to make it less brittle. Frequently, the camphor has evaporated through the effect of heat and light, which has caused objects such as combs to become brittle, and the teeth to break off. Polymers are generally susceptible to discoloration and embrittlement caused by humidity, light, and heat, and in some cases, oxygen. Polymers from the mid 20th century onward are not necessarily intended to last for more than a few years and consequently they may be vulnerable to degradation.

Rubber, whether natural or synthetic, eventually reacts with oxygen and chemicals used in the manufacturing process, and can dry out, crumble, or become sticky.

*Some early synthetic polymers, or plastics, such as Bakelite, are readily identifiable by color and application: Bakelite was widely used for radios. Because the plastics varied in stability, it is helpful to know what they are, but all are sensitive to heat and light.*

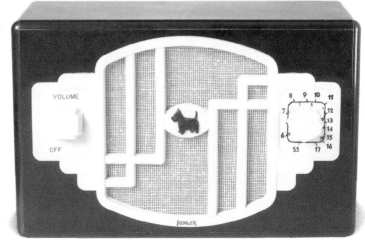

# INORGANIC MATERIALS

Inorganic materials have a mineral origin, and among those traditionally used in the manufacture of the decorative arts are metals, stone, ceramics, and glass.

In the case of metal artifacts, it is important to identify the type of metal used, since some are more prone to corrosion than others. Copper and copper alloys, such as bronze, corrode in conditions of high humidity, forming a green surface coloring or verdigris, typically found on bronze sculpture. Many bronzes were given a green patination at the time of their creation and to remove this would be to devalue them greatly. Iron is a highly unstable material that corrodes easily if it is not looked after properly. Lead oxidizes over time, but like silver, only corrodes in extreme conditions. Particular care should be taken of items made from zinc, since it oxidizes if exposed to the atmosphere. Inexpensively produced diecast metal toys can become brittle,

*Glass in itself is unlikely to deteriorate as a result of atmospheric conditions such as humidity or light levels, but extreme fragility combined with delicate surface decoration make this Bohemian vase (above) at extreme risk of physical damage.*

*The copper tray (above right) shows surface patches of characteristic green verdigris where the lacquer coating has exposed the copper to the elements. It should be carefully cleaned before the corrosion begins to eat into the metal.*

particularly if they are exposed to damp conditions and if the zinc used in their construction is impure. Gold neither tarnishes nor corrodes if it is relatively pure, but 9 or 10-carat gold may tarnish as there is a high content of other metals. The purer forms of gold alloy are very soft and prone to wear and abrasions.

Ceramics, glass, and stone are unlikely to be affected by atmospheric conditions in a normal home because of their non absorbent surfaces. They are far more at risk from physical damage in the form of knocks, being dropped, careless use, and staining. Once weaknesses such as

crizzling (a fine network of cracks) on ceramics, or glass disease (excessive sodium leaching from early soda glass identified by a flaking iridescence) have set in, however, damp conditions will accelerate deterioration. Surface decoration applied to decorative objects in these materials, such as gilding or enameling, tends to be very easily worn.

## MultiMedia

Many antiques are made of a combination of several materials, some of which may be incompatible with its neighbor and cause or accelerate the process of deterioration in another. A classic example is the effect of metal or glass beads combined with delicate silk and cotton embroidery threads and canvas. Not only can both metal and glass corrode, leading to stains and ultimate fiber breakdown in the textile, but their weight and sharp edges can sever the fibers. From the medieval period until the 1800s, artifacts such as caskets were made of wood, covered with leather, and had iron fittings. In extreme conditions, acids used in the tanning process leeched out, caused corrosion in the iron, which in turn rotted the leather.

Cleaning presents a problem too. The application of a commercial furniture polish to a gilt metal-mounted item of furniture, or a glass cleaner to a mirror bordered by a delicate, painted or gilded wood or composition frame could leak onto the material it is not intended for and destroy surface finish, or lodge in crevices. Environmental factors

*Some metals corrode more than others. Cast iron (above) rusts quickly and the corrosion eats into the metal, leading to pitting and flaking. Sturdy household iron pieces, such as the lamp base (above), can have loose rust brushed off, and be treated with a commercial rust remover, but most important is to keep them in a dry atmosphere.*

*This early 19th-century French console table (right) is a medley of materials, including amboyna (a hard, durable wood), easily worn gilt mounts, patinated bronze, and a marble top, each of which has different environmental, restoration, and cleaning requirements.*

*Many materials of different strengths merge in items of jewelry as in this 20th-century collectible by the American Miriam Haskell. It combines high-quality faux baroque pearls, whose luster is only skin deep, and harsh metals. Jewelry generally needs to be stored carefully so that the different elements do not knock or rub against each other.*

*In beadwork (above) the cutting edge of damaged glass beads can gnaw at the delicate embroidery threads and backing. A too humid atmosphere may cause glass disease, but a too dry atmosphere may embrittle the fabric.*

*The organic lining material of the cutlery case (below) is prone to moth attack; wood and the bone knife handle are organic too, and may warp or split with changes in temperature. The inorganic brass hinge is tougher, but may corrode.*

affect different materials in different ways: wood and metals, or even different metals, expand at different rates, which can lead to buckling if two such materials are combined in an inlaid surface, for example. Furniture or musical instruments with mother-of-pearl inlay should be kept out of direct sunlight or heat sources, and maintained at a constant level of relative humidity. But often it is a matter of reaching a compromise when considering a suitable environment for an object made up of different materials.

Sometimes, the process of restoration can introduce new and incompatible materials, which may result in additional deterioration. Fragments of Classical statuary were transported from Italy in the 1700s and 1800s to cold, wet, northern climates. They were built up into complete figures, using new marble, and the limbs joined with iron dowels, and placed outside. The iron dowels corroded, which in turn led to splitting and discoloration in the marble.

*Clocks are notorious for their complexity of construction and materials. Even within the movements are often found different metals which expand, contract, and wear at different rates. This c.1700 bracket clock is a cleaner's nightmare of ebony veneer with gilt mounts and a glass panel.*

# A HEALTHY ENVIRONMENT

THERE MAY BE NO APPARENT OR SERIOUS FLAWS IN AN ANTIQUE, BUT THE CONDITIONS IN WHICH IT IS KEPT MAY BE SLOWLY CAUSING DETERIORATION IF THE ENVIRONMENT IS HOSTILE. EXCESSIVE DRYNESS OR DAMPNESS, HEAT OR COLD, POLLUTION FROM TRAFFIC OR SMOKE, CAN ALL CONTRIBUTE TO THE ILL HEALTH OF SENSITIVELY CRAFTED OR AGED ARTIFACTS, ALTHOUGH SOME MATERIALS ARE MORE SUSCEPTIBLE THAN OTHERS. A SUDDEN CHANGE IN ATMOSPHERIC CONDITIONS CAN CAUSE EVEN MORE SIGNIFICANT DAMAGE.

*An antiquity like the earthenware Tang figure may have been in an underground tomb for hundreds of years. The shock of surfacing into a completely different environment would put enormous stress on the friable medium, so it is displayed in the protected environment of a custom-built case.*

An extreme case of how an object can react to a change of environment occurred on a recent excavation in Israel. The lid of a 7th-century B.C. Philistine ivory mirror case was uncovered in cool, damp soil, and within an hour of exposure to the hot dry air, it cracked into several pieces. On a less dramatic scale, it is worth considering what the effect of air-conditioning might be on an object that has spent a length of time in a damp, unheated auction room

## TEMPERATURE AND HUMIDITY

Humidity, or the level of moisture in the air, may lead to corrosion in metals and encourage the development of mold. Because organic materials such as wood and textiles, have a cellular structure, they are hygroscopic—they absorb or desorb water according to the relative humidity in the environment. Relative humidity (RH) is the amount of water which a given volume of air can absorb before reaching saturation point at a given temperature. The quantity rises with increase in air temperature. Levels can be monitored by the use of paper strips or digital indicators, and maintained with humidifiers and dehumidifiers, all of which are available from specialist suppliers. Sachets of self-indicating silica gel are useful to control humidity in a small, enclosed area such as a coin cabinet; they are blue when dry, and turn pink when moisture has been absorbed.

With organic materials, it is crucial to avoid persistent, sharp fluctuations in RH levels, whether overnight or at different times of the year. An acceptable RH level is considered to be 45-60 percent for most artifacts. Most organic materials react slowly to moderate change: a 20 percent fluctuation may result in damage such as cracking or warping, but a 10 percent (or 5 percent for painted wood) fluctuation is unlikely to be harmful. During a 24-hour period, there should be ideally no more than 5 percent variation, while a 15 percent can be harmful. Bear in mind that though the overall RH level in a room might be acceptable, a heat source such as a radiator or powerful lighting may dehydrate an item placed nearby. If an organic object is to be moved from one environment to another, such as from a cold, damp cellar to an air-conditioned room, this should be done gradually; a small object, for example, could be kept in an enclosed container with its own midway microclimate; a larger item could be placed in a "buffer zone" which is midway in temperature and humidity, such as a lobby, and a bowl of water can be placed near or under the item.

## LIGHTING EFFECTS

Many inorganic materials, such as metals and glass, are not sensitive to high levels of exposure to light (as long as they are not painted), but organic materials, especially paper and textiles, are very vulnerable. The heat and ultraviolet radiation from natural sunlight and the heat generated from artificial lights are both potentially damaging, causing colors to fade, embrittlement, and breakdown of fibers. Ultraviolet-reducing film or coatings can be applied over windows, but they do not reduce the heat from the sun's rays, and blinds may be a more practical and flexible alternative.

Dimmer switches for general lighting near sensitive objects such as a wallhanging, are useful for keeping light levels down to approximately that of a bedside table lamp.

Fluorescent lights are cooler than tungsten but do emit ultraviolet radiation, and although the bulbs are cool, the starting units are not; if they are fitted into a display cabinet, there should be adequate air circulation. With fiber-optic lights the control unit can be outside a cabinet, but the lights are very expensive.

## POLLUTION

Exhaust fumes from traffic, emissions from industrial sources, and other pollutants form gases such as sulfur dioxide that combine with moisture in the atmosphere to create acids that can eat into the surface of all kinds of materials. The most exposed victims are outdoor architecture and statues in a city, but this atmospheric cocktail is hard to evade even within the home environment, and even with sophisticated filtration systems or air-conditioning. Pollutants accelerate the process of tarnishing on metals such as silver, and the deterioration of many organic materials, but their effects can be kept at bay if artifacts are kept in sealed cabinets, or if

*Cabinets can protect items from dust, pollution, and light, but they must be stable and of non acidic wood.*

doors and windows leading onto busy streets are rarely opened. If this conflicts with the need for room ventilation to guard against dampness, it may be necessary to move particularly sensitive items to a more protected area.

Charcoal filters for cooking appliances found in most hardware stores can be usefully adapted for displays of sensitive antiques. They should be discreetly and centrally positioned and not in direct contact with the objects, so that the absorbed gases are not concentrated around one particular site. A practical method of reducing levels of sulfur dioxide and nitrogen dioxide is by carpeting the floor and putting a fabric covering on the walls to "soak in" the acids. But do not use your antique textiles for this purpose!

In addition to external pollution, some materials can cause deterioration in others placed nearby. Sulfides given off by vulcanized rubber items, as found in late 19th-century mourning jewelry, trigger tarnishing in silver objects, for example, and some low-quality chemical dyes can cause fiber breakdown in a textiles.

It is important to know what your display cabinets are made of too. Oak, particularly if it is relatively fresh, but even after 600 years, emits organic acids, and some manmade reconstituted boards give off formaldehyde and other fumes, all of which may trigger corrosion in metals. Elm, fir, and spruce are among the most stable woods.

The touch of a finger can deposit a trace of corrosive acids on a highly polished metal surface which will induce tarnishing in that area. For this reason it is a good idea to wear cotton gloves when handling.

For longterm storage, it is especially important to use materials such as acid-free tissue paper, which will neither stain, like newsprint, nor induce tarnishing or degradation. It is unwise to wrap metal objects in bubble plastic as a microclimate is created, and tarnish forms leaving the impression of bubbles on the metal.

*Above the mantelpiece is a classic place for hanging a picture, but if there is a working fire beneath, it is a potentially damaging area, because of rising heat, smoke, and dust.*

## BACTERIAL AND PEST DAMAGE

If objects and display areas are kept free of dirt and dust, and the environment is within acceptable parameters of temperature and humidity, pest and fungal attack can be largely prevented. Mold and fungus growth normally take place in damp, dark conditions, and are accelerated by warmth and lack of ventilation. Many organic materials

The ivory panel (above) has radically discolored because it was kept in a cloth or leather bag over a long period and absorbed the dyes.

Dolls were meant for children to play with, but many, such as this bisque, swivel-headed Parisienne, are very fragile.

are particularly susceptible to bacterial action, and it is important to check them carefully before introducing them into your home.

Pests such as woodworm beetle can attack whatever the environment, but major infestations are more likely to occur in cold, damp conditions. Other pests in different climates may thrive in different conditions. Silverfish, a common problem in large book and manuscript collections, thrive in damp and dusty environments.

If insect activity is suspected, it is vital to isolate any object immediately, preferably by wrapping and sealing in polythene, and to seek professional advice. Clothes moths can be effectively treated by freezing an object twice at a temperature of –30°F (–22°C).

## PHYSICAL USE AND ABUSE

The most common cause of damage to artifacts is from physical handling, and an owner needs to cultivate a special state of awareness when handling antique or precious items. Fragile objects should be displayed out of the reach of children or pets, on stable shelves or in display cabinets. If too many objects are displayed close together, there is an increased likelihood of accidental damage caused by an item being dislodged when a neighboring one is being handled.

When you carry an object, it should be carefully supported from underneath unless its condition or structure (for example, a Tiffany lampshade whose rim is the most fragile part) mitigates against this. Some objects are deceptively fragile.

Consider taking photographs of your more valuable objects as photographs can provide valuable reference for the restorer in the event of damage. They can also be useful if any object is stolen.

Wearing cotton gloves when handling highly polished metal surfaces like that of the sword (below) will prevent acids from your skin being deposited on the surface, which would cause localized tarnishing.

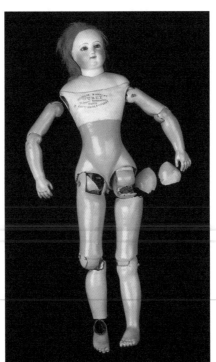

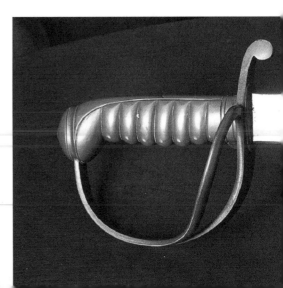

*Textiles are particularly sensitive to light, humidity levels, and insect and fungal attack.*

*The solid appearance of some objects belies their fragility. This marble-clad model (right) of an arch is very heavy, but much less robust than one cast in bronze. Some of the marble veneered sections have given way to reveal a marble core where it was presumably lifted by its sides.*

# FINDING A GOOD EXPERT

THE DIFFERENCE BETWEEN A CONSERVATOR AND A RESTORER IS NOT MERELY ONE OF TERMINOLOGY. THE KEY DIFFERENCE IS THAT A RESTORER WILL REPLACE OLD OR DAMAGED PARTS OF AN OBJECT, WHEREAS A CONSERVATOR WILL TREAT THESE AREAS TO STABILIZE THE OBJECT BUT WILL NOT ACTUALLY REPLACE THEM. EACH DISCIPLINE HAS ITS OWN CODES OF PRACTICE, AND IT IS INSTRUCTIVE TO BE AWARE OF THEM BEFORE DECIDING ON A COURSE OF TREATMENT.

*The value of sculpture and statuary depends a great deal on the quality and condition of the detail, such as the facial features, especially as discreet repair is often difficult.*

*Marble is a porous material and absorbs dust and other pollutants; here a restorer cleans a statue with a controllable, high pressure steam jet.*

Andrew Oddy of the British Museum explains the currently accepted museum policy on restoration this way: after reconstruction of a conserved object, it should appear complete from a distance of 6 feet (2 m), whereas from 6 inches (15 cm) the expert can clearly see what is old and what is new.

Whatever work a conservator carries out on an artifact should be reversible. This also applies to minor or temporary repairs done at home, such as regluing a piece of molding which might otherwise get lost.

For most private owners there will be two main considerations as to whether to choose a restorer or a conservator. First, if the object is functional rather than solely decorative, such as a tallcase (longcase) clock that the owner wishes to keep in working order, parts will wear out and need replacing, and in this case a restorer rather than a conservator will be required. Second, although this may not be a prime consideration, the owner may be concerned as to what effect any work carried out will have on the value of an object, both at the present time and in the future. It is not always possible to predict whether what appears to be stable restoration at the time will still be so in the future. The ultimate deterioration of the 18th-century restoration of Classical statuary could not have been predicted given the level of knowledge at that time. Consequently, if restoration is carried out on an object, it should be reversible wherever possible and include materials consistent with the original. Increasingly, collectors are keen to acquire pieces that are

One way to detect previous retouching to the decoration on ceramics is to tap the suspect area with your teeth (above). A dulled sound suggests a repainted surface, while the original, glazed decoration will respond with a sharper sound.

It is important not to destroy the patina on a bronze statue (above right), but spots of corrosion eat into the metal, and are here being scraped off with a scalpel.

A furniture restorer deals with the wood parts of a piece of furniture, but you need to go to an upholsterer for the soft parts. If the two experts communicate, all the better, for upholstery may conceal constructional flaws that are not obvious until it is removed.

*The interior of a general restoration workshop (above).*

unaltered or in original condition, and if future sale is contemplated, it should be stressed that the cost of restoration will not always be reflected in a consequent increase in market value. All undamaged objects in good condition will fetch more than one that has been restored, however well it has been done, with very few exceptions such as a particularly rare example, or one with an exceptional provenance.

If an object is in good condition and the correct techniques and materials are used to clean it, a collector should have the aim of preventing harmful tarnishing and corrosive or bacterial action rather than changing the appearance of his collection.

Where an owner wishes to change the appearance of an object by remedial cleaning, or to stabilize it or treat for bacterial or pest damage, specialist advice should be sought.

If you are thinking of buying an item of significant value, particularly ceramics or glass, where flaws or repairs may not be obvious but could decrease value, it is worth consulting an expert first. It is possible to engage a conservator to produce a formal condition analysis, and the seller should not object to this if the artifact is genuinely as described. In the case of clocks and other mechanical antiques, which may have been operational for over 200 years, a clock conservator's report is essential in establishing which elements of the movement are replaced. The best sources for restorers and other experts are one of the professional organizations (see Directory) or personal recommendation.

## Making a commitment

When selecting specialists, ask to see examples of their work and if possible their workshop. Obtain a written estimate, or at the very least, an indication of their scale of charges. Usually such experts are in high demand and may not be able to carry out the work immediately, although an indication of the projected timescale should be given. If urgent treatment is required, the stabilization part of the process should be carried out as soon as possible. Conservators and restorers will normally charge on a time basis, and apart from insurance and materials used, the cost will be unrelated to the value of the item. However, if an object has been attacked by outside infection or is facing imminent deterioration, the cost of inaction should be fully taken into account.

*A Staffordshire figure receives a new neck (above).*

*Ultraviolet photography can pick up areas of restoration (left).*

A SIMPLE CHAIR OR TABLE, AN ELEGANT WRITING DESK, OR A VOLUPTUOUS SOFA...ALL HOLD CLUES TO THE PAST: TO THE TYPES OF WOOD THAT WERE AVAILABLE, THE CRAFT SKILLS AND TECHNOLOGY MASTERED, AND THE LIFESTYLES OF THOSE WHO USED THEM. THE ORGANIC NATURE OF WOOD ABSORBS ALL THE SIGNS OF AGE AND EXPOSURE TO THE ATMOSPHERE, OF YEARS OF POLISHING, AND OF USE OR EVEN ABUSE BY GENERATIONS OF PREVIOUS OWNERS.

THIS IS WHAT GIVES ANTIQUE FURNITURE SO MUCH OF ITS APPEAL; THE NATURAL AGING PROCESS PRODUCES COLOR AND TEXTURE IMPOSSIBLE TO REPLICATE IN A MODERN FACTORY. AN INKSTAIN OR A CANDLE BURN MAY EVENTUALLY ADD CHARACTER AND VALUE—UNLESS REMOVED BY ILL-CONSIDERED CLEANING OR OVER-RESTORATION. DAMAGED JOINTS AND SURFACES WHICH DIMINISH THE FUNCTION OR ATTRACTION NEED ATTENTION, IF ONLY TO PRESERVE FOR THE FUTURE. BUT THE GENERAL RESTORATION RULE MUST BE TO DO THE MINIMUM, AND TO ENSURE THAT THE TECHNIQUES, JOINERY, FINISHES, AND HISTORY ARE CONSERVED.

# FURNITURE

# THE WRITING DESK

WRITING DESKS AND CHESTS OF DRAWERS ARE BOTH ESSENTIALLY FUNCTIONAL ITEMS OF FURNITURE, SHARING MANY ASPECTS OF CONSTRUCTION AND VULNERABILITY. BUT THE WRITING DESK INCORPORATED EXTRAS SUCH AS WRITING SURFACES AND PIGEON HOLES FOR WRITING EQUIPMENT, AND ALSO HAD TO LOOK ELEGANT IN A DRAWING ROOM OR STUDY.

In the late 1600s most writing desks were made entirely in oak or walnut, except for the coarse backing boards. As a wealth of exotic woods became available from the 1720s—from San Domingo mahogany, figured maple, and fruitwoods to boxwood and ebony for decorative stringing—they became a canvas to display the cabinetmaker's veneering and decorating skills. The new styles may have been more elegant, but they were also more vulnerable since veneer is particularly susceptible to changes in temperature and humidity.

*Fall lock and housing:* Impatience, lost keys, or malfunctioning lock mortices can wreak damage here over time, quite often leaving an ugly hole or gash.

*Fall:* Usually made of one of two planks with cleated ends and is prone to warping and shrinkage; remedial work is expensive, especially on a veneered piece.

*Secret drawers (above) may be concealed as pillars on each side of the stationery fitment door or behind a pelmet at the top of each pigeon hole. Another clue is if the length of the official drawer is noticeably shorter than the depth of the writing desk.*

*Locks:* May have suffered from forced entry or corrosion. The fall and the desk's small internal drawers and cupboards may have had locks at one time.

*Feet:* May not be original. The examples here are Victorian replacements. Early writing desks normally had solid walnut bun or bracket feet that were prone to woodworm and damp rot, and often replaced.

EARLY GEORGIAN WRITING DESK, *with later handles and feet. It is to be restored as close to its original appearance as possible.*

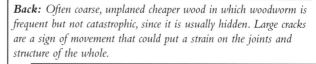

**Back:** *Often coarse, unplaned cheaper wood in which woodworm is frequent but not catastrophic, since it is usually hidden. Large cracks are a sign of movement that could put a strain on the joints and structure of the whole.*

**Top surface:** *Should be a complete piece apart from decorative banding. Rear corners are often subject to damage. Minor water marks and ink stains are to be expected and do not diminish value.*

**Sides:** *Often a single piece of veneer, prone to cracking with changes in temperature or humidity. Remove the bottom drawer to check the base timber for splits, which indicates movement in the whole piece, and will need attention.*

**Handles:** *Look inside the drawer where the handle is attached. Are there signs of earlier holes which have been plugged, suggesting replacements? Original handles display a degree of wear, patina, and verdigris that is virtually impossible to fake. The face of the drawer where the handle has knocked against it should be worn or dented. There may also be a stain around metal handles and locks where they have been cleaned; neither diminishes the value of the piece.*

**Fall hinges:** *Prone to splitting if the fall is dropped without the lopers extended. Hinges are commonly replaced when the writing surface needs repair. Clumsy repairs, such as the use of screws that are too large in diameter, forcing their way through the wood, devalue a piece. Height packing can often be seen under the hinge to reduce the strain on the fall when open. If this hinge is not reset accurately, further damage may occur.*

**Lopers:** *Pull-out action should be smooth, but lopers may warp and foul with their runners or the carcass side. Check that the backstop has a piece of timber pinned and glued to the inside of the carcass at the back of the loper to prevent it from being slammed, which would progressively crack or dislodge the backboards.*

**Drawers:** *Joints loosen, bottoms shrink and split, the drawer lifts out of its housing groove, wears the runner, and wears its own lining runner. However, it may have taken 200 years for this to happen, so properly restored it should last another two centuries. Failure to remedy worn runners leads to problems such as damage to the lower edge of a veneered rail and damage from forced opening and closing.*

# PRACTICAL ADDITIONS

Writing desks are basically chests of drawers with a drop-down, sloped writing flap or fall on top. Both evolved from the family dower chest in which clothes were kept. But it was troublesome retrieving items from the bottom of a chest, and from the early 1600s easier access was achieved by raising the chest on legs and suspending boxes beneath it. By 1650 more boxes had been added, and eventually these developed into drawers.

Early examples of writing desks in the late 1600s were in two pieces, the seam covered by a decorative molding. Later still, from the start of the 18th century, bookcases or cabinets were added to the top of writing desks and continued to be made into the 1900s. Some later copies of earlier styles are now almost as valuable as the originals. As with any compound piece of furniture, it is important to check that the base and upper part agree and are not of different ages and designs. A "married" piece is worth very much less. Writing desks and chests of drawers produced in the first quarter of the 1700s are rare, highly sought, and expensive. They may have been veneered in walnut, which is fragile and was often replaced later wiith an alternative veneer such as mahogany—if this has happened, it lowers the value of a piece. An expert will be able to tell you if the style and veneer are authentic. Mahogany writing desks and chests of drawers became the norm toward the middle of the century, and are more sturdy, but are valued in thousands of dollars rather than tens of thousands. The richness of the wood does not necessarily make a great deal of difference to price, although condition, of course, does.

## The strength of the joinery

Joined furniture in the 1600s and 1700s was made without glue, which allowed the timber a certain amount of movement. If solid wood is set into a rigid frame that does not allow any movement, it will split, as so many cabinet pieces do when exposed to a dry atmosphere. Dry construction (without glue) has ensured that many fine examples of early chests of drawers have survived. However,

*Bow, serpentine, or bombe-shaped fronts (left) can develop major problems, especially if exposed to low levels of humidity in centrally- heated apartments. The complex construction which underlies the veneered surfaces can cause them to tear and split, involving extensive, specialized restoration.*

these firmly pegged mortice and tenon joints were eventually replaced with flat, dovetailed boards veneered with walnut, producing pieces that were more elegant but also more fragile.

Applied geometric moldings decorated the drawer fronts of English and American examples, with extensive use made of split turning in contrasting woods such as bog oak, dyed fruitwood, or maple. In continental Europe, cabinetmakers pioneered the use of veneers in pictorial and geometric designs in the 1700s. Dutch floral marquetry in particular has to be treated with special care to preserve the intricate inlays.

Drawers gradually became much lighter, and their sides ran on their bottom edges. Corners were dovetailed and heavy moldings replaced with delicately lipped and molded—but easily detached—edges. Lipped fronts, fashionable from the end of 1600s, gave continual trouble. The stops that should have prevented the drawer from shutting against the lipping often failed, causing the lipping to split. In many cases, this has been replaced with cocked beading that is out of period and devalues the piece. Look for this especially on vertically veneered drawer fronts decorated with a chevron or feather inlay and cross-banding.

Continental pieces, such as Louis XV French Rococo *bombe* commodes, were often elaborately veneered, and embellished with ormolu mounts, often laid on a cheap pine carcass that tended to put stress on the veneered surface. In France the small, decorative *bonheur du jour* writing desk is characterized by the use of cross-banded veneers, often in light, attractive woods which proved particularly prone to splitting with changes in temperature and humidity.

## GENERAL CARE

The most fundamental rule for writing desk owners is to make sure that the lopers are extended before lowering the fall. If the fall should drop without them in place, the hinges could be torn away, and the veneer, planks, and joints could split. Do not use ballpoint pens on the writing surface as the impression will come through the paper into the wood. Dry, cracked leather writing surfaces can be revitalized with a

*This 18th-century highboy (right) graphically illustrates the grace of the American cabinetmakers' art, its decorative finials emphasizing the fine proportions. The cabriole legs, though light and slender, are strong enough to take the weight of this delicate piece.*

lanolin and beeswax preparation available from specialist suppliers. Allow the dressing to be absorbed for twenty-four hours before buffing gently with a clean soft cloth.

Make sure the drawers always run smoothly; rub candle wax on the runners, and avoid ramming them home against the stops as this can weaken joints, allowing the rail to move and breaking the veneer at the junctions. A restorer can replace damaged veneer, but it is expensive.

To remove a fresh stain, try dampening it slightly and apply a touch of lemon juice, using a fine paintbrush. Leave the solution to dry for a few minutes and then dab with a tissue. Persistent stains need to be dealt with by a restorer.

When buying chests of drawers and writing desks, look for telltale signs of woodworm; remove the drawers and inspect the softwood carcass for flight holes and wood dust (known as frass) in the feet and back, especially if the piece is made with either walnut or maple since these woods are particularly susceptible. Woodworm can be treated chemically or by the process known as "thermo lignum," by which the wood is heated while maintaining constant humidity. Deal with any infestation before you take the piece home as it may spread to other pieces.

### TIPS FOR LATER STYLES
*Later writing desks and chests of drawers often had cock beading—an applied molded strip along the drawer edge (left). Although decorative, and a mark of quality, this also protected vulnerable veneered corners. If the drawers are going to foul, due to runner wear or carelessness, the cock beading takes the punishment, not the veneer, and if sections are missing, it is worth having them replaced. Bracket feet (left) were fitted on writing desks and chests of drawers from c. 1760, and sometimes were fitted in place of earlier bun feet. They are particularly vulnerable to splitting, if a piece of furniture is dragged rather than lifted when moved.*

### CHANGING HANDLES
*Handles and keyhole covers (below) have often been replaced due to changing fashions, lost keys, or damage, so they are not reliable indicators of date. Until about 1700, wrought iron was a common material. Brass rim locks were introduced toward the end of the 1600s. Elegant brass handles were often accompanied by elaborate backplates echoing the elaborate escutcheon plates of door furniture style. If the original handles have been replaced, and you want the piece to look as authentic as possible, a restorer may be able to make a cast from period originals and produce replicas.*

*Visiting burglars did not extend the lopers on the writing desk (below) before they raided the contents; the fall dropped violently, causing the wood to split, and the knuckle of the hinge was strained creating an unsightly gap beneath fall and writing desk carcass.*

## THE RESTORER'S BRIEF

The owner of the writing desk featured on page 30 wanted to continue to use it as a functioning piece of furniture, and for it to be restored to its original style and beauty. If he had wanted to sell it to a dealer, he would have been advised not to restore beforehand, as many dealers prefer to have items "as found." Nevertheless, this particular writing desk might have fetched around $35-50,000 (£20-30,000) unrestored, and its value is likely to be doubled when finished, although this is partly because it is a particularly rare and valued example from the early 1700s. Individual pieces must be judged on their own merit and value.

If you are going to use an item of furniture, it is worth having any restoration done that prevents further damage, such as to drawers and runners, lopers, hinges, or fall. The ideal is to return the piece as much as possible to its original condition; this may involve deciding whether to replace the feet, handles, and moldings. Ask the restorer if he has access to casts of handles and lockplates made from period originals.

Badly cracked and warped veneer or a damaged fall will affect value and be expensive to restore. If a burlwood veneer has become dulled by years of waxing, which in turn has absorbed dust and soot, ask the restorer to clean the surface to bring back the translucent quality of the original. If you are tempted to remove surface blemishes, bear in mid that you will also be removing the patina of age.

Restorers should be asked not to glue the joints of chests originally made using the dry construction method; this would devalue the piece and might cause the wood to split, making any later restoration more expensive.

A competent restorer can replace missing drawer lipping, but this would only be commercially viable on an exceptional piece, as it is a lengthy process which involves the careful removal of all the cross-banding, which has then to be replaced once the new cross-grained moldings have been fitted. Loose beading should never be nailed back, but stuck with a reversible hide or fish glue, or, if you are unsure, keep the pieces together in a safe place.

*Furniture with metal banding or inlays combined with wood veneer (above) should be frequently checked as different rates of expansion and contraction can cause the metal to buckle away from the surface—a sharp edge that can easily be caught while dusting.*

*Most restorers (below) have a selection of old veneers which can be used to match lost pieces; always keep detached pieces of veneer or banding safely until restoration can take place.*

# THE DROPLEAF TABLE

T ABLES ARE INVARIABLY SOME OF THE MOST UTILITARIAN ITEMS OF FURNITURE IN THE HOME—THOUGH THEY CAN ALSO PLAY A DECORATIVE ROLE—AND INEVITABLY BEAR THE SIGNS OF EVERYDAY USE THROUGH THE AGES.

The dropleaf table may be a practical working table—such as an oak gateleg— or a more elegant drawing room design reserved for lighter duties such as writing. But its relatively complex construction, incorporating leaves (or flaps) and hinges, and sometimes drawers, mean that it encompasses in one most of the potential problem areas a table is likely to present.

The manner in which the top is supported on usually four, sometimes more, legs is the principal difference between the many table styles. In some cases, elegance is sacrificed for greater strength, but generally the reverse is true. With the development of joining techniques, the possibilities for decoration increased, but certain features, such as hinges, introduce weak points. The more complex tables became, the more weak spots they had.

**Drawer:** *These particular tables have a drawer fitted into one end of the underframe, and a "dummy" drawer front at the other end to balance the design. Look inside the drawer front for holes that do not relate to the handles currently fitted. Replacements may detract from the value of your table, though well-made copies using historically correct alloys are available from specialists and are almost indistinguishable.*

**Knuckle joint:** *The joints on which some dropleaves pivot. They function well when used for the wings that support the shorter and lighter leaves of Federal and Neoclassical Pembroke or sofa tables, but are put under considerable strain when incorporated in a heavier dining table.*

**Legs:** *Examine the joints that connect the legs to the underframe and test for any movement by gently pushing them to and fro. Saber legs, as in the featured piece, are always cut from one piece of timber, which inevitably have areas of short, weak grain that will fail, especially if the table has been dropped onto them or leaned on. Look for a quick-fix repair made with screws underneath the leg and for loose joints where the leg joins the pine or maple frame members.*

**Top:** *Signs of use such as staining and bruising may enhance a table's value; removal of a patina could seriously devalue. Buckled and split veneers are more serious. Check that the top has been properly attached to the subframe with old slothead screws or wood glue block. If the top forms a fixed center section with leaves on each side, check it has not shrunk so that the leaves no longer hang vertically.*

**Rule joint and hinges:** *The convex part of this joint, formed on the edge of the central section, hides three or four hinges. If the leaf is strained upward, this timber covering will be broken and will probably fall away. Look for botched hinge repairs or brass hinges used as replacements, which lack the strength of iron butterfly hinges.*

**Wing:** *Failure of the delicate knuckle joint, which allows the wing to rotate through 90 degrees, causes the leaf or flap to sag. Swing the supports to see the action of the knuckle joints in case they are badly worn, and check the wings for excessive wear or woodworm.*

**Center column:** *Tenoned into a large, square block known as the bed, which is then screwed to the underframe of the table. Any excess pressure that is exerted on the tenons via this block—such as by someone sitting on one end of the table—will cause the table top to loosen. Check how firmly the top is attached to the base.*

GRECO-ROMAN-STYLE DROPLEAF TABLE *of the later Federal or Regency period (c. 1815)—it incorporates most of the potential problem areas a table is likely to encounter.*

## EVOLUTION OF TABLE STYLE

The introduction of a table with a leaf or flap that extends the surface area brought flexibility of use, and as cabinetmaking techniques developed, a greater degree of elegance. Often, however, dropleaf designs lost the structural stability of earlier, simpler tables.

Early dining tables consisted of a number of boards laid over trestles so the table could be removed. These were gradually replaced by long and heavy oak refectory tables that were not designed to be moved at all. Later came draw tables, the predecessors of the dropleaf, with two ends that could be pulled out and supported on sturdy, bulbous legs. The earliest form of folding table was made from a thick slab of timber with a leaf attached to each side and supported by lopers (pullout supports). The weight of this table compromised its usefulness because it was so cumbersome. However, toward the middle of the 1600s, the gateleg became popular as a dining table because of its lighter, joined construction. Practical and thoughtfully designed, it could be folded down and placed away from the center of the room to create space for social occasions such as musical evenings.

From the mid 1700s, the use of a stretcher to stiffen the underframe was dispensed with, doing without the gate

*The slender legs of this 1805 Federal dropleaf table support 14 feet (4.25 m) when the leaves are fully extended—dragging the table along an uneven floor or undue weight on the table top would put them under enormous strain. The middle hinged section can be used as a separate table.*

*Stretchers between the legs, like those of the English c. 1670 table (above), not only strike a visual balance between the table top and the floor, but also have a steadying influence on what would otherwise be a top-heavy construction. Flat stretchers like these need to be checked for lost veneer because of dampness and abrasion.*

support for the wings, as the gate used the stretcher to provide the lower pivot point.

## The enduring dropleaf

Dropleaf tables have been in continuous production since the 1700s, and from the mid 1800s more attractive and expensive styles were reproduced or faked.

English and east coast American cabinetmakers produced mahogany and walnut dining tables with large drop leaves supported on cabriole legs which pivoted on knuckle joints, but when these joints were used for heavier-leaved tables they tended to be overstrained.

Compared with gateleg tables, Chippendale or Federal period dropleaf tables had uncluttered subframes, but replaced

structural stability with elegance. The great weight of the mahogany tops supported on just four legs put tremendous strain on the subframe. The heavy top, supported on a turned column with elegant sweeping reeded legs could, without careful use, loosen from the column. The legs often split away, and the lion's paw castors become worn, refusing to rotate through 360 degrees.

A turned underframe can give a clue to the possible date of manufacture; for example, an English barleytwist design indicates a table that is post 1660, whereas in France at a similar date, the fashion was for straight tapering legs with gadrooned capitals and scrolled stretchers. In the second quarter of the 1700s, European cabinetmakers opted for mahogany rather than walnut; it was more resistant to woodworm attack, denser, and could be crisply carved. In America, mahogany was used from much the same period; the other main woods used were cherry, walnut, and maple.

The most durable table tops were made from dense timbers such as oak and mahogany. Walnut, birch, and pine surfaces tend to be soft and mark very easily. Turned wooden knobs replaced earlier brass handles on drawers, and these in turn are often changed back to the original style. To check for changes, look for threaded holes covered over with the brass back-plate of a retrofitted or later handle.

## Lightweight variations

The lightweight Pembroke or breakfast table was used for games, intimate meals, or tea. However, the turned edges concealing the hinges have often been stressed, resulting in cracks or splits. An early 18th-century space-saving design was the folding or "tuckaway" table which comprised two rectangular underframes that pivoted to form an X frame to support the top when required. The simple joined frame folds flat to allow the top to fold down, thus taking up very little floorspace. To stop the frames from rubbing against each other as they are opened or closed, turned wooden washers were inserted between both pairs of horizontal rails. It is important to check that these washers are intact or that well-made wooden replacements have been fitted. This form was still made in the 1750s by some of the finest English and American cabinetmakers for use as a folding tea table. They were made from mahogany with elegant cabriole legs, but were no less robust than the earlier versions. Nineteenth-century interpretations of the style use turned legs for support, initially in delicate proportions but becoming more ponderous toward the late 1800s.

*Surfaces that are designed to be written upon have a leather or baize covering as on a writing desk. This beautifully polished table top carries the impression of a ball pen where no protection was inserted between the document and the wood. The only remedy would be to lift the veneer and steam the indentations out, but as this would destroy some of the original finish—which would then have to be recreated—the owners may be better advised to live with the scars.*

## GENERAL CARE

Before you invest in an antique table, examine it thoroughly. Have it turned upside down so that you can see whether woodworm has attacked the softwood underframe. If so, the table should be treated before it is introduced to your home.

Careless operation of the leg, gate, or wing that supports a dropleaf can result in expensive repair bills, so make sure you shut it flat against the underframe before letting the leaves drop. Extending the supports beyond 90 degrees strains the delicate knuckle joints on which they pivot. Sitting or leaning on the top strains the legs to the point where a joint could fail, or in the case of a pedestal base, the top will loosen from the column

When eating at an antique table, cover the surface with a heat-resistant cloth or use place mats. Resist the temptation to put a flower arrangement or houseplants on it as water spills can do irreparable damage to finely patinated surfaces. Any spills should be wiped immediately.

Polish vigorously with a pure beeswax polish (not "polish that contains beeswax") three or four times a year. Overpolishing can dull the surface. Attempting to clean wood surfaces with "revivers," which contain a cocktail of solvents, could dissolve the surface finish. Similarly, the use of oil over shellac or waxed surfaces can lead to permanent scarring of the underlying wood. Between waxings, remove dust from surfaces with a soft cloth, using a soft brush for molded or carved areas.

Be very careful with veneered surfaces; if liquid seeps into cracks it may hasten buckling and lifting of veneered sections; it is safer to dust these with a soft-bristled brush.

*The gateleg (below) has been swung to the optimal position for supporting the massive oak leaf. Anything less than this 90 degree optimal could start to put unbearable stresses on the hinges and hinge fixings.*

## THE RESTORER'S BRIEF

A skilled restorer will be able to stabilize an unsteady frame, remake joints, and copy missing metal hardware that looks original and will add value.

Drop or falling leaves are by necessity hinged to a fixed center section. These pivotal points are where stresses manifest themselves as splits, cracks, or areas bereft of a timber covering, all of which should be dealt with to prevent further deterioration. The leaves of a dropleaf table have to be supported either with a leg that swings out from beneath the fixed center section or by a wing that is attached to the main table frame and is flipped out to support the extended leaf. Tables with large drop leaves have a leg to support them, whereas the narrower leaves as in the featured table have wings. Both support systems can fail, but can and should be repaired.

All original table tops carry some honorable battle scars. Remove them and you take away something of the table's history. This raises the question of how much restoration is a good idea; structural weaknesses obviously have to be addressed, but the "improving" of a table top by the removal of rings, scratches, or ink stains will not dramatically improve your table's value, unless the staining is particularly severe; over-restoration may decrease it, especially now that conservation as opposed to restoration is increasingly popular.

Faded colors and heavy wax patinas can be restored, given time and a generous budget. If you are unsure of the type of finish on your table top, ask a restorer to make some solubility tests on a hidden area to identify the nature—and originality—of the finish.

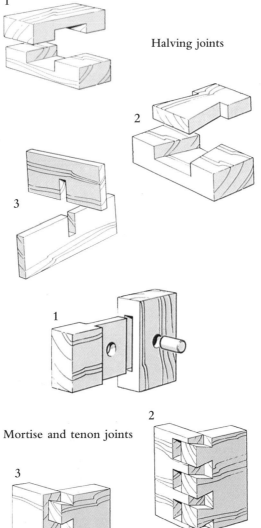

Halving joints

Mortise and tenon joints

## LOOKING AT JOINTS

*The soundness of a joint was not only a mark of the original cabinetmaker's skill, but vital for the long term survival of the piece of furniture. Joining is a "dry construction" method (without glue), and while joints do swell, contract, and distort with changes in humidity, if they are well made, they are still the strongest and most reliable method of joining sections of furniture.*

*Halving joints* are basic construction joints generally used in the carcass.
1. Cut from the middle of a piece.
2. Dovetail halving.
3. Joint cut into the thickness of the piece.

*Mortise and tenon joints* were in general use by the end of the 1400s. The projecting tenon fits into a matching cutout section called the mortise.

1. Tenon secured by pegging.
2. Through dovetail join at a right angle. As this creates a slight unevenness on the outer surface, veneering can lift at this point.
3. Stopped or lapped dovetail, which does not show through on the outer surface and is suitable for veneers.

*To treat live woodworm, flood each hole separately (left). Wear gloves for safety. As a deterrent against future infestation, wipe the fluid over the backs and bottoms of the carcass, but keep it away from polished or decorated surfaces.*

# THE COUNTRY CHAIR

**P**ROVINCIAL VERSIONS OF STYLISH URBAN DESIGNS, MADE FOR EVERYDAY USE AS DINING AND GENERAL PURPOSE CHAIRS, HAVE ENDURED, BECAUSE OF THEIR STURDY JOINED CONSTRUCTION, TO BECOME DESIRABLE ANTIQUES.

Some of the most basic chair designs, originally made for everyday use in kitchens and taverns, have been upgraded to become collectors' items today. The more sophisticated and elaborate relatives of simple country chairs were the dining chairs of upperclass urban homes, crafted from exotic hardwoods such as Cuban mahogany. What characterized the country versions was a sturdy joined construction and the use of locally available woods. Country carpenters adapted styles from the design sourcebook of the time, Thomas Chippendale's *The Gentleman and Cabinet Maker's Directory*, published in the mid 1700s, to suit their own skills and traditional materials. An original Chippendale version of the chair featured would have been upholstered; in the country version, ash has been used for the main frame for its strength and flexibility, while the seat is elm for its resistance to splitting and ability to expand and contract in length as well as width.

When buying country chairs, generally check for hasty repairs such as inappropriate gluing that could be expensive to put right, and for signs that chairs have been dipped in caustic soda to remove the original coating. This corrosive treatment discolors and dries out the wood, weakens the joints, and often leaves harmful chemical residues which could injure children or pets.

SHAKER ROCKING CHAIR, 1840: *The North American Shaker communities believed in economy of design combined with strength and practicality. Chairs were usually designed to be hung upside down from pegs when not in use, but this would have been difficult in the rocking form (right) as the rockers extend well to the rear of the chair to prevent its falling backward.*

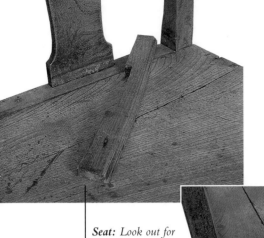

**Cresting rail:** *Always look for damage in this area—especially for signs of alteration that suggest the cresting rail has been broken and reshaped rather than restored to its original shape by the replacement of any missing wood.*

**Splat:** *This form of splat may split due to severe shrinkage but is unlikely to become detached from the frame.*

**Seat:** *Look out for shrinkage of the seat boards, which causes original wood nails to pull loose. Sometimes cheap repairs have been made with iron nails instead of wood pegs.*

**Frame:** *To check if a chair has been weakened, place one hand on the rail which runs across the front of the seat, the other on the cresting rail, and gently flex the frame, to see if there is any significant movement. Check that the chair stands without rocking. Badly repaired frames are often glued out of square.*

**Patina:** *Two hundred years of abrasion and exposure to ultraviolet light have worked together to produce the mellow appearance, but when the chair was delivered to its first owner, the color of the wood would have resembled mahogany, achieved by stain overlaid with copal or shellac varnish. Most owners of today would not wish to restore this effect.*

**Stretchers:** *The bracing bars which give the chair its strength of construction. Check for cheap replacements which are too thin or which have been made with different wood.*

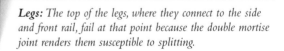

**Joints:** *Look for hasty repairs, such as inappropriate gluing or nails and screws, which could involve further expense to put right. The original joints would not have been glued. The main potential weak spot is where the seat joins the frame—this was traditionally done with tapered wooden nails known as "trenails." If the nails have snapped, a restorer will know how to "rive" and fit slightly oversized replacements.*

**Legs:** *The top of the legs, where they connect to the side and front rail, fail at that point because the double mortise joint renders them susceptible to splitting.*

A LATE 18TH-CENTURY COUNTRY CHIPPENDALE *chair displays its enduring qualities.*

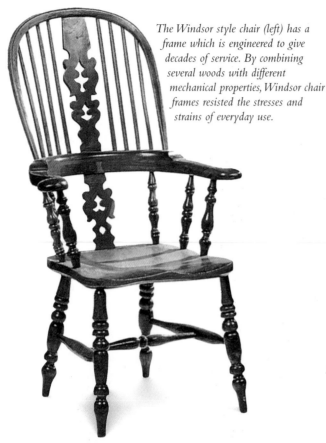

*The Windsor style chair (left) has a frame which is engineered to give decades of service. By combining several woods with different mechanical properties, Windsor chair frames resisted the stresses and strains of everyday use.*

earliest wooden upright, side, or pullup chairs were "backstools" which evolved from stools in the 1600s; the back was simply an extension of the back legs, with cross stretchers between the legs to provide stability and strength, and a solid, square wood seat. The back was often surmounted by a carved crest or cresting rail that was easily damaged if the chair fell over backwards; many will have been repaired. Over time the back and back legs acquired a certain independence from each other: by the early 1700s advances in joining and a movement toward greater elegance favored curvaceous cabriole legs, and supportive stretchers were largely abandoned, at least for elegant dining chairs.

## Designs for everyday use

Practical styles for everyday use continued to be made in the country, however. Turned chairs of stick construction evolved into various forms of Windsor chair, including the gothic and hoop-back styles, in the late 18th century. The legs, anchored by stretchers, slotted into the seat, and stick uprights or pierced splats formed the back. These were often glued or

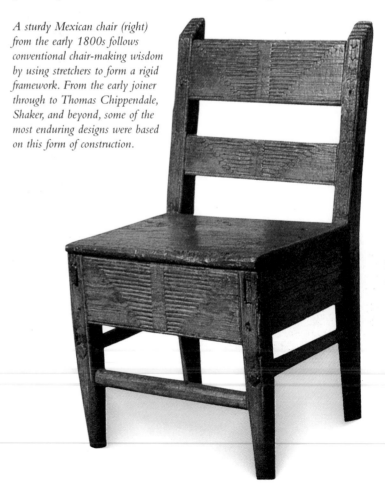

*A sturdy Mexican chair (right) from the early 1800s follows conventional chair-making wisdom by using stretchers to form a rigid framework. From the early joiner through to Thomas Chippendale, Shaker, and beyond, some of the most enduring designs were based on this form of construction.*

# EVOLUTION OF THE SIMPLE CHAIR

If style, shape, comfort, and practicality determine a chair's success both in its own day and as a collector's item, the country versions of Chippendale's designs are a good investment. Thomas Chippendale became London's leading cabinetmaker in the mid 1700s. His stylistic innovations were much imitated throughout England and dominated American furniture design 1760–1780; designs were still being copied in the late 1800s. The publication of *The Gentleman and Cabinet Maker's Directory* meant that local carpenters could follow his designs. Chippendale used the same basic constructional techniques that ordinary joiners or carpenters had been using since the mid 1600s; a sturdy structural underframe made up of bracing bars and stretchers, using mortise and tenon joints to connect the bars to the legs.

Joined chairs developed from the concept of a framed and paneled box from which some of the panels had been removed to leave the frame with a seat and back added. The

wedged into slots for extra strength as they tended to work loose with shrinkage of the wood. If a hoop shape splits or becomes detached, a restorer can steam it to make it pliable enough to repair.

The technique of steaming or soaking wood was used from the 1850s to make curvaceous bentwood chairs, the best-known exponent being the Austrian Michael Thonet. They were solid wood, but lightweight, strong, and low priced—and were soon to be seen in homes and cafes all over Europe.

## GENERAL CARE

Many chairs show damage which arises through inappropriate, thoughtless use. Use the chair for its intended purpose: to sit on. Standing on a chair seat puts your entire body weight on the frame, and holding the cresting rail as you step up strains the frame toward you and weakens the joints. Do not rock back on a chair to the point where the front legs leave the floor, as this puts an enormous strain on the legs; and if the chair falls over backward, the back rail may well break. Dust regularly and polish with a pure beeswax polish three or four times a year.

## SETS OF CHAIRS

*Most 18th- and 19th-century dining and hall chairs were made in sets, and an original set will command a premium. A "set" may have been expanded from three genuine chairs to six or even eight with modern handmade copies, and these can be hard to identify. To check before buying, arrange the set in a line and stand at one end so that you can view all the backs in relation to each other. The "rake" or angle should be the same for the whole set. If the set includes an arm, elbow, or carver chair, the seat on these should be wider than the others. Lift each chair in turn and check that all are of a similar weight: a modern chair will probably be lighter. Variations in wood coloration or seat covering material are not necessarily an indication that the set has been expanded.*

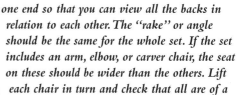

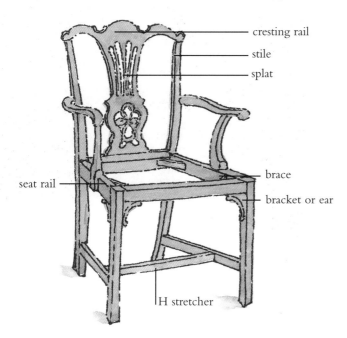

- cresting rail
- stile
- splat
- brace
- bracket or ear
- seat rail
- H stretcher

## THE RESTORER'S BRIEF

Simplicity of construction often tempts amateurs to make repairs on an upright or country chair, and these can be fatal or difficult to rectify. You should go to a restorer who will have proper clamps and reversible wood glues, and who understands the original construction techniques. Loose joints are often poorly repaired either by the addition of metal brackets and plates or the use of epoxy gap-filling glues, both of which can be reversed—at a cost. Ask the restorer to plug and patch holes made by nails and screws to regain value. Glued joints that have worked loose should be dismantled completely before cleaning and regluing. Original joined construction should be repegged, not glued.

# A CHESTERFIELD SOFA

A COVERED FRAMEWORK CAN CONCEAL A HOST OF PROBLEMS FOR THE UNWARY COLLECTOR: POORLY MADE, BADLY REPAIRED, OR SEVERELY WEAKENED FRAMES MAY LURK BENEATH A PADDED SURFACE.

The chesterfield was a true sofa, with arms and back on the same level, both rising from a strong, rectangular seat frame. It brought sofa design full circle after the curvaceous and often structurally weak drawing room furniture of the mid 1800s, and marked a revival of quality in upholstered furniture, with a structurally sound framework and a high degree of comfort. The deeply buttoned upholstery introduced by the Victorians mirrored the coachbuilders' style for upholstering carriages and gave a room a sense of comfort and well-being that had been lacking since the first quarter of the 19th century.

But such a luxuriance of upholstery can disguise problems within the framework. When buying 18th- or 19th-century upholstered furniture, it is necessary to inspect the framework from underneath, or even consider selecting a sound, bare, period frame from an upholsterer and have it covered yourself in keeping with its original period. Only then can you be assured that the upholstery is not hiding a potential hazard.

*Buttoning:* If the buttons are loose or missing because of rotting of the twine or rusted metal rings holding them in place, it is a major upholstering task to replace them, involving removal of the back covering material and the use of special long needles.

*Cover:* Chesterfield sofas with their original leather covering in good condition are very rare and expensive; most have been reupholstered. Any upholstered furniture with its original cover will be worth an enormous amount more than its re-covered equivalent. Earlier sofas originally covered with a delicate material such as silk damask are almost bound to have been re-covered unless they are museum pieces.

*Legs:* Missing castors can be replaced with period originals or reproductions. Back legs are often held in position only by three dowels bored right through the leg, creating a weak structure before the sofa is put to work.

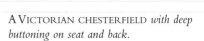

A VICTORIAN CHESTERFIELD *with deep buttoning on seat and back.*

**Seat:** *Sit down and move around, lean on the arms and against the back. Listen for muffled creaks. Are the noises in harmony with the movement? When viewed from the front and the side, does the piece as a whole lean or sag? Anything out of order may be a sign of unsound framework.*

**Frame:** *The straightforward chesterfield frame does not have the problem of the curving love seats and other frivolous mid- to late-19th-century sofa styles, in which curves were sawn out of straight-grained timber, leading to later fracture, but it is still worth checking the joints. The greatest stress points are where the legs meet the bottom rails. If the upholstery hides the frame, sit and move around to hear any groans of strained joints.*

**Back and arms:** *Some chesterfields were equipped with a drop end operated by a cast-iron ratchet mechanism (see p. 49). If it is in working order, the sofa will be about 10 percent more valuable than a fixed arm equivalent. Be careful of mid- to late-19th-century sofas with no wood visible on the backs and arms; they may have been formed with bent steel rods and straps, providing a structure that is too flexible and unsteady, and which cannot be replaced.*

**Stuffing:** *The deeper the padding, the more expensive the reupholstering process. Check what the stuffing would have been on the original sofa; restoring it in keeping will help restore value, too.*

**Underframe:** *Lay upholstered furniture on its back to inspect the underframe. On a chesterfield, for example, if it has been upholstered in the correct period style, you should be able to see the underframe that connects the legs. Unfortunately, many pieces were badly reupholstered and burlap (hessian), linette, or calico (muslin) was tacked or stapled to the underside of the frame, possibly masking botched repairs, or major frame replacements have left very little genuine woodwork intact.*

# STYLE, COMFORT, AND STRENGTH

Early sofas of the 1700s consisted of a rectangular frame with arms and back of a similar height to form a strong, rigid box constructed with conventional joinery methods—mortise and tenoned, dovetailed, or lap-jointed together (see p. 41). The result was elegant but strong: a rectangular frame which was covered with delicate silk damasks or elaborate, finely woven needlework. Examples with original coverings are rare. The rectangular form was retained until the mid 1700s, but with upholstered backs and arms. In North America, the most elegant forms were made in Philadelphia, their sensuous lines covered with damask.

Glamorous Greco-Roman, French Empire, or Regency sofas of the late 18th and early 19th centuries brought the art of upholstered furniture to the pinnacle of perfection. Frames were constructed with the greatest craftsmanship using the most expensive materials, and were the most strongly built

*The high back of this settee from the early 1700s illustrates the fundamental difference between a sofa and a settee. A true sofa has a back which is the same height as the arms. This settee has evolved by linking two armchair or easy chair frames together. Note the considerable difference in seat heights.*

*A well-made sofa of the Regency period (above) illustrates the strength that a rectangular form allows the frame-maker to build into upholstered furniture. This piece has been sympathetically reupholstered by someone who understands the importance of applying historically correct methods to period frames.*

frames of any period. Rich coverings such as Aubusson tapestry often concealed most of the frame, sometimes leaving only the legs showing.

With the advent of the Federal or late Georgian period in the 1810s, more of the frame was exposed, with delicately inlaid or painted wood backs and arms influenced by the designs of English furnituremakers Hepplewhite and Sheraton. The square sofa with exposed, turned-front arms became one of the most popular designs in Federal North America; it was beautifully made and has been much copied since. Frames were more delicate, and although some were supported by eight legs, examples from this period are more easily strained through misuse. The oval, round, or curved frames with higher backs and shallow arms required a different constructional approach, and the frame members were linked with butt joints—simply pinned with dowels—rather than secured by traditional joints.

From the 1840s, industrialization and massproduction techniques tended to take precedence over craftsmanship, with an overall decline in the quality of construction and materials. Springs, introduced in the 1840s, brought a greater degree of comfort, and deep-buttoned velvet or brocade upholstery became fashionable.

## GENERAL CARE

Buff wood parts with wax polish occasionally, taking care not to let the polish go on the upholstery. Dust painted or gilded wood lightly with a soft, dry cloth. Lightly vacuum upholstery as long as it is in reasonably stable condition, putting a net over the nozzle of the vacuum cleaner to reduce suction power if necessary. Protect fitted upholstered covers from everyday usage by covering with a loose throw. Some spray dry-cleaning products can be used to lift spots but only with great care as they may cause bleaching; always do a spot test on an inconspicuous area first.

Treat leather covers with hide food and saddle soap as soon as they show signs of becoming dry—how frequently this happens will depend on the humidity level in the atmosphere.

*To hold the framework of the Victorian tub chair (below) together, wooden dowels are driven through the top of each leg and into the end of each curved seat-frame member. The inherent weakness of this construction can be seen in the collapsed leg (left).*

## THE RESTORER'S BRIEF

The furniture restorer deals with the frame, and an upholsterer with stuffing, covers, and buttoning.

A chesterfield with a sound frame, but which needs to be completely reupholstered, will only be worth a few hundred dollars, and because of its luxuriance of padding, it will be very expensive. With careful reupholstering, however, the sofa will be usable, and a considerable amount of value regained, especially if it is an early example which cannot reasonably be expected to have retained the original cover. Materials and stuffing need to be in keeping with the period to maintain the line and the value; some upholsterers universally apply bulky 19th-century upholstering techniques, even to earlier, flatter styles.

Weakness or breakage in the frame, arms, or legs should be professionally

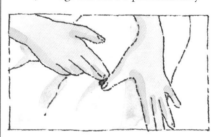

*Before replacing deep buttoning, new wadding is put in place if necessary and small holes are torn in it at each buttoning point.*

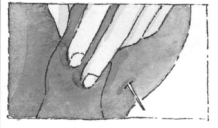

*A long mattress needle is pushed through the back of the frame and the covering fabric. Strong twine is threaded through the needle, picks up the button, and loops back through to the back of the frame.*

*Drop-end sofas can usually be adjusted for position by a simple ratchet mechanism. The mechanism (above) ceased to function as the fixing points became loose. This is caused by screws loosening in their holes as timber has shrunk, but is easily repaired.*

fixed immediately, especially if the sofa is in use. Missing castors, or metal ornamentation can be replaced from copies cast from existing originals.

Early 19th-century furniture with inlaid brass ornament, gilded metal mounts, elaborate castors, and exotic wood features is very expensive to restore. Availability of exotic woods may be restricted and hard to replace, but the restorer may have supplies in stock, or be able to simulate the original finish. Painted or gilded wood sofas that have been chipped or scratched can be carefully retouched to maintain their value.

Slot-in upholstered seats and backs should never be recovered over the old upholstery and cover, as this adds to bulk and strains the frame. If only part of the upholstery is worn, do not only have that section replaced—the result will be an unfortunate "Harlequin" effect—leave well enough alone, or go all the way.

# THE CANE CHAIR

C ANE OFTEN PROVIDED A CHEAPER, AND IN SOME WAYS A MORE VERSATILE AND PLIABLE ALTERNATIVE TO UPHOLSTERED FURNITURE.

In the 1600s, craftsmen in the West picked up a technique from Asia that was to prove a practical alternative to expensive upholstery. It was also a means of making chair seats and backs more pliable by weaving split canes at angles between the frame members. By the end of the century, cane chairmaking was established as a separate trade in the West. But the technique made inroads into the luxury market, too, for even the new, specialized trade of cabinetmaking experimented with cane, setting delicate panels into the seats of beautifully turned and carved frames of oak or walnut. Fundamentally, though, cane was a cheap, lightweight option that could be produced quickly; as a result, many pieces have inherent weaknesses.

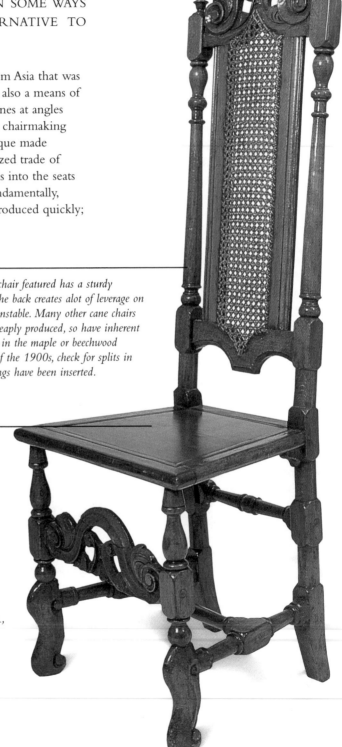

*Frame:* The caned, high-back chair featured has a sturdy construction, but the height of the back creates alot of leverage on the joints, which then become unstable. Many other cane chairs are light in weight and were cheaply produced, so have inherent weaknesses, such as woodworm in the maple or beechwood frames. In bentwood furniture of the 1900s, check for splits in the frame, especially where fixings have been inserted.

*Seat:* Where the seat is caned, and even if the caning appears to be the original 17th-century work, if a cane is fixed around the frame to cover the entry and exit holes— this indicates re-caning or repair executed in the 1800s.

BOSTON–STYLE HIGHBACK CHAIR, *late 1600–early 1700; a sturdy construction with decorative cane.*

**Front stretcher:** *The broken carving has been re-glued out of register and will have to be reassembled. Fortunately the previous repairer had not attempted to re-profile the carving to hide the mistake.*

*English canework (left) is more open-meshed, with wider strips than the Chinese cane that inspired it. Seat rails on a cane seat are prone to splitting where the forces exerted by the cane have made the wood fail between the weaving holes.*

**Joints:** *Failed joints between seat and legs may have botched repairs—look for bore holes filled with wax or epoxy, beneath which may lurk more sinister remedies in the form of large screws and nails.*

*Though the rush seat of the carved and painted chair (right) produced by the Hitchcock company, has some protection from damage by the addition of a bentwood facing, it is no defense against cats who might use it as a scratching mat!*

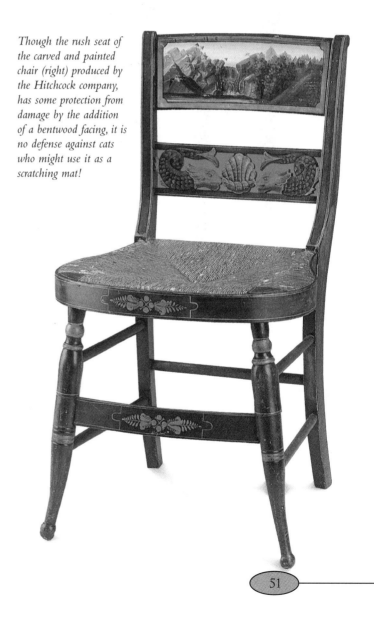

**Cresting rail:** *The carved rails on this style chair are often severely damaged when the chair falls backwards. Check for repairs or recarving.*

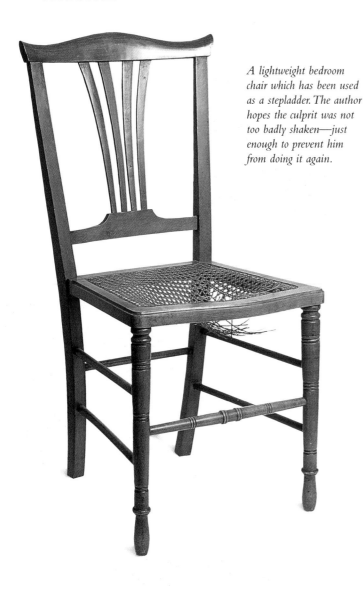

*A lightweight bedroom chair which has been used as a stepladder. The author hopes the culprit was not too badly shaken—just enough to prevent him from doing it again.*

## CANE, RATTAN, AND WICKER

Light, flexible cane began to replace upholstered chair seats and backs from the 1660s. It is made by splitting thin strips from the outer bark of rattan, a type of palm. Rattan is a vine, and in the wild supports itself by climbing stronger plants. It grows tall and thin, bends easily, and is strong and water resistant.

The Chinese work that inspired the Western trends for cane is more delicate and finely meshed than the wider-stripped, open mesh of the Europeans. The development of the drop-in and stuff-over seat, and solid wood back splats in the 1700s put cane out of fashion, but it returned in the early 1800s with the Greco-Roman revival in Europe and North America, with its lighter, Classical chair lines. Frames were often painted with Classical motifs over a yellow ground that blended well with the natural color of cane. There was a simultaneous revival in chinoiserie, and japanned and gilded frames provided a natural canvas for broad brush-strokes of cane to chair backs and seats. Wicker made use of the coarser inner fiber of the rattan vine. In the United States in 1844, Cyrus Wakefield started to develop a technique for enveloping chair frames with the rattan wrapping material that had been discarded by cargo handlers. Within ten years, the inner waste parts of the rattan vine were being used to produce furniture that could be painted or stained and was pliable to work, and cheap to produce. Decorative cane wrapping is often unraveled or missing, but usually can easily be replaced. At about the same time, a power loom was invented that wove rattan into sheets that could be fixed into channels around a bentwood frame. Splits can develop in the frame, especially where fixings have been inserted.

In the 1920s "Lloyd Loom" furniture, an invention of Marshall B. Lloyd, mimicked wickerwork. The material was created from wires covered with machine-twisted paper known as fiber art or fiber cane; it was stronger than its natural predecessors, but less water-resistant—it swells or even disintegrates with overwetting.

## GENERAL CARE

Avoid placing caned chairs in areas of your home where they might sustain damage through continual use. Small 19th-century caned chairs were destined for the bedroom where clothing was the only thing to be draped across them.

Before you attempt to clean wicker or cane furniture, make sure you have the genuine article as opposed to fiber imitations. For natural cane or rattan, use a dry paintbrush to remove as much loose dirt and dust as possible. Then dip the brush in warm soapy water to remove the remaining dirt. Rinse with clean water and leave to dry in a warm, airy place. Maintain with an occasional wipe from a damp cloth.

## THE RESTORER'S BRIEF

The highback chair frame featured on page 51 would have originally been stained to represent walnut or painted black to simulate ebony. Unfortunately, this particular chair was very poorly restored using nails, screws, and epoxy resins. The final insult was to "French polish" it to a toffee-apple shine. The chair is to be completely restored in the correct period style; this will ultimately double its value, but the cost of restoration will absorb any increase. Nevertheless, the owner will have the satisfaction of a sound, usable piece of furniture that has been restored to its original condition, even down to the vegetable based stain and period varnish.

Because of the nonporous nature of rattan, staining and coloring new work to blend with original caning can pose problems for the restorer. There is nothing worse than new strands of cane making an ugly contrast with the original, or a new seat staring up beneath a beautifully patinated back. Always ask to see examples of a weaver's work before committing yourself, and make sure that an historically correct style and type of caning is going to be used.

Hand stripping heavily overpainted cane or rattan furniture is a life sentence—there are companies that specialize in this work. Spray painting is the most effective way of refinishing. Chemically stripping fiber art or fiber cane is not recommended.

*The verandah or garden chair (right) from the early 1900s has lost much of its cane bindings, but these can be replaced at home. Find matching bindings from a craft or upholstery store, and first dampen the cane to make it pliable. Then apply PVA glue to the underside of the binding and wrap it back around the bamboo frame, holding it temporarily in place with strips of elastic or rubber.*

## CANING A CHAIR

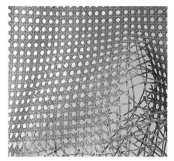

*Re-weaving a cane seat can be expensive. Most weavers price the work by the number of holes in the seat frame, so count the holes and request some quotes.*

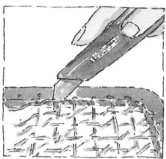

*The old cane is cut away following the inside line of the frame. The fringe of old cane that is left is pulled out with pliers, and the frame is wiped clean.*

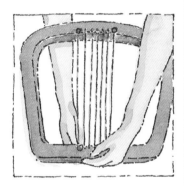

*The first and second layers of cane, at right angles to each other, are temporarily anchored with golf tees.*

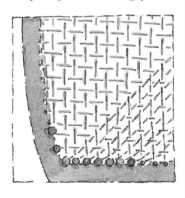

*Two diagonal layers are woven through the first two layers; the golf tees are removed, and the canes are anchored with custom-made pegs which are sunk beneath the surface.*

# A LACQUER CABINET

ORIENTAL STYLE LACQUERED DECORATION WAS APPLIED TO MOST TYPES OF EUROPEAN FURNITURE, FROM CLOCKS TO CHESTS. UNFORTUNATELY, NOT ONLY WERE THE LACQUERS THEMSELVES OFTEN A MIX OF INCOMPATIBLE SUBSTANCES, BUT ANY MOVEMENT IN THE UNDERLYING TIMBER AGGRAVATED THEIR INSTABILITY.

Introduced via Venice in the late 1500s and inspired by pieces of Chinese lacquer, the fashion for collecting lacquered objects continued intermittently in Europe until about 1770. "Japanned" furniture—the Western imitation of Chinese lacquer—was imported from England by wealthy traders living on the east coast of America, and the style was revived toward the end of the 1800s. European lacquer differs from its Oriental counterpart in both the materials and motifs used. Oriental lacquer uses the sap of the tree *Rhus vernicifera*, while in Europe almost the same transparent effect is achieved with layers of spirit-based varnishes. Both are equally fragile, but European lacquer has a greater range of ground colors.

*Surface: Look for cracks and chips in the decoration in all areas where there is likely to have been movement, such as the doors, the drawers, or the fall in a writing desk. These should be stabilized to prevent further deterioration. Although sensitivie retouching in small areas is possible, a damaged varnish cannot be retouched; it has to be completely removed and revarnished, a process which could devalue, and complete stripping and relacquering is not advised.*

*Gilded decoration: Dull areas could indicate a hasty repair with gold paint. These should be stripped and regilded with gold leaf to regain value.*

QUEEN ANNE RED LACQUER ESCRITOIRE: *Gilded chinoiserie motifs can be sensitively retouched to maintain value.*

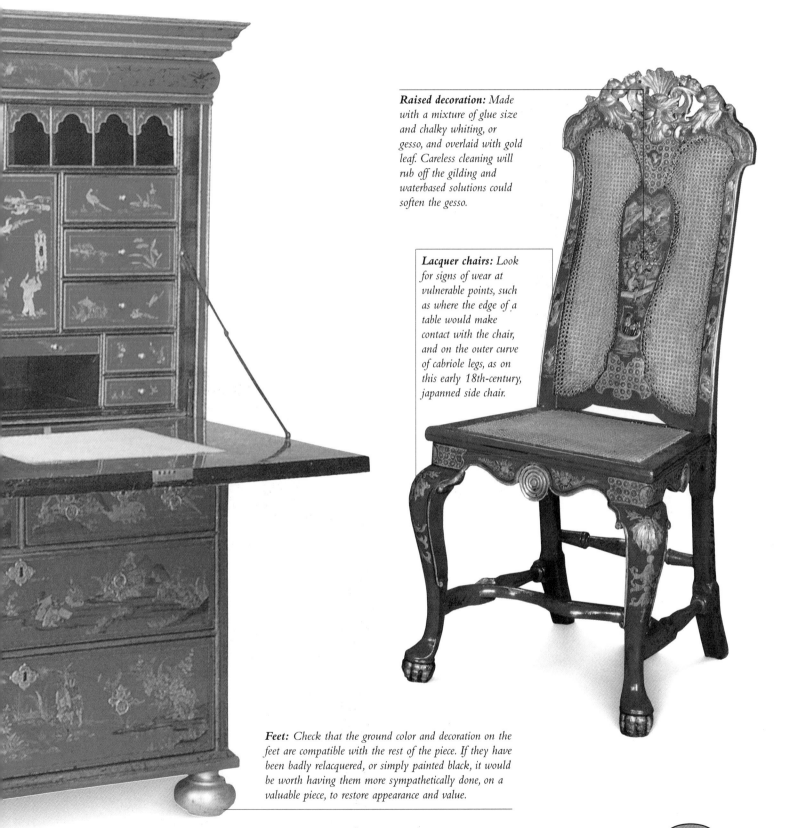

**Raised decoration:** *Made with a mixture of glue size and chalky whiting, or gesso, and overlaid with gold leaf. Careless cleaning will rub off the gilding and waterbased solutions could soften the gesso.*

**Lacquer chairs:** *Look for signs of wear at vulnerable points, such as where the edge of a table would make contact with the chair, and on the outer curve of cabriole legs, as on this early 18th-century, japanned side chair.*

**Feet:** *Check that the ground color and decoration on the feet are compatible with the rest of the piece. If they have been badly relacquered, or simply painted black, it would be worth having them more sympathetically done, on a valuable piece, to restore appearance and value.*

*One form of the 19th-century revival of lacquer imitation was oil-painted papier maché (right), which lacks structural integrity and loses its lamination under stress. Lasting repairs are virtually impossible.*

painter in France. In 1730 he was granted a patent for a method which could not be distinguished from Oriental lacquer. His family continued to decorate furniture in this way until the end of the century, and "Vernis Martin" became a term loosely used to describe many forms of lacquer produced in France in that period.

The endless demand saw Oriental-style decoration applied to most types of European furniture, regardless of style; even plain household furniture was enthusiastically decorated by amateurs. Western lacquered furniture looks like what it is: European with superimposed Oriental designs.

*Genuine lacquered bracket clocks, such as the c. 1720 example (below) are highly sought. But look closely at any chinks in the decoration; they may reveal a pearwood veneer that suggests lacquer decoration has been superimposed upon a case that was originally ebonized. If this has happened, it would reduce value, but it would probably be uneconomic to revert to the original.*

## ORIENTAL GLOSS

Many Western furnituremakers tried to imitate the expensive Chinese and Japanese lacquer imports, but climatic and material limitations made it impossible for the techniques to be copied exactly. English cabinetmakers had been attempting to copy lacquer since the 1620s, with varying degrees of success. In 1688, John Stalker and George Parker published *A Treatise of Japanning and Varnishing*, complete with naive illustrations of Indian subjects to fuel the enthusiasm for the style. They developed a technique which incorporated a black, red, yellow, green, or blue background together with simulated tortoiseshell. Decorative detail was raised with gesso (a combination of animal glue and chalk) and became known as Bantam work. The most successful imitation was developed by Guillaume Martin, a coach

*This genuine Chinese lacquer throne chair, c. 1775 (above), is unmistakenly Oriental in shape, and has more complex and fragile joints than its European counterparts.*

## GENERAL CARE

If you are buying lacquered furniture, avoid examples of well executed, gilded work patched with gold paint that lacks the reflectivity of pure gold since it is only brass dust suspended in lacquer. Reversing this will be very expensive.

On no account allow any cleaning procedure which incorporates abrasive methods or the use of water based solutions. Fragile coatings will flake if rubbed and gesso will expand or lose adhesion if impregnated with water. Any deterioration in the surface is best treated by a restorer.

## THE RESTORER'S BRIEF

The materials used to create the illusion of oriental lacquer are animal glue, chalk, resin, shellac, gold and silver leaf, vermillion and lamp black. Over time, the incompatibility of these materials together with movement from the underlying timber have combined to create some major headaches for restorers.

Some owners of lacquer pieces have been ill-advised by overzealous restorers to have all the original decoration stripped away and the whole piece redecorated using modern methods. Many fine pieces have been devalued by this treatment.

Conservation with minimal cleaning and redecoration and then only with historically correct or reversible materials should only be attempted by specialists. Many new techniques allow for existing work to be stabilized without sacrificing or masking the original decoration. Specialists in this field are held on data bases by museums and galleries in both the United Kingdom and America.

Do not attempt to clean or revive these extremely fragile surfaces yourself. Liquids can dissolve the delicate bond between paint and the underlying timber, causing irreversible damage.

*The japanned surface of an early 18th-century tallcase (longcase) clock (right) was originally painted with pigments bound in shellac. The restorer will retouch small areas of color with reversible, waterbased acrylic paints. If shellac-based pigments were replicated, they would bond too well to the original surface and make later restoration impossible.*

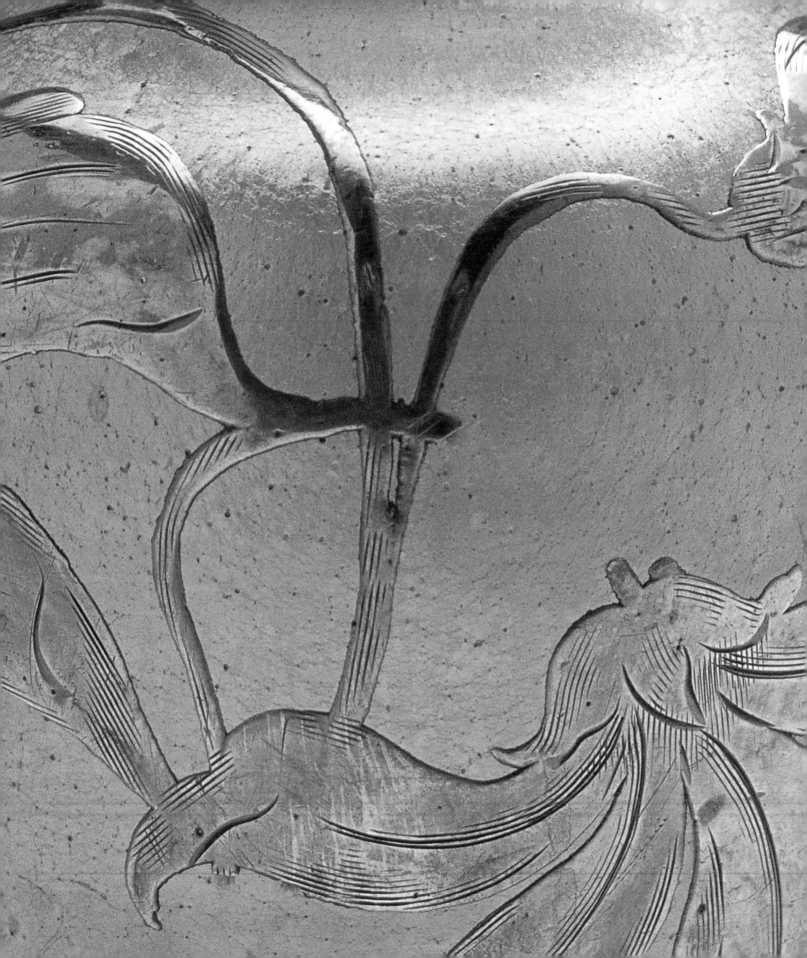

AGE AND THE ENVIRONMENT DO NOT HAVE SIGNIFICANT EFFECT ON THE HARD, GLOSSY, RESILIENT SURFACES OF CERAMICS AND GLASS, BUT THE MENTAL ATTITUDE OF THE OWNER MAY. ANY DAMAGE IS LIKELY TO BE INSTANT, SERIOUS, AND DIFFICULT TO RESTORE, AND THE MOST COMMON CAUSE OF IT IS HUMAN CARELESSNESS. THE CLEARER THE MEDIUM, THE MORE DIFFICULT IT IS TO REPAIR UNOBTRUSIVELY, AND WITH THE EXCEPTION OF ANTIQUITIES, A GLASS OR CERAMIC ITEM THAT HAS BEEN BROKEN AND THEN RESTORED WILL BE CONSIDERABLY DEVALUED, ESPECIALLY IF IT IS DECORATIVE. A FUNCTIONAL PIECE, ONCE BROKEN, CANNOT BE SENSIBLY USED AGAIN. HOWEVER, SKILLED BONDING AND FILLING WITH RESINS, AND INTRICATE RETOUCHING TECHNIQUES CAN AT LEAST RESTORE APPEARANCES, AND PRESERVE THE ESSENTIAL FORM AND ARTISTRY.

# CERAMICS & glass

# A TANG FIGURE

ALTHOUGH NOT IN THE PRICE RANGE OF MOST CERAMIC COLLECTORS, POTTERY OF THE CHINESE TANG DYNASTY (A.D. 618-907) IS IDEAL TO ILLUSTRATE THE PROBLEMS AND DIFFICULTIES THAT ARE COMMON TO UNGLAZED EARTHENWARE.

With something as ancient as a piece of Tang pottery, restoration at some stage of its life is to be expected, and assuming that this has been properly done, it will not affect the value, unlike most collectible ceramics. Indeed one has reason to be cautious of a "perfect" piece. Restoration is highly skilled and the correct materials and adhesives should be used. Incorrect or unsightly restoration affects the value of any ceramic object and will, if not irreversible, be very expensive to put right. Unglazed earthenware generally is very conducive to effective restoration, as on the matte surface it is easy to hide areas that have been built up and matched, something that is much more difficult to hide on the reflective surface of a glazed object. Most restored pieces will be suitable for display only.

*Surface: It is probable with antiquities of this date that the surface has a network of traveling cracks which are often tiny and difficult to see, but they do diminish the strength of the whole figure. It is vital that such a surface is consolidated immediately as any movement may result in damage or destruction. The surface may also be friable (crumbly) and tiny pieces may come away, resulting in loss of surface detail. The friability can be stabilized by a restorer.*

*The clay: The color of the clay can provide a clue to identity. Tang figures were fired in an airy environment— "oxidized" firing—and tend to have a chalky appearance with a pink or yellow tinge. Han funerary figures, on the other hand, were "reduction" fired, in a smoky, airless kiln and tend to be gray. Han is slightly less crumbly, though Tang is more finely potted.*

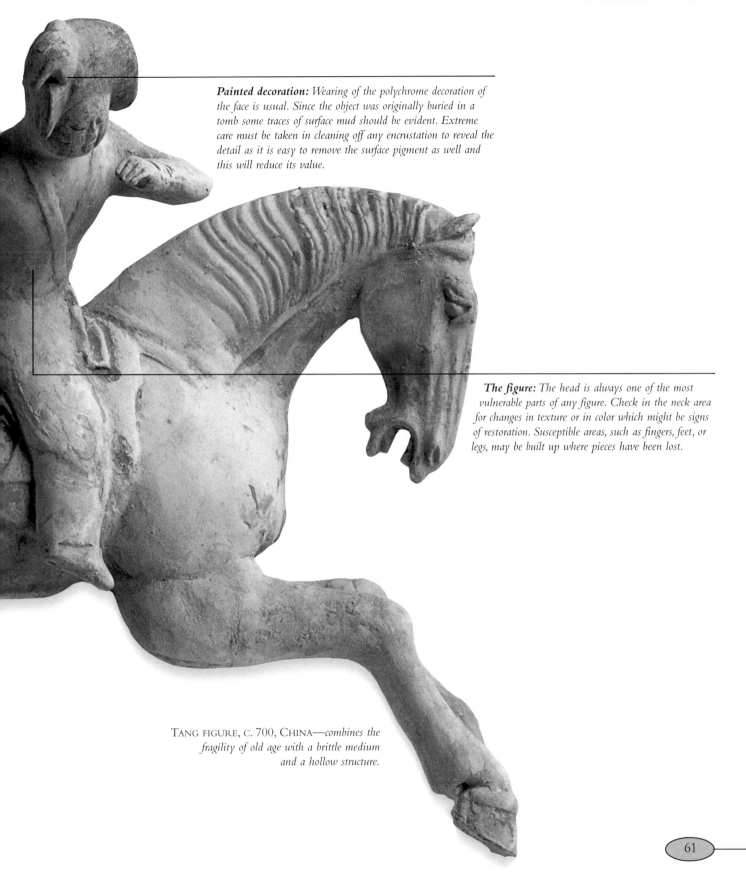

**Painted decoration:** *Wearing of the polychrome decoration of the face is usual. Since the object was originally buried in a tomb some traces of surface mud should be evident. Extreme care must be taken in cleaning off any encrustation to reveal the detail as it is easy to remove the surface pigment as well and this will reduce its value.*

**The figure:** *The head is always one of the most vulnerable parts of any figure. Check in the neck area for changes in texture or in color which might be signs of restoration. Susceptible areas, such as fingers, feet, or legs, may be built up where pieces have been lost.*

TANG FIGURE, C. 700, CHINA—*combines the fragility of old age with a brittle medium and a hollow structure.*

## UNGLAZED STYLE

The Tang figures were created as funerary objects for the tombs of the powerful and wealthy. The variety of tomb artifacts, both domestic wares and figures—soldiers, courtesans, sportsmen, musicians, and animals—reflect the lifestyle of the deceased.

Earthenware was made from fairly coarse clays compared to porcelain, and can be fired only at relatively low temperatures which are enough to harden the clay but not to fuse it into an impermeable body. Earthenware is brittle and friable. Unless it is glazed it remains porous and likely to absorb dirt, and it degrades more quickly. Glazes have therefore been used throughout history to seal and preserve the surface and, of course, for decoration.

*Earthenwares and stonewares are left unglazed for the decorative effect of their matte surface finish even in 20th-century collectibles, as in the Joan Miro plate (above).*

*The polychrome detail and friable surface on the face of this Tang courtesan must be consolidated to preserve them.*

Unglazed earthenware antiquities from many ancient cultures are collected today, from pre-Columbian, Egyptian, and Mediterranean pottery dating back to 2,000 B.C., to the tribal pottery of Africa and southeast Asia, and Indeed, the medium has continued to be used for all kinds of collectable, mainly decorative wares to the present day. All suffer from the same problems of being low-fired and unglazed with a permeable, friable surface. For practical use, earthenware had to be made water resistant by the application of a glaze, such as redware, the simple and functional low-fired earthenware of early colonial America.

Stoneware, which is generally made of a finer-textured clay than earthenware and can be fired at a higher temperature, is water resistant even if it is left unglazed, and was used for sturdy tankards and flasks in Germany from the 1500s, and in Britain from the 1600s. These robust, coarse stonewares are grayish in color, although brown stoneware fires brown at the surface because of iron content in the clay.

## GENERAL CARE

Antique pottery like the Tang pieces, that have been buried and excavated, are particularly fragile because of their low-fired, unprotected body and should be moved as little as possible. Once a piece has been restored, consolidated, and put in a stable condition, it should be kept safe from possible environmental damage, in a stable display cabinet.

Be aware of the areas where restoration has taken place and never pick the object up at these points. Wear gloves when handling unglazed earthenwar, since moisture and grease from the hands can be absorbed into and stain the surface. As it is porous, clean with a soft, light brush, never water. Stoneware is more resilient and less likely to stain.

*The Cypriot painted terracotta jug (below) is a museum piece dating from the 6th or 7th century B.C., but later examples of similar work would require the same degree of care to preserve such a delicate, unglazed paint surface.*

## THE RESTORER'S BRIEF

Tang pottery is perhaps the most extreme example of the problems besetting unglazed pottery. The material is both brittle and friable, yet the figures are often complicated and usually hollow; the resulting structure is very weak. It is usual therefore for Tang pieces to have been conserved, often immediately after excavation, and as long as this process is carried out correctly, the value is not greatly altered. Such skills are highly specialized, demanding knowledge of the correct adhesives and materials, and are vital, as bad work is almost impossible to reverse. However, if a rare and beautiful piece can gain a safer future as a result of being restored, it is probably worth going to the trouble and cost of finding the right specialist to do it correctly. On antiquities it would be worth seeking the advice of a museum conservator before taking any action.

Since the pigment is not fired onto the surface, it can easily come away with the mud. However, a restorer works with a microscope and can remove the mud while consolidating the pigment; he may be able to sympathetically enhance the detail. Retouching is done with reversible acrylic-based paint; fine surface filler or plaster is used to fill cracks (the resins used on porcelain would be too strong).

Problems can occur where stainless steel dowels have been used, for example to peg a broken leg, since the dowel is stronger than the pottery and a knock may cause a further break next time at the end of the dowel. This can be corrected by the insertion of longer dowels. The restorer should be able to spot previous restoration and "marriages" of disparate fragments of different figures, and this can be confirmed by viewing the object under ultra-violet light.

It is unusual for restoration to have such a minimal effect on value as in the case with Tang figures, but rarity and the absence of many completely unrestored examples are the main reasons for this.

Restoration of other pieces of unglazed ceramic can be very successfully carried out. The nature of the material is conducive to good restoration because repairs are easily hidden on the matte surface. However, the cost of the restoration must be taken into account in relation to the value of the object. Restoration can be carried out for sentimental reasons on items of little value, but is not recommended if the purpose of the restoration is to increase the value of the piece for sale.

*Earthenware for household ware such as these medieval jugs (left and above), was partially glazed to make it waterproof.*

# BLACK BASALT TEAPOTS

FINE-GRAINED STONEWARES, SUCH AS JOSIAH WEDGWOOD'S BLACK BASALT AND JASPERWARE, TOGETHER WITH BISCUIT PORCELAIN AND PARIAN WARE, WERE LEFT UNGLAZED FOR DECORATIVE EFFECT, AND USED AS ELEGANT YET AFFORDABLE ORNAMENTAL PIECES. HOWEVER, WITHOUT A GLAZE TO PROTECT THEM, THEY ARE EASILY STAINED, A PROBLEM WHICH CAN SERIOUSLY UNDERMINE VALUE.

**Body:** *Look for chips; their level of visibility determines their effect on value: in Jasperware, a chip reveals whether the piece has been dipped to provide surface color, or whether the body itself is colored. Chips are much more visible on dipped ware. The most vulnerable parts of the body are those which are usually made separately and then applied, such as the handle, the knop, and the spout.*

**Decoration:** *Enamel decoration (above) stands slightly off the surface. A degree of wear is acceptable, although chipped colors can be filled and matched quite successfully. Sprigged decoration typical of much Wedgwood and Parian ware consists of applied molded motifs which detach easily, and because they are so characteristic of the style, this would diminish the piece's value, but they can be filled with resins.*

**Spout:** *Usually of the same material as the body; the metallic end of this example may be original for additional strength at a vulnerable point, or may conceal later damage.*

**Surface:** *Fine, unglazed stonewares are easily stained, which will devalue. If water has been absorbed, this may weaken the body, but both problems can be restored to a certain extent. The feel of the surface can help you to identify the material. Mass-produced Jasperware after the 1800s tends to be a little coarser than the early pieces. Parian is very smooth and was designed to imitate marble. Biscuit porcelain is very hard and dry, and has an eggshell-like texture to the touch.*

BLACK BASALT TEAPOTS, C. 1870—*victims of unskilled restoration: excessive glue had to be removed before any further work was done.*

Josiah Wedgwood's "black basaltes" or basalt, a fine stoneware stained with manganese oxide, developed around 1768, was hard enough to be cut and polished on a lathe. In 1774, Wedgwood discovered that the addition of barium sulfate to clay originating from South Carolina produced a particularly fine, hard, white body. The result was Jasperware, a white stoneware that could be thinly potted and easily colored by the addition of metal oxides. It could also hold crisp detail and was ideally suited to the hallmark bas-relief decoration of Classical motifs and figures. The new improved stoneware could be fired at a much higher temperature than earthenware so that it is sometimes almost vitrified, producing a body similar to biscuit (fired but unglazed) porcelain.

By the 1780s, Wedgwood had instituted a cost-cutting technique for some of his wares which involved dipping the pieces to give surface color rather than incorporating color within the body. On early pieces of Jasperware the decorative moldings were fired directly onto the body, but this caused staining and they were later fixed with a layer of slip (liquid clay) before firing. Only an expert would be able to tell the difference but the earlier method is more likely to stay in place.

From 1753, the French porcelain factory at Sèvres produced statuettes in biscuit (fired but unglazed) porcelain and other factories throughout Europe and the United States followed suit. Porcelain firing is at a higher temperature than that of stonewares, with the result that the white brittle body is harder, less porous, and less liable to chip.

Parian is a white, unglazed porcelain that aimed to capture the smoothness of marble. It

*The maintenance of a pristine white finish to the Sèvres biscuit softpaste porcelain depiction of Leda and the Swan, c.1765 (right) is all important to the ardent collector.*

*The interior of the Jasperware jug (below left) is glazed so that it can hold liquid. The characteristic relief decoration can be built up with resins if lost or chipped.*

was first produced at the British factories Copeland and Minton in the mid 1800s, and used mainly to produce busts and statuettes (see pp.74, 202).

## GENERAL CARE

Store or display unglazed fine stonewares and porcelain in a stable unit. Keep any pieces with applied decoration out of range of direct heat, such as away from a fire, as this could cause the slip used to hold the decoration in place to expand and loosen. Wear gloves when handling any unglazed ceramic, and dust clean with a soft brush only, never water, since the body is porous. When packing, use acid-free tissue—never newspaper—around the piece to protect from staining.

## THE RESTORER'S BRIEF

Chips, cracks, and staining can all greatly reduce value, especially if they are obvious. But the fine-grained, matte surface of unglazed stoneware and porcelain is easier to repair than a glazed surface. It is worth having loose pieces secured invisibly, and as the motifs are usually repeated, missing sections can be

replaced by taking a mold from another section. Alternatively they can be built up using resins. Staining is a particular problem since the bodies are porous and many are light in color. Once a liquid has penetrated, the surface may become friable (crumbly) and should be stabilized.

Ornamental pieces require top-quality restoration, but if repair is so drastic that it is going to obviously alter the

appearance of the piece, it may be better left alone.

If it is expertly restored, and as much as possible of the original secured with the appropriate materials, a piece does regain some of its former value. Make it clear that if any surface areas are retouched when trying to hide a seam, for example, no original areas of decoration are overpainted unnecessarily.

# AN IRONSTONE DINNER SET

D O NOT BE COMPLETELY FOOLED BY TOUGH-SOUNDING NAMES SUCH AS IRONSTONE AND WHITE GRANITE. THESE ARE TOUGHER MATERIALS THAN EARLIER EARTHENWARES, BUT STILL SHARE THE FUNDAMENTAL WEAKNESSES OF ANY POROUS BODY COVERED BY A GLAZE.

Strong household ceramics such as "ironstone" were introduced in 1813 by Charles James Mason in England, and predominantly used for dinner and tea sets. Similar stonewares were used by various American makers between 1860 and 1900, and at other factories in Staffordshire, England. Because they are functional rather than decorative, many pieces surviving today bear the signs of having been subjected to heat (crazing of the glaze), eaten from (worn and scratched), and washed (chipped, and worn decoration).

Mason's "Patent Ironstone China," and its competitors have become very collectible, especially earlier examples, and complete dinner sets in mint condition command a premium, so it is worth thinking twice before you use them.

**Ladles:** *Frequently become separated and lost. Tureens and gravy boats with original ladles are particularly prized. Because of their slender form, ladles tend to break, or chip easily when knocked. Look for stains and signs of wear in the bowl of the ladle.*

**Inner surfaces:** *Look for cracks and lines where two pieces may have been joined and oversprayed to cover a repair (overspraying yellows with time).*

**Body:** *An ironstone body is opaque. Check for cracks and chipping, although these can be restored for display purposes, if not for use. Run your fingertips over the surface; changes in surface texture may indicate repair.*

**Decoration:** *Blue and black decoration was applied under the glaze, and so had some protection from wear, but any overglaze painting—which feels slightly raised from the surface—is more vulnerable. Previous restoration can be identified by slight changes in color and texture. Run a pin lightly over the surface to check for a sudden change in texture, or tap your teeth against a suspect spot. True glaze produces a sharp, clear sound, compared with a slightly dulled sound on the unfired, softer paints of a restored area.*

**Staining:** *Check for damp-looking stains near cracks. Water or grease can penetrate cracks in the glaze and weaken the body. Stains can be very successfully removed by a restorer, but do recur if the piece is used again.*

**Knops:** *Do not use to pick up the weight of a lid or cover without being sure that it has had no previous restoration, and always support the lid from below with your other hand.*

**Glaze:** *Often has a blue-gray tinge. Look closely to see if the surface is uneven—a sign of poor quality—or cracked. The condition of the glaze affects the value of the piece, even though it does not necessarily diminish the underlying strength or usability, unless it reflects a flaw in the actual body. Breaks or cracks in the glaze mean the piece has lost its impermeability, and is likely to absorb stains if used.*

**Handles:** *Never pick up a piece by its handles—they are frequently weakened by the stress of lifting a heavy vessel—and are particularly unreliable if they have been restored, which many of them have.*

IRONSTONE CHINA DINNER SERVICE, c. 1910, with underglaze blue ground and easily worn, overglaze gilding.

## SETTING THE SEAL ON EARTHENWARE

Strong "stone chinas" are earthenwares reinforced with ingredients such as pounded iron slag and flint, and were indeed stronger than the simple earthenwares which preceded them. These earlier pieces could only be fired to a temperature that was high enough to harden the basic material, but not to fuse it together to make it nonporous. Ironstone china could be fired to a higher temperature, but one that was still not high enough to completely eliminate the tiny air spaces that make a ceramic body porous. Like all glazed earthenwares, ironstone was given a firing at a slightly lower temperature to fuse the glaze onto the surface and so make the clay body waterproof. An allover glaze renders earthenware practicable for household items, especially those which need to be cleaned in water. But any chink in this glassy armor breaks its impervious seal, and exposes the porous body beneath, which absorbs not only water but grease and other stains, all of which can travel beneath the surface and

*The brown stain in this gravy boat (above) could possibly be drawn out by a restorer soaking it in deionized water, using a poultice of pulp or Fuller's earth, or by bleaching, but there is no guarantee.*

weaken the body as a whole. Glazes are also used decoratively, usually to add color. Initially, they were sprinkled on by hand in dust form (which then liquified during firing to run over the body), and later, the clay bodies were dipped into the glaze. There are many different types of glaze which give different finishes. Salt glazes used from medieval times

on household pottery, to clear lead glazes—that tend to absorb bright colors—and the opaque tin glazes that formed a white background for decoration on maiolica, faience, and Delft. Tin glazes tend to be brittle, and splinter and chip easily at the edges.

Ironstone was often decorated with fanciful Oriental patterns, which were printed in outline under the glaze in blue and then the colors, such as the reds, which could not withstand firing temperatures, were painted in by hand over the glaze. These are consequently more vulnerable: overglaze colors on any ceramics present a broader palette of color, but are more likely to be worn away with use and washing. Gold decoration is the most delicate of all.

## GENERAL CARE

If you want to use your glazed earthenware, keep it for special occasions, treat it with great care, and alternate the pieces you use to ensure even wear over the whole of the service. If any item is chipped or cracked, the glaze is crazed, or it has been previously restored, do not use it at all. Do not

*The decoration (below) was mercury gilded, a process not used today; retouching would be watergilded or using bronze or mica pigments which are not as hardwearing, and the match would not be as exact.*

immerse it in water, and never put any glazed earthenware in a dishwasher. It is important to establish whether the decoration is underglaze or overglaze, so that you can judge how resistant the decoration is likely to be. If in doubt, seek an expert opinion.

If plates are displayed in a cabinet, make sure the furniture is stable, that there is a rack to prevent the plates from sliding forward, and leave a gap between each piece. Keep restored pieces out of direct sunlight or in complete darkness, as both situations hasten the yellowing of the resin. Stack no more than four plates at a time, since more than that could put breaking-point pressure on the lowest plate, and interleave the plates with a protective cloth or paper. To clean damaged, restored, or decorative pieces, lightly dust them with a soft brush, or for more persistent marks, use a cotton swab (bud) dampened with saliva.

Decorative pieces were generally produced in large quantities, so you may find replacement items in better condition. Keep your eye open at markets and in antique shops for odd pieces which may fill gaps in your own service.

## GLAZED EARTHENWARE FIGURES

*Although made of glazed earthenware, Staffordshire figures do not suffer the same problems of heavy use as household china. But because they were mass-produced, readily available, and not regarded as precious items, they were handled a great deal. They are hollow, molded figures and many of the breaks on pieces that survive today are almost as old as the figures themselves. The figures are usually painted with overglaze gilding and enamel colors which are often badly worn by now. This example's head and right arm had been knocked off, and the horse's leg was missing. By the time the restorer had replaced the head and arm, and remodeled a new leg in plaster, nearly 10 times the value of the restored piece had been spent on piecing it together. But then it was completely worthless beforehand, even for display only.*

## THE RESTORER'S BRIEF

As pottery is generally less expensive than porcelain, the cost of restoration tends to balance the value of the object. Household pieces with minor scratches or staining are often not worth restoring. A badly stained piece can have an facelift, using a poultice—which is the restorer's equivalent of a face pack and draws the stain out—or bleach. However, neither method is guaranteed, and the item would only be improved for display purposes rather than use. Cracks and chips will only be rendered impermeable once again if the piece is refired with a new glaze, but this is not generally recommended, as it destroy the integrity of a collectors' item and reduces value.

*Iron rivets (above) can be a valuable indication of authenticity and age, and should not be removed unless they are causing stress; then drill holes can be filled and the area restored.*

# AN ENAMELED PORCELAIN COFFEE SET

A COFFEE SET MADE IN JAPAN FOR EXPORT TO THE WEST IS A 20TH-CENTURY COLLECTIBLE RATHER THAN AN ANTIQUE, BUT PROVIDES A USEFUL IF FLAMBOYANT EXAMPLE OF ENAMELED AND GILDED PORCELAIN, AND OF QUASI-FUNCTIONAL WARE WHICH ALSO HAS AN IMPORTANT DECORATIVE ROLE TO PLAY.

From the late 1800s to the first half of the 20th century, tea and coffee sets like this were mass-produced in China and Japan in a Western style specifically for the Western market. Some, such as Satsuma and Kutani, borrowed the names from earlier centuries (1600s), of far superior, finely crafted, and precious wares. Nevertheless, the modern versions have become collectibles in their own right, and are still relatively easy to find. Despite being apparently functional, many were designed to be purely ornamental. Quality and materials vary, however (Satsuma, for example, is glazed earthenware, and Kutani is always porcelain). As with any ceramic, it is worth identifying your patient and its condition, before making a diagnosis as to care and restoration, and deciding whether the items should be used or not.

The Japanese set illustrated is made in a fine, translucent, but intrinsically tough porcelain, although its thinness gives it a certain fragility. It is decorated in bright enamels and gilding applied over the glaze. A subsequent firing then fixes the colors and offers sufficient protection for judicious use as long as individual items are not cracked.

*Interior:* Check for staining, which can usually be removed. The tough, white glazed interior of the jug in this set was fine, but the softer, gilded interior of some of the cups was badly scratched; it had obviously been scoured to remove obstinate stains. This kind of damage can be very difficult to restore and reduces the value.

*Rims:* The most likely place for minor chips and cracks, but unless these are disfiguring, they are better left than restored, to maintain maximum possible value. Chipping generally has a greater effect on value and desirability of the service as a whole than fading of decoration. Serious chips can be invisibly mended or retouched, increasing value to some extent in comparison to the damaged state.

**Decoration:** *Gradual wear and fading is to be expected, especially in useful ware. Establish how the decoration has been applied (see panel p. 73); this has a bearing on care. Loss of value depends on the degree of fading and abrasion: a print is very difficult for the restorer to retouch, but enamel decoration is easier. Underglaze enamel colors are relatively tough, especially on Satsuma ware. Transfer-printed designs may rub off if they are on top of the glaze, but if overglazed are more resistant. Sets with overglaze decoration or metallic finishes (which scratch easily) should be used sparingly, if at all. Missing areas of decoration can be retouched if appearance is seriously affected.*

**Appendages:** *Spouts and finials are prime spots for breakage and previous restoration; they stand proud of the body and are also likely to have been made separately. The greatest stress point is near the join, where the ceramic is narrowest.*

**Handles:** *The narrowness of the ceramic, and the fact that the handle is made separately from the main body making the join a common breaking point. Judge whether the handle looks as though it is designed to hold the piece when full of liquid, or whether it is simply a decorative extra. Cracks in the handle itself or in the body near the joins should be treated, and the piece not used. Handles are high profile, and unsightly chips on them affect value.*

**Surface:** *Check carefully when buying, for large areas of surface damage are expensive to repair and the cost may outweigh the value of the piece.*

**The body:** *Strike the body lightly; porcelain should resonate. If there is a dullness to the sound, the piece could be cracked. To establish whether the body is porcelain or pottery, hold a piece up to the light; porcelain is usually translucent. Look inside to check for traveling cracks which need to be consolidated immediately to prevent further deterioration.*

**The base:** *Look for unglazed areas on the base of footrims; it may help identify the medium: porcelain has a smooth, hard finish that is difficult to scratch. Check also for any marks which might aid identification—these should be preserved, so take care they do not become worn away by washing and wear.*

PORCELAIN COFFEE SERVICE, JAPAN, 1940s
*Useful, decorative, and collectible, but not valuable enough to justify costly restoration on purely economic or investment grounds.*

# THE QUEST FOR PORCELAIN

Porcelain is made from fine white clay (kaolin) and other raw materials such as ground feldspar (also known as china stone or petuntse), which can be fired to a higher temperature than earthenware or stoneware. This means that the minute particles of clay fuse together to form a hard, vitreous body distinguished by its translucency. Porcelain is compact, almost completely impermeable, intrinsically tougher than pottery, and can also be crafted into more delicate forms, which in turn gives it a greater degree of fragility.

The Chinese were making porcelain some 800 years before the technique was first mastered in the West at the Meissen factory in Germany in 1710. The breakthrough was crucial since tea, coffee, and chocolate were fashionable drinks for smart society from the late 1600s, and had to be served in vessels that could hold very hot water without cracking.

Slightly coarser softpaste porcelain had been known in the West since the 1500s, but it was not widely used until the 1700s. It was not used for teawares; fashionable society would have used imported Chinese porcelain.

Eggshell porcelain, made by the Chinese from the Ming Dynasty (1368-1644) onward, and in the late 1800s and early

*Softpaste porcelain, like this basket from Bonnin and Morris, Philadelphia, c. 1769-72 (above), imitated the Chinese porcelain imported by the Americans from the 1780s, but was not as tough and water-resistant.*

1900 by the Japanese, at Beleek and Minton in Britain, and in East Liverpool, Trenton, and Baltimore in the United States, is particularly delicate. Portraits are sometimes incorporated in the base of teacups which are only visible when the piece is held to the light. Bone china, a white porcelain modified by the addition of bone ash to the paste, was developed at the Bow factory in London around 1747 and later taken up by Spode in the 1790s along with other factories; it was not commonly produced in Europe and America. The bone ash acts as a flux promoting the fusion of the ingredients.

Bone china appears slightly softer and creamier and is less crisp than hardpaste porcelain; when it chips it is possible to feel the slightly denser texture of the body.

## Pattern, style, and shape

The date of a piece can provide a clue to material and consequently its use, care, and the advisability of restoration. Much domestic china produced in the West during the 1800s is unmarked because in the highly competitive china market, the retailer did not want his source revealed to the buyer. Much can be gleaned from pattern, style, and shape, but it is worth seeking expert advice to establish identity, date, and value. As an example, Satsuma wares of the late 1800s tend to be of a higher quality (though there are exceptions) as they were more finely potted, had better quality decoration, and were more delicate than those produced later, when the emphasis

*The porcelain produced by the Philadelphia company of William Ellis Tucker (below) was known for its bright floral patterns and lavish gilding.*

was on mass-production in which the refinement is lost, the relief decoration exaggerated, and the potting is sometimes thicker. The paintwork tends to wear.

Today, people generally do not require the huge sets often seen in the 1800s, but a setting for six or eight is to be expected and anything less than this is undesirable unless it is particularly special. The values of sets are dramatically affected by missing pieces. Look out in antique shops, auctions or markets for replacements.

## GENERAL CARE

A restored item should not be used; the resins used in restoration are toxic, and the piece is weaker. If restoration on some pieces in a set has been carried out, and this is not immediately obvious, mark them to ensure you do not use them by mistake. Valuable antique sets, or those clearly made for decorative purposes only, should not be used at all. Use items in rotation so that wear is even throughout the whole set. Do not put boiling water directly into fine china or porcelain as it may expand rapidly and crack; in the 1700s it was found that if cold milk was put in first it prevented the porcelain cracking, which how the custom of drinking milk with tea began.

Never wash decorated china in a dishwasher, only by hand in warm water with mild detergent. If a piece is cracked or chipped keep it away from any liquid.

## IDENTIFYING DECORATION

*Establishing how decoration has been applied gives an indication of its durability.*

*Hold the piece to the light; if a highlight falls over the pattern onto a glaze that has been applied over it, the decoration is underglaze, applied after the initial firing, but before a final glaze. The decoration seems to merge into the body, and sometimes has slightly fuzzy edges. A design applied after the final glaze can be felt by running your fingertips over it. Enamel colors are used on ceramics or glass and are made from powdered glass and metal oxides and suspended in an oily medium. When the piece is fired, the oil burns away, leaving the enamel colors fused on the surface. On underglaze firing, the colors, which contain metal oxides, are restricted to pigments (cobalt blue, iron red, manganese purple, copper green or red, and chromium yellow) which can withstand the high firing temperatures required to fuse the glaze to the surface. With overglaze decoration, a greater range of colors is possible as colors with different levels of resistance to heat can be applied and fired individually at different temperatures to fuse them to the surface, but it is more likely to wear and fade.*

## THE RESTORER'S BRIEF

Always go to an expert to mend broken or cracked porcelain. Using super-strength modern glue could cause irreversible damage and staining. The restorer has to remove even the tiniest speck of glue, identifiable only under a microscope, to ensure that a join is true, and this process can waste a lot of time and your money.

A restorer can clean a piece, bond broken pieces, consolidate cracks, fill and remodel missing areas, remove stains, and take apart and redo old or clumsy previous restoration. You can discuss with the restorer whether you want the repair to be invisible (overspraying) or not (color fills),

but be aware of the ethics involved in completely concealing a repair, and ask how much of the original is going to be lost. Many restorers now feel that a break should be repaired and camouflaged (so that it would be unoticeable at a distance but visible if closely inspected) rather than invisible. You may be able to live with small areas of damage, especially if it is to only one or two pieces.

Eggshell porcelain has the same properties as very thin glass, and it is very difficult and expensive to restore.

*A ceramics restorer has to try and match pigments and glazes exactly to restore a piece in keeping with the original.*

# FINE CERAMIC FIGURES

ECORATIVE PORCELAIN AND FINE CERAMIC FIGURES ARE FOR DISPLAY, RARELY FOR PRACTICAL USE—WITH THE POSSIBLE EXCEPTION OF WATCHSTANDS—SO PRISTINE APPEARANCE IS OF PARAMOUNT IMPORTANCE, AND ANY DAMAGE OR RESTORATION WILL REDUCE VALUE.

**Facial features:** *Fine features are a mark of quality and of origin, but because they are proud of the surface are likely to chip. Check for signs of touching in where the features may have been enhanced, in particular variations in color, quality, and texture. Look for areas of paint which are on the surface if the rest of the decoration is under the glaze.*

EARLY 20TH-CENTURY CERAMIC FIGURE—*with a poorly retouched neck.*

**Hands and feet:** *Poorly restored hands which look out of proportion, the wrong color, or badly misshapen can ruin the whole appearance of a figure and increase the cost of restoration as the old repairs will have to be undone and cleaned. Always keep broken pieces; it is better to use what is salvageable than to model replacements in resin or plaster. To test for restored parts, knock your teeth against the suspect area very lightly; it should feel hard and crisp; if restored, slightly sticky.*

**Base:** *Can be glazed or unglazed depending on factory tradition. Light scratches and general dirt are acceptable signs of wear and age. Look for signs of previous restoration in the hollow interior of the figure-any signs of respraying are suspicious. A chip at the back of the base is not a problem as it does not affect the appearance of the piece.*

*The base is also where you may find a factory mark, but even this may have been tampered with. Telltale signs are patches which appear to have been scratched away, or a mark that has been added over the glaze. Some pieces were deliberately faked such as the Chelsea pieces produced by Edmé Samson in the mid 1800s; an expert would certainly be able to tell.*

**Head and neck:** *Particularly prone to being knocked off, and even if replaced by skillful restoration, this would have a major effect on value. But a head sensitively replaced is preferable to no head at all! A glued crack or join may have been disguised by overpainting or spraying with resin; look and feel for a change in color (resin yellows with age), texture, or temperature—resin is warmer than porcelain.*

LATE 18TH-CENTURY MEISSEN FIGURE of St. Theresa of Avalon, whose fingers (above left) needed some attention.

Although decorative figures and groups have been made from earthenwares, the finest examples are of porcelain. Porcelain figures are usually hollow and made of the finest china clays. This medium, combined with an extremely high firing temperature, creates a hard, brittle object that is fragile and easily shattered. The models for most figures were made by a master modeler. Molds were then taken of the model, sometimes in sections, and the separate pieces bonded and fired; but figures rarely break at these joins.

Porcelain was developed in China over 1,000 years ago but it was mainly for domestic ware. The European tradition of decorative porcelain figures dates only from the early 1700s. The Meissen factory, near Dresden in southern Germany pioneered the production of the first hardpaste porcelain outside the Orient in 1710. By the end of the 1700s, fine quality figure production had spread throughout Europe. English factories, unable to make hardpaste porcelain until the discovery of a fine china clay and china stone in the 1760s, continued to use the slightly offwhite, coarser softpaste porcelain which they had been produced in Europe ince the 1500s. This relied on adding materials such as ground glass, bones, or flint to the clay to encourage it to fuse, or vitrify, into a hard, impermeable paste. It could not be fired at as high a temperature as hardpaste porcelain and could not be as finely modeled; it is equally fragile.

In the 1800s, mass-production techniques led to an increase in quantity of figures produced, and in many cases, quality of detail and decoration decreased. However, factories such as Meissen and Worcester continued to produce handmade figures of the finest quality.

*Use a soft-bristled cosmetic or lens brush to dust fine ceramic figures; dust cloths could catch on the details.*

## GENERAL CARE

Porcelain figures must be displayed in a secure place; the most common causes of damage are from children, cats, and careless cleaners. When handling a figure alwayfis hold it from the base, never from by fragile extremity. Do not reach round other items to pick up an object; move them out the way first. Roll up loose sleeves and guard against knocking the figure on the shelf above.

Although porcelain is water resistant, the decoration may not be, and you should only use water if the decoration is under the glaze. Use a cotton swab (bud) dampened in a very mild, warm, soap solution to treat isolated areas. These objects are too fragile to risk immersing in a wash bowl.

## THE RESTORER'S BRIEF

Firing cracks, which occur most frequently at joins during firing, look dark and are covered with glaze; it is not necessary to have them repaired. Similarly, a chip incurred during manufacture may have been colored and glazed over at the time and such flaws are part of the history of the piece and should not be changed. If damage spoils the whole appearance, skilled restoration is worth considering, but it will be expensive.

Ask a restorer to undo a poorly executed previous repair. This will restore its aesthetic appearance and enhance value, though never to the level of a perfect piece.

Missing parts can be made up in colored resins and attached, though they eventually yellow with age, a process which is accelerated if the object is left in sunlight, or totally in the dark, or in an overlit and hot display cabinet.

*Building up a finger tip (left) with epoxy putty, which matches the strength of porcelain, holds its shape, and can be finely carved.*

# THE DECANTER

**D**ECANTERS WERE INITIALLY A PURELY PRACTICAL MEANS OF SERVING CASKED WINE AT THE TABLE, BUT THEY CAME TO FULFILL AN EVER MORE DECORATIVE ROLE, AND THE DECISION TO RESTORE IS OFTEN A MATTER OF MAINTAINING APPEARANCES.

Serving wine from expensive glass bottles or decanters was generally the preserve of the upper classes during the 1700s, but in the following century, the increasing prosperity of the expanding middle class combined with technological advances in glassmaking to bring about a boom in decanter production. Gradually the custom of decanting fortified wines such as vintage or crusted port, as well as Madeira and sherry, became established, and later still, toward the end of the century, spirit decanters were introduced.

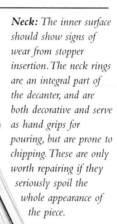

*Neck:* The inner surface should show signs of wear from stopper insertion. The neck rings are an integral part of the decanter, and are both decorative and serve as hand grips for pouring, but are prone to chipping. These are only worth repairing if they seriously spoil the whole appearance of the piece.

*Body:* Deep cut glass surfaces are a sign of quality; hold the decanter from the base to feel the weight: cut glass is generally heavier than pressmolded glass. The thicker the glass body is, the stronger it is; any relief decoration is susceptible to being chipped. Neglected pieces may have dirt or mineral deposits in the crevices, which, if obstinate, are worth having cleaned professionally.

*Interior:* Stains from liquids, including water, that have been left inside for too long are inaccessible and difficult to dislodge. If home tactics do not work (such as using a bottle brush and a denture-cleaning substance), it is worth having them cleaned professionally.

*Base:* Small scratches due to normal wear are perfectly acceptable. More serious are internal cracks that have occurred when the decanter has been put down too forcefully. Pontil marks indicate a handblown decanter; some are sharp and uneven; others are rubbed to an even, generally circular, finish. Pontils are not necessarily a guide to quality, simply to the tradition of the glassblower. Use an eyeglass to check for a signature or factory mark on pieces of the second half of the 1800s and later.

BLOWN GLASS DECANTER, EARLY 1800S, *after a major cleaning operation.*

**Stopper** *If stoppers are broken, lost, or separated from their host decanters, the piece as a whole will be significantly devalued. Many were hand-ground to fit each decanter neck and it is difficult to find a matching alternative to fit, though a specialist glassmaker could make a new one. An old stopper could be found in an antique shop or market and made to fit either by grinding or building up with resin. Scratches and wear at the point where stopper and decanter neck meet are generally a good sign of fit and use, and though chips are less desirable, they are rarely worth repair.*

*The set of c. 1800 decanter bottles (above) have a brass-bound, mahogany carrying case, but should still be wrapped in tissue and any open space padded out, for safe transportation.*

## CLASSIC DECANTER SHAPES

*The strength of any particular decanter design depends on the thickness of the glass. Ship's decanter's are particularly stable and often have a thicker base than other shapes, and claret jug handles can be very fragile.*

claret jug

shaft and globe

shouldered

tapered

club

cruciform

ship's

*The painted and gilt decoration on the 19th-century blown glass bottle (above) is extremely delicate and shows some wear; it should never be immersed in water. A chip at the top has been filled with resins.*

## THE QUEST FOR STRONGER GLASS

The process of gently "canting" wine from its original bottle to another container became an essential part of serving red wine, perhaps to reduce sediment reason, from the early 1700s. Early decanters, really still only bottles, were of soda glass, a slightly cloudy glass that was easily worked, though it is less brilliant than lead glass and also less thick and strong. They were purely functional since soda glass is not suitable for cut or engraved decoration and were stopped with corks if any wine was left unfinished. They are rarely seen.

In the 1670s, English glassmaker George Ravenscroft developed a clear flint glass, otherwise known as lead glass, which was used for wide-mouthed bottles for serving at the table. Lead glass was strong and brilliant; it could not be blown thin, and so it provided a thick strong body which, some fifty years later, proved ideal for cutting since it was an excellent refracter of light. These early decanters tend to be heavy to hold, but they were also tough and could be cut, etched, engraved, or enameled, and so decanters began to fulfill a decorative role.

High-quality engraving, etching, and enameling increase a decanter's worth, and if worn or damaged will reduce its value. Hand-cut glass is more desirable than machine-cut, but it is often difficult to tell the difference. A hand-cut surface tends to feel sharper to the touch. Enamel or gilt decoration can be retouched, but little can be done to restore scratched engraving or a chipped body.

All decanters up to and throughout the 1700s were handblown by skilled artisans and are thinner and therefore more fragile than the molded decanters of the 1800s. The introduction of pressmolded glass in America during the 1820s paved the way for the mass production of cut-glass lookalikes. Sometimes the products, created by pressing the hot soft glass into iron molds, were hand finished by glass cutters to give a finer effect, but they can be identified by the seam running from top to bottom where the two halves have been joined. Pressmolded glass marked a decrease in the quality of the glassware and its decoration, which was usually simply cut, however, it was often stronger and more robust. Fine hand-blown cut glass was still produced.

The engraved signatures and factory marks introduced in

the second half of the 19th century are useful in establishing original and quality, even for pressmold factories, and provide one good reason for not having scratches rubbed out.

## GENERAL CARE

Hold a decanter around the neck and support the base. Remove the stopper vertically from the neck. Never apply force but if it is stuck, try smearing olive oil around the join between stopper and bottle. Leave it for about an hour to let the oil seep into the neck, then submerge the decanter in hot water (though not if it has any gilded or painted decoration, which should never be washed) to expand the body. Then remove the stopper vertically without twisting.

Do not leave alcohol in a decanter for any length of time: if it starts to reduce, it leaves an unsightly and inaccessible stain. Clean with warm soapy water but bear in mind that it will be slippery. Use a medium-textured, long-handled bottle brush for the inside. Never try to insert a cloth; you may never get it out again. A weak solution of scale remover or denture cleaner can be used to soak off interior stains.

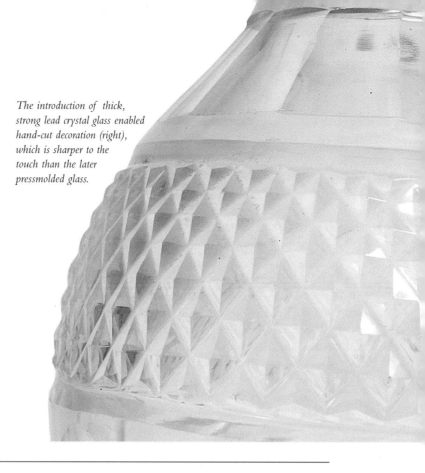

*The introduction of thick, strong lead crystal glass enabled hand-cut decoration (right), which is sharper to the touch than the later pressmolded glass.*

## THE RESTORER'S BRIEF

A decanter with a large crack, chip, or hole is not only impossible to use but worthless and beyond repair. Small chips to stopper, neck, or cut or applied decoration are not important. Repair to the interior, which is in contact with liquid if the decanter is to be used, should be avoided, as the resins used by the restorer are worn down by alcohol and restoration will fail. A restorer can remove bad staining on most types of glass, unless it has actually eaten into the glass.

The story of the decanter on page 76 encapsulates the most common decanter problems. The stopper had snapped off, leaving the stem firmly lodged in the neck. The alcoholic contents had reduced to leave a dark stain. Commitment to each stage of restoration came only after the previous stage had been successful. First the stopper was released by careful soaking in an ultrasonic tank in which some form of detergent and water is submitted to high-frequency sound waves. It was not bonded until it was certain that the staining could be removed.

The money spent on the restoration would not be reflected in the sale price (the piece in good condition would fetch $200-300 (£125-200), but before restoration it was unattractive and valueless.

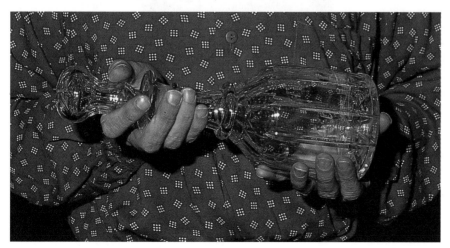

*Always support the decanter from the neck with one hand and beneath the base with the other. The stopper should be pulled out straight, never twisted or forced.*

# A STEMMED DRINKING GLASS

THE STEMMED GLASS IS THE ULTIMATE IN VULNERABILITY, COMBINING EXTREME DELICACY OF CONSTRUCTION AND MATERIAL WITH INEVITABLE BUT POTENTIALLY HAZARDOUS USE AND WASHING.

Glass has the light, hard, waterproof, and hygenic qualities ideal for a drinking vessel, but was not widely used as such until the 1700s, and then only by the wealthy. It was not until the following century that drinking glasses were in general use.

Venetian glasses dominated the European market from the 1400s onward. They were made in easily worked but fragile soda glass and, later, soda-lime or the clearer cristallo. Venetian technical expertise gradually extended throughout Europe, and in the 1700s, the invention in Bohemia (now the Czech Republic) of a thicker, tougher glass made with potash and lime made glass cutting and engraving possible. Although the basic material may have improved by the late 1700s, with the more substantial and clearer flint and lead glass, the principal weakness of a stemmed drinking glass is in its construction, and that fundamental weakness remained. The stemmed glass is usually made in three parts: the bowl, the stem, and the foot, which are skillfully joined by the glassmaker. This structure has evident weaknesses. The stem, supporting the bowl at one end and the foot at the other, is the main stress point because it subjected to careless handling when the glass is held.

With the introduction of the more versatile lead glass came a variety of engraved, enameled, and gilt surface decoration, whose value for the collector of today stands or falls by its condition. An elaborately engraved 18th-century glass can command a very high price—as long as it is absolutely perfect.

## THE RESTORER'S BRIEF

Glass restoration is costly, and it is almost impossible to make invisible repairs. A restorer can grind down a chip or fill a crack with resins, but neither is recommended on a valuable or rare glass, as original glass is lost in grinding down, overall shape and balance is spoiled, and value plummets. It is straightforward having minor flaws in gilt or enamel decoration retouched, but in order to retain the value it has to be well done. Original decoration in good condition pushes up the value.

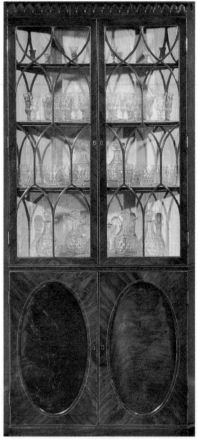

*Valuable glassware can be attractively displayed in a stable cabinet, rather than risked in use.*

## GENERAL CARE

Few other collectibles combine such intrinsic fragility with such a potentially high rate of use and frequent cleaning as drinking glasses. Precious glasses, and those with enamel or gilt decoration which wears off all too easily, should be preserved only for display. Cleaning need be no more than a dust with a soft cloth or brush; place the glasses in the center of a firm table that is not slippery—a rubber mat is a good idea, but not a tablecloth, which may slip or be pulled off. Support each glass from its base, keeping it held securely but not too tightly, in your hand.

If you do use your glasses, and as long as they have no applied enamel or gilt decoration, wash them one at a time in warm water with a little mild household detergent added. For extra security, place a cushioning material such as a towel in the washing sink and wrapped around the faucets (taps). Wash and rinse, then drain for a couple of minutes on a towel, and dry immediately.

**Rim:** *Run your finger around the rim to check for slight uneveness, and see if the decoration overruns or comes very close to the edge; both suggest that earlier chips have been ground down. A restorer can grind down existing chips to make it safer to use, but this always affects the value of the piece and may spoil its balance as a whole.*

**Stem:** *The weakest part of the glass, through which all the stresses pass. While the repair on a stem will remain fragile, restoration may extend the display life of a glass appreciated for its appearance. When buying a glass, hold it up to the light to check for signs of previous repair. Look for a flaw across the stem as if it had been snapped off, or there may be a color variation where resins have been used. Run your finger over the surface; if there is a break, you will feel a difference in surface levels or a change in texture*

**Foot:** *A network of fine scratches on the base is a good sign of age and use, as long as it is not too even, which may suggest sanding, with the aim of deceiving. Existing chips should not be ground out as this could spoil the proportions of the foot. Run your finger along the edge to check for slight bevels indicating previous grinding; even if the edge seems perfect, it is possible that the whole edge could have been ground to iron out any blemishes.*

*Despite exciting 20th-century developments in glassmaking, as in the examples by American companies Tiffany, Steuben, and Quezal (above), the fundamental weak points of the stemmed glass remained the same.*

SCHWARZLOT GLASS, LATE 18TH-CENTURY: *the painted decoration is very susceptible to wear, and touching in or consolidation of flaking areas are highly skilled tasks.*

# THE PAPERWEIGHT

PAPERWEIGHTS AND SPECIALTY GLASS ARE COLLECTED ABOVE ALL FOR THEIR DECORATIVE VALUE, AND THE SLIGHTEST FLAW IN THEIR APPEARANCE CAN SERIOUSLY AFFECT THEIR VALUE ON THE COLLECTORS' MARKET.

Paperweights are tactile; they present an invitation to be picked up, handled, and admired. They are made from solid lead glass, and so are heavy and likely to have been dropped. They do not shatter easily, but do chip and crack.

Although they are now collected for their decorative appeal, paperweights were originally also designed to be used, especially the multifunctional examples like the Whitefriars inkpot paperweights of the early 1900s.

As with any decorative glassware, visual perfection is the ideal, and the guiding rule for or against restoration is the degree to which the damage affects or interferes with the appearance. In many cases it is better to live with minor chips or scratches on a paperweight than to attempt restoration which, on glass, is rarely invisible.

In the early 1820s, the technique of pressing soft, hot glass into patterned iron molds was taken up in the United States, but peak paperweight production was in France between 1845 and 1855. Although there are many different styles, the basic construction technique was perfected at the three French factories of Clichy, Baccarat, and Saint. Louis, and was picked up by glassmakers around the world, so there is no great variation in standard or strength between one solid glass paperweight and another.

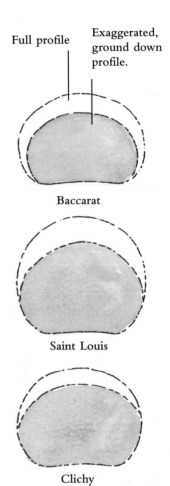

Full profile · Exaggerated, ground down profile.

**Baccarat**

**Saint Louis**

**Clichy**

*Typical paperweight shapes (above) with the effects of extreme grinding down. In reality, only very thin layers are likely to be ground away, so if you do come across an example shaped like the shaded areas above, avoid it! Better to live with a slight flaw than to have a piece ground down, as this grossly devalues the piece.*

*Canes (left)—long strands of colored glass grouped together and then sliced to give a pattern across the grain like the inside of a candy stick—are used for decorative effect in paperweights.*

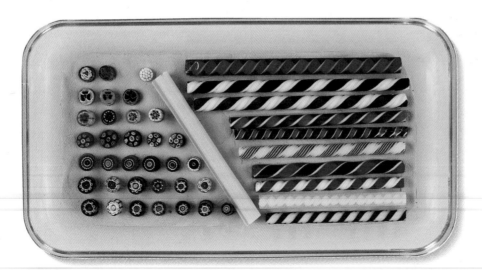

**Surface:** *Look out for tiny chips and scratches—the more prominent they are, the more the value is reduced. Check for uneven surfaces as a sign of previous restoration by holding the base of the paperweight firmly in one hand and turning the paperweight in the palm of your other hand. If a specialist glass worker has not turned it well, you will feel undulations in the surface. Early paperweights came in three sizes, so it is possible to check against a similar one to see if glass has been lost by grinding down.*

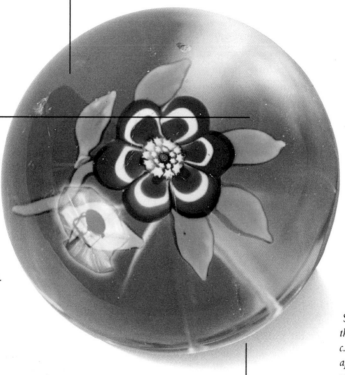

**Internal appearance:** *There should be a clear view across the transparent section of the glass; internal cracks are incurable and cannot be restored but can be improved. Resin with the right refractive index is run into the crack so it reflects less light; some will still be reflected and so the flaw will still be visible. Often the crack is too tight to take in the resin.*

SPECIMEN PAPERWEIGHT *from the Baccarat Factory, France, c.1850, which retains its visual appeal despite a minor chip, and was not restorerd.*

**Base:** *Some bases were traditionally not ground down but left rough; all antique examples are likely to have some degree of wear, so a flawless base suggests a modern or reproduction paperweight.*

*A concentric Saint Louis mushroom paperweight style shows the use of canes.*

*A 19th-century patch box decorated with a sulfide might appear at an auction as a "paperweight-related article."*

*An extremely rare Saint Louis paperweight known as an "upright bouquet," with a faceted top.*

# THE DEVELOPMENT OF DECORATIVE GLASS

Although glassware for decorative, rather than practical, purposes, was made by the ancient Greeks and Romans over 2,000 years ago, the most creative and experimental period of production in modern times was not until the 1800s.

From the 1300s the Venetian glassmakers of Murano developed cristallo (a form of soda glass) that was soft in its molten state and therefore easily worked into elaborate, decorative shapes. It was too brittle to cut, but was suitable for diamond-point engraving. Venetian glass was exported all over Europe until the 1600s when glass factories began to be established elsewhere to supply their domestic markets. Venetian glass is often highly decorative; and for special occasions, such as weddings, much enameling was used. Latticino glass, developed in the 1500s, is decorated with a pattern of white or colored glass threads. Venetian glass is vulnerable to crizzling, a "disease" or "glass sickness" caused by a faulty balance of ingredients and characterized by a network of fine cracks and deterioration of the glass: this cannot be treated but the condition can be stabilized by keeping the affected item in a controlled, dry environment. Special display cases can be made and the antiquity of a piece usually justifies the expense. George Ravenscroft's addition of lead oxide to the ingredients cured the problem.

In Bohemia (now the Czech Republic), also during the 1600s, the technique of painted enamel decoration was fully developed and applied, usually in bold colors, to plain glass shapes, but it has tended to wear off. In the mid 1700s a glass tax in England forced glassmakers to make lighter and cheaper glass; but the

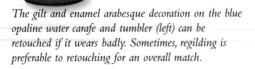

*The gilt and enamel arabesque decoration on the blue opaline water carafe and tumbler (left) can be retouched if it wears badly. Sometimes, regilding is preferable to retouching for an overall match.*

product was also more fragile. Of English makers, John Lucas opted for a less highly taxed bottle glass to make cheap, enameled glassware decorated with, for example, white flecking for perfume bottles and flagons, but the fact that few survive is testament to their fragility.

In the 20th century, pioneering Art Glass manufacturers such as Emile Gallé, Auguste and Antonin Daum, and later René Lalique in France and Louis Comfort Tiffany in the United States, extended the boundaries of decorative glassware techniques, with acid-etched, enameled, and dramatically colored, sometimes iridescent glass. They reinvented *pâte de verre*—glass ground into a paste, molded into the desired shape and then fired to produce translucent, soft-edged glass that feels very hard to the touch. Both Gallé and the Daum brothers also used *marquetries de verre*, a technique that entailed incorporating preformed glass motifs into the piece while it was still hot.

Cameo glass, though made in Roman times, was revived in Europe in the 1800s, and highly developed in the late 1800s by glassmakers such as Webb, Stevens and Williams, Gallé, and Daum, and in the early 1900s at the Orrefors factory in Sweden. It is made of two differently colored layers of glass, one encased within the other; the outside layer is then cut or etched through to reveal the layer beneath. For top price on the collectors' market, pristine condition is essential.

*Cameo glass, like the Stevens and Williams plaque (below) was the ultimate in decorative glassware, and its value depends absolutely on immaculate appearance.*

## GENERAL CARE

Purely decorative glassware should be displayed on a stable shelf or in a cabinet, where it cannot be easily knocked. Paperweights, some early examples of pressed glass, and solid glass figures are heavy for their size and should always be supported from the base when handling.

To clean decorative glassware, place the article on a flat, easily accessible, non-slip surface such as a rubber mat. Maintain a polished surface on paperweights by dusting with a clean cloth, or wipe with a clean damp cloth to remove smudges. Never use anything at all abrasive, as even the finest of scratches will matte the surface and reduce value.

Particular care should be taken not to put pressure on relief surfaces such as cameo glass. If stubborn dirt remains in crevices, soak the item in warm water in a small plastic basin with a towel in the bottom and try to remove it with a cotton swab or soft brush.

*Relief decoration as on much of Emile Gallé's work (above) may become chipped, but small pieces can often be successfully bonded back into place.*

## THE RESTORER'S BRIEF

The enjoyment and value of a paperweight for the collector depends on its decorative qualities and its clarity and sparkle. A French paperweight from the peak period 1845–1855 in good condition can sell for as much as $5,000 (£3,200), so if you do decide on restoration, make sure it is done by a specialist glass worker. Minor scratches and chips can be rubbed out, but must result in a completely even, highly polished surface withe highly specialized machinery. However, rubbing out damage alters the shape and size of the piece, and the restorer should also be asked what effect there will be on the interior image.

Good, undiscernable restoration on decorative glass can substantially increase the value, but many restorers are unhappy about such radical intervention, and in many cases it may be better to live with the chips or to fill them with resin. Structural cracks can be consolidated with resin, which can strengthen the piece, but does yellow over time. It is reversible, however, and the process can be repeated. The decision to repair a damaged piece of specialty glassware may depend on where the damage is. Invisible repair is almost impossible, but helped by the use of water-white resin adhesive compatible with the refractive index of the glass. Ask the restorer how obvious finished restoration will be and how exactly the quality of finish, texture, hardness, and color can be matched. Sections of relief decoration on cameo glass can be very successfully built up in resin, although value is affected.

Matte glass scratches very easily and the original surface is then difficult to reproduce. Surface smudges can be removed with a mild detergent solution.

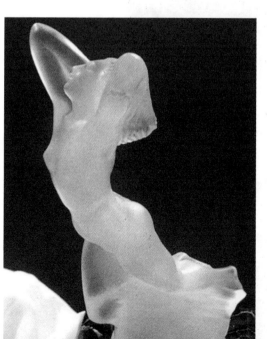

*Repairs on matte or frosted glass like the 1929 automobile mascot (left) can be barely visible because less light passes through, but scratches appear white. The Apsley Pellatt scent bottle (above) contains a sulfide, in which a preheated cameo has been inserted into an envelope of glass.*

# THE CHANDELIER

G LASS, METAL, HEAT, AND LIGHT COME TOGETHER IN CHANDELIERS, LUSTER LIGHTS, AND LAMPS. RESTORATION HAS A PART TO PLAY, NOT ONLY IN REPLACING AND RESTORING FRAGILE OR LOST PARTS, BUT IN KEEPING THE ITEMS SAFE TO USE.

Many chandeliers have been considerably altered, if not completely rebuilt, to suit prevailing fashions and lighting technology; others, such as French Baroque designs, have been much copied, which makes them difficult to date. But possibly more important for the owner of a functioning wall or ceiling light, is whether the lighting fixtures are in harmony with the overall design…and whether the often-considerable structure and weight are adequately supported. If a chandelier breaks free from its mount, it not only will probably be severely damaged itself, but could seriously damage anyone or anything beneath it.

*Pins:* Usually of brass or silver plate; they should be checked regularly and kept free of corrosion. Pins with any signs of corrosion should be replaced. A broken pin could undermine whole sections which could then fall on other sections, with disastrous consequences. It is not unusual for a chandelier to have new wire links, which do not affect value as long as the appropriate materials are used (not pieces of bent wire!), and are in the right style.

GEORGE III 12-ARM CHANDELIER, *c. 1790. The size—it is nearly 6 feet (2 m) high, and nearly 4 feet (over 1 m) in diameter—means that it would need heavy-duty supporting chains and hooks secured into a ceiling joist for it to be secure.*

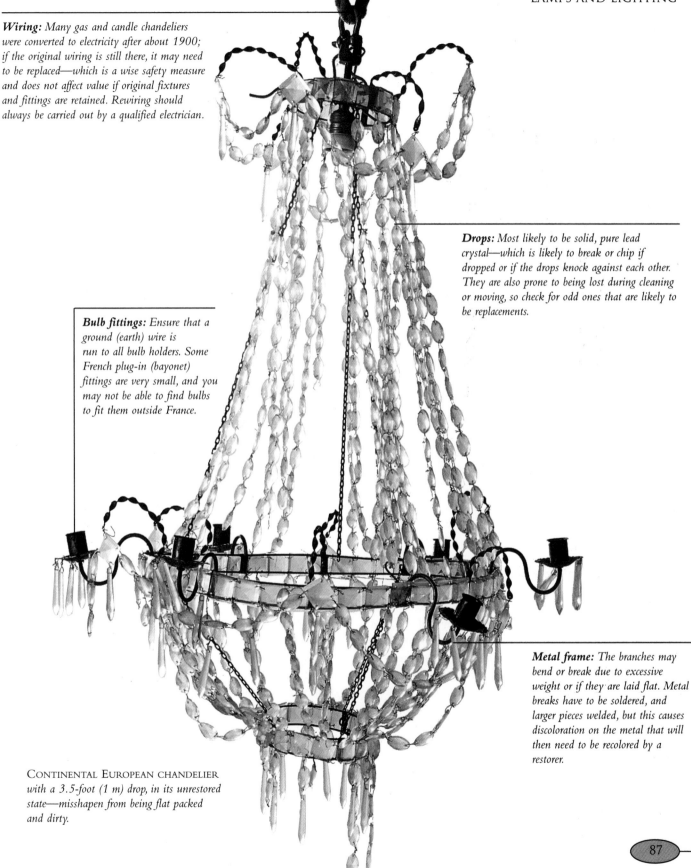

**Wiring:** *Many gas and candle chandeliers were converted to electricity after about 1900; if the original wiring is still there, it may need to be replaced—which is a wise safety measure and does not affect value if original fixtures and fittings are retained. Rewiring should always be carried out by a qualified electrician.*

**Drops:** *Most likely to be solid, pure lead crystal—which is likely to break or chip if dropped or if the drops knock against each other. They are also prone to being lost during cleaning or moving, so check for odd ones that are likely to be replacements.*

**Bulb fittings:** *Ensure that a ground (earth) wire is run to all bulb holders. Some French plug-in (bayonet) fittings are very small, and you may not be able to find bulbs to fit them outside France.*

**Metal frame:** *The branches may bend or break due to excessive weight or if they are laid flat. Metal breaks have to be soldered, and larger pieces welded, but this causes discoloration on the metal that will then need to be recolored by a restorer.*

CONTINENTAL EUROPEAN CHANDELIER *with a 3.5-foot (1 m) drop, in its unrestored state—misshapen from being flat packed and dirty.*

*The small, late 19th-century chandelier (above) is one of a pair that will have to be taken apart for a thorough cleaning; matching replacements were found for missing drops.*

## PRACTICAL LIGHTING

The earliest chandeliers were made of wood and were suspended from the ceiling on a pulley system so they could be raised and lowered for new candles or tallow lights to be put in. They were a practical way of lighting a large area which could not otherwise be illuminated. By the 1400s, many were painted and decorated with gilt. They suffer from all the problems associated with wood, such as woodworm, and any painted decoration or gilding is likely to be worn, although it can be sensitively restored.

In the 1600s, brass chandeliers became fashionable, originally in Holland, and then in England and the rest of Europe. The polished brass reflected the candle flames and gave an attractive light.

The Venetian, Giuseppe Briati, is usually credited with exploring the reflective quality of glass for lights when he introduced blown glass chandeliers in 1739. As lead crystal glass became the norm, and glass-cutting techniques more advanced, makers added cut glass lusters or drops to their designs. These were then linked to form swags, and by the end of the century the glass ornament almost concealed the underlying framework, and made the whole structure enormously heavy. Gas light from the 1860s brought conversion of chandeliers and new "gasoliers" with hollow glass arms through which the gas was piped (these are now rarely found outside museums). From the early 1900s, purpose-built "electroliers" were introduced. Sometimes the gas or electric fixtures are out of keeping with the original chandelier design; if so, you can decide to convert it back to candles (or non-drip, oil-filled mock candles), or even gas. As the main value of a chandelier is in its structure, rather than the type of light fixture, this will have little effect on value, and may even enhance it.

## GENERAL CARE

The obvious first precaution for a chandelier in use is to make sure it is securely mounted—that the ceiling and means of attachment are strong enough to support the weight; a chain from a joist may be necessary for heavy pieces. Lighter chandeliers can be suspended just from a hook, or a purpose-made electrical fixture into which the hook slots, which makes it easier to take down the chandelier for cleaning.

Wall and ceiling lights in use gather dust very quickly and need regular light dusting. Do not stretch up to clean as it is easy to dislodge the lusters, but stand on a stepladder or stable, raised surface.

For more serious cleaning, or if you are moving, you will have to take down the chandelier. Call in someone to help. Take the drops off first, while the chandelier is still hung, as they may chip if knock against each other. Do devise a system of labeling so you know where each piece came from. A black-and-white photograph can be useful for reference when you reassemble it. Chandeliers should not be laid down on the floor, as not only are the drops likely to unclip and knock against their neighbors, but the metal framework may become bent or scratched. To clean the drops use a mild detergent or glass cleaner and dry immediately with a clean cloth. If wax needs to be removed, glass and metal parts can be soaked in very hot water, the wax taken off, and then they can be cleaned in the normal way. Try to keep the links dry, but if they do get wet, use a cool hairdryer to dry them. Metal parts can be cleaned with a commercial metal polish, unless it is gilded (as with ormolu), when it should not be polished at all. Rehang the chandelier before putting back the drops; start at the top and work down.

When transporting a chandelier, if you are not going to disassemble it completely, devise a method of keeping it hung—such as a wooden crate (tea chest) with a bar across it. Use packing around the sides to prevent it from swinging and wrap the drops individually in acid-free tissue paper.

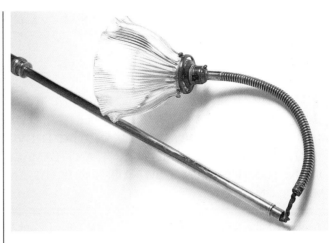

*A flexible upper stem adds to the versatility of this early 20th-century standard lamp (above), but regular re-angling has weakened the join. A metalworker will have to replace the screw threading, and the owner will have to resist making too much use of the angle-poise feature.*

*The ormolu (mercury gilded bronze) mounts on the 1790s chandelier (above) should be slightly tarnished; if they are not the chandelier has been over-restored or is not as old as it purports to be.*

## THE RESTORER'S BRIEF

Chandeliers and other lights usually sustain damage because they have fallen or because they have been packed and transported without due care. Small areas of damage, such as a few chipped drops, as long as they do not threaten the safety of the whole, are not a problem, and in a complicated chandelier will not be noticed at all. A restorer can bond and consolidate such damage with resins and although this is not invisible, the repair is less noticeable in a chandelier than in ornamental glassware. Missing drops can be replaced—ask the restorer if he knows any specialist stores that keep stocks of spare drops and lusters. Normally the cost of having a drop made and cut in glass would not be justified in relation to the value of the light. Alternatively, a cast could be made in resin for around half the price of glass, from a mold of one of the existing drops; ask the restorer how closely he can match the glass color; it will feel warmer to the touch and eventually yellow with age.

Bent or broken armature should be straightened by a restorer using clamps and special bending tools. Worn or corroded pins should be replaced immediately.

# A TIFFANY LAMP

THE HIGHLY STYLIZED OVERALL DESIGN OF TIFFANY LAMPSHADES, AND THE COMPLETE INTEGRATION OF MATERIAL AND DECORATION MEAN THAT THE VISUAL IMPACT OF THE WHOLE IS ALL IMPORTANT; ANY DAMAGE NOT ONLY DIMINISHES THIS IMPACT BUT RESTRICTS USE, AND HAS A BIG IMPACT ON VALUE.

The stained glass-effect lamps developed by the Tiffany Glass Company in New York in the 1880s are prime examples of mixed-media objects. They incorporate materials, such as glass, enamel, metal, and sometimes even precious or semiprecious stones, that react to environmental factors such as heat and cold in different ways. However, it is less these environmental factors, but how the different materials combine, react with, or come into contact with each other, that tend to result in damage.

Louis Comfort Tiffany, one of America's most influential designers, originally employed outworkers to make the lamps, resulting in a great variety of form and color. He was inspired by the iridescence that ancient glass acquired from the corrosive action of metals in the soil in which it had been buried for centuries, and he experimented with metal oxides. Later, production-line methods were introduced, and whole runs of particularly successful designs were produced in a range of sizes, but there is no marked deterioration in quality. However, the style has been extensively copied, and it is worth looking for a maker's mark to establish top Tiffany quality.

*Glass sections:* The join between the two different materials—glass and lead (above)—has moved due to heat and the weight of the piece, resulting in lost glass sections; this is not a problem unless they are likely to fall out. The glass is strong and not particularly thin, but is often curved, which makes it difficult to replace. Missing sections can be closely matched and replaced with colored resins, or replacements may be found from a similar shade.

## GENERAL CARE

Always make sure an antique lamp stands flat, and that the cord (flex) is not likely to be tripped over. The heat from a light bulb is not strong enough to affect lead solder, but it is advisable to use a low-power bulb and not to leave the lamp on for long periods, especially if resin has been used for restoration, as this might yellow over time.

When picking up the shade, support the whole of it and the glass from inside from the top, not from the rim, which could buckle; it may be worth asking someone to help, especially if the shade is heavy or large. If more than a regular light dusting is necessary, wipe lightly with a nearly-dry sponge—which picks up the dirt without corroding the metal. Use a short, cropped, stiff-bristled stencil brush to reach into crevices and seams between metal and glass.

Before packing a lamp, dismantle the shade from the stem with great care, and pack separately. Invert the shade in the box so that the weight is spread evenly and not pressing down on the bottom edge. When removing the shade from the box, put your hand beneath it and lift it from its top. There should be no weight put on the box once it is packed, and no vibration.

**Frame:** *A lead or copper frame is heavy and can be bent by a knock, throwing the whole shade out of alignment and loosening the glass. The lead filets do not bend unless pressed hard, but they are fragile and need to be supported from the inside during cleaning. Look for evidence of soldering (color variation) indicating previous restoration and consequent weak points.*

**Base and stem:** *The stem takes the entire weight of the shade and can be bent or broken; anything that renders the lamp less stable, such as an uneven base, should be rectified. Look for solder in places where it should not be, such as halfway down the stem—which should be continuous and unbroken. Tiffany lamps have a dark patination applied at manufacture which is sometimes mistaken for dirt; attempts made to remove it would devalue the lamp, though it can be replaced by a restorer.*

**Supports:** *These are the point where the shade is connected to the top of the stem and may include stretchers from the rim of the shade. If they are bent by external pressure, the shape of the shade is affected.*

TIFFANY LAMP, WITH ROSE BOWER GLASS, 1900, *and a sturdy metal base.*

## THE RESTORER'S BRIEF

With an object made from different materials, restoration needs to be carried out by specialists trained in the different media. Depending on the complexity of the lamp, it may also be necessary to have the pre-restoration dismantling done professionally.

Ask a glass restorer to repair any chips, cracks, or loose areas in a valuable shade or lamp that may further deteriorate with continued use or movement. Cracks can be consolidated and missing sections filled with resins or with glass taken from broken shades, which will restore strength. To maintain value, however, it is vital that copper foil and glass similar to the original be found. Resins are detectable, lack the brilliance of the original glass, and yellow with age.

A metal specialist should reshape or solder bent or damaged metal. Though the shade must be dismantled, such procedures and should have minimal effect on the value if properly done.

**Wiring:** *Check that this is in the correct place by comparing it with other similar lamps or consulting an expert. There should be a purpose-made hole at the side for the wire or a channel under the foot. If the wire covers decoration it is unlikely to be in the right place.*

# A CLOISONNÉ VASE

WHEN ENAMEL DECORATION IS APPLIED TO METAL, IT INTRODUCES RICH, LUMINOUS COLORS, BUT IT IS FUNDAMENTALLY GLASS, AND, THEREFORE, FRAGILE.

Enameling is the art of decorating a surface using a glass or vitreous paste colored by metal oxides which is fused to the surface by heat. When combined with metal, the enamel is an integral part of an object rather than a surface decoration, and if it is seriously damaged, value can be drastically reduced.

*Cloisonné* is made by the creation of *cloisons,* or partitions, of strings of flat or twisted metal wire applied to the metal surface, creating compartments for the enamel paste. A knock can cause the enamel between the cloisons to "ping" off. *Champlevé* (literally, raised fields) work is a little more resistant since depressions hammered or pressed into the metal body are filled with larger areas of enamel. *Plique a jour* ("applied to the hole") is like cloisonné but with the backplate removed to produce a stained-glass window effect, and is extremely fragile.

The fundamental problem with all enamel work on metal is that metal flexes to a certain extent if it is knocked, whereas enamel does not, and will crack, chip, or split at any stress point caused by distortion of the metal. It reacts just like glass, but is also more likely to shatter and crumble.

*The Russian jeweler Carl Fabergé used basse taille enameling for his decorative eggs (above). The design is chased, engraved, or stamped onto a metal body, and flooded with clear enamel.*

## GENERAL CARE

The delicate glass of the enamel dictates the level of care: dropping, knocking, or rough cleaning may cause cracking, and pieces to break off. Dust regularly with a soft brush, using a stencil brush to remove dirt from the cracks. Never soak in water, but a cotton swab (bud) dipped in a mild solution of mineral-scale remover can be used for obstinate stains. Dab dry immediately and thoroughly. Do not use a duster which may catch, or an abrasive cleaner. If the metal needs cleaning, ask a restorer for advice as some commercial cleaners remove gilding or patination.

## THE RESTORER'S BRIEF

Individual enamel "compartments" can be restored or replaced, though because damage is contained within a small area, restoration may not be essential. Loose or unstable pieces should be secured since they are easily lost. If the piece as a whole is friable it should be handled as little as possible and consolidated. The featured cloisonné vase fell off a shelf and landed on a hard floor on the edge of its top rim, hence its squat appearance. The value of the vase did not, in the owner's view, justify expensive restoration.

Because enamel work combines two different materials, check that the restorer is skilled with both metal and with glass and resins, or that different specialists are used. Ask about the techniques to be used: a specialist enameler would use new pigments to produce new resins, but the objects would have to be refired and this is not recommended for valuable antiques, as it puts stress on the remaining enamel. Better to ask if a glass restorer can fill in missing pieces with matching resins, though these may not have the same luminescence as the originals. Ensure that only the damaged or missing areas are treated; the original decoration must be left intact.

Enameled metal objects are not among the most highly priced antiques, and the cost of intricate restoration tends to outstrip the value of the item, but on pre-1600s items, restoration would always be worthwhile. It is worth having seriously tarnished and dirty pieces professionally cleaned as any unnoticed corrosion is detrimental to the piece as a whole and can push the enamels off or stain them.

**Tarnishing:** *Exposed metal next to cracked or lost enamel may tarnish or corrode, causing discoloration.*

**Framework:** *If a piece is knocked or dropped, the metal framework and the ground metal on which it is laid will be dented or distorted, putting pressure on the enamels which may crack, crumble, or "ping" off.*

**The enamel:** *Enamel is intrinsically more friable than glass and crumbling can result from natural aging. Chips and cracks are the most common problems; they can be stabilized with resins, or even filled. With cloisonné the pieces of enamel are separated so damage to one piece will have no effect on another if the metal ground is not dented. The expansion and contraction of the metal in response to temperature changes puts pressure on the brittle, inflexible enamel, causing it to crack.*

**Base:** *Dents at the bottom of slender-necked vases can often be pushed only from the inside using a special, long-handled tool, or by drilling through the metal to insert the tool. Either way risks further loss of enamel, and it may be better left alone.*

CLOISONNÉ VASE, JAPAN, C. 1880: *a combination of tough metal and fragile glass.*

THE STRENGTH AND RESILIENCE OF METALS AND GEMS VARY ACCORDING TO THEIR CHEMICAL MAKEUP, CRYSTALLINE STRUCTURE, AND HOW THEY ARE SUBSEQUENTLY CRAFTED OR USED. THE APPARENT HARDNESS OF METALS CAN BE MISLEADING; SURFACE PLATING CAN ALL TOO EASILY WEAR AWAY, AND WAFER-THIN METAL SHEETS CAN SPLIT AND TEAR; MOISTURE AND OTHER ELEMENTS IN THE ATMOSPHERE LEAD TO TARNISHING AND CORROSION. THE KEY TO PRESERVING SILVER AND OTHER METAL IS TO POLISH AS LITTLE AS POSSIBLE SO THAT THE METAL ITSELF AND ITS DECORATION ARE NOT SLOWLY BUT SURELY WORN DOWN AND DEVALUED.

# SILVERWARE
# & *jewelry*

# A SET OF FLATWARE

A NTIQUE AND "ESTATE" SILVER OR SILVER PLATE FLATWARE
SETS ARE A PLEASURE TO USE BUT MUST BE REGARDED AS
SETS AND THE CONTENTS USED ROTATIONALLY TO AVOID
DETRIMENTAL UNEVEN WEAR TO INDIVIDUAL PIECES.

Eating implements, or flatware, have long been made of precious metal
because it is hygienic and has a more pleasant feel in the mouth than base
metal. The soft metal can also easily be engraved with personalized devices
such as initials or family crests. Methods of construction include casting,
hand-fashioning from sheet metal, and die-stamping, while additional
decoration may be added by engraving or chasing. Strength primarily depends
on thickness of metal employed. English silver is decorated on both sides and
is thicker than Scottish flatware, which is single struck—with the
decoration on only the upper side. American and continental European
flatware can be either double or single struck.

Plated flatware is less pliable than solid gold or silver, but the
thin layer of precious metal wears relatively quickly and it is not
always economic to replate. It is also less pleasant in the mouth and,
when worn through to the base metal core, imparts a distinctive taste
to some foods. To reduce distorting the taste of fruits, solid silver
dessert sets are sometimes gilded.

*Forks:* Bent tines
(prongs) must not be
bent back by the owner
as fracture may result,
or at best the prong will
not end up perfectly
realigned. The job
should be given to a
professional.

**Silver plating:** *Wears away in time with
extensive use, especially on fork prongs and
spoon bowls. Replating is really only
economically viable for pieces of a complete set,
not for individual assorted pieces.*

**Engraving:** *Personalized engraving should
be left in place on sets of solid silver flatware.
It is not possible to remove engraving from
plated flatware. It is considered acceptable,
however, to remove disparate engraving when
assembling a matched-up solid silver flatware
set from different sources.*

**Case:** *Usually of oak or pine and often veneered with show woods, this should be treated like an item of furniture. It is generally sturdily built but subject to stress at joints and hinges—which should be repaired promptly if damaged. Tempting though it may be to lift by the handles, these should not be relied upon; support from the base, as a case filled with flatware can be very heavy.*

**Handles:** *Bone handles are glue-fixed to the blades and may become loose, especially if immersed in hot water, and must be professionally refixed. Cracking becomes terminal and the handles will need to be replaced. Cleaning with milk may revive dulled bone handles.*

**Baize-lined divisions:** *The cloth is prone to moth attack, and should be sprayed with a proprietory spray at the first signs of attack. Minor cases of loose dividers may be reglued in position by the owner. Lost dividers and areas denuded of lining should be replaced by a professional case fitter to maintain both practical and economic value.*

MAHOGANY BOXED, SILVERPLATE FLATWARE SET, 1930S. *The association of different materials demands a varied approach to care and restoration.*

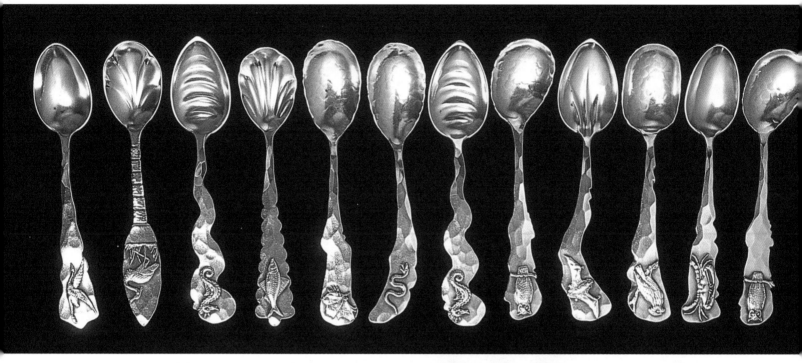

## MATCHING SETS

The different pieces that make up a set of flatware did not all evolve at once. The introduction of forks followed some time after knives and spoons, and sets of matching knife, fork, and spoon for a single person's place setting only originated in the mid 1600s, following the development of rolled sheet metal. Full sets for several place settings are rare from before about 1800, but even then families often bought piecemeal, assembling a set gradually, with the result that there are likely to be slight differences in style or pattern. The great advantage of many earlier pieces of flatware is that they are generally fashioned of thicker-gauge silver than in the 1800s and later, so they wear better, even though they have been in use for longer. Additionally, it will not matter if one or two pieces are matched replacements, because so few full sets survive from before the early 1800s. The main drawback in earlier pieces is the uneven wearing down of fork prongs, although this problem will also be found on forks from the 1800s that have been subjected to extensive use.

While silver plate flatware originated with the introduction of sheffield plate (see page 108), examples are very rare and the real flowering of plated flatware and sets came with the invention of electroplating in 1840 (see page 109). Plated

*Care must be taken to use parts of a set—like the silver gilt novelty spoons (above)—in rotation so that wear is even.*

*The spoon bowl (left) has been crudely repaired with a "let-in" patch. If the spoon forms part of a set, a repair would have to be of a higher standard if value were to be maintained.*

wares were vastly cheaper, but the thin outer layer of silver gradually wears away to reveal the base metal core. This results in unsightly blemishes that cannot be polished and makes the piece of flatware less pleasant to use. The other disadvantage of silver plate is that since the layer deposited by electrolysis is pure silver, articles tarnish more readily, needing more frequent cleaning—which aggravates the wear problem.

American and continental European sets tend to be "longer" than their British counterparts, including such extra pieces as cocktail forks and iced tea spoons.

## GENERAL CARE

Use all the pieces of a particular type in the set equally or in rotation. Otherwise, some items will start to show considerably more wear than others, which would devalue the set as a whole. If a selection is kept in a drawer for everyday access, make sure these pieces are swapped with others from the set on a regular basis. It is, however, accepted that less frequently used elements of the set, such as soup spoons or fish forks, show less wear than ordinary spoons and forks.

Certain foods such as eggs, salt, and brassica vegetables (cabbage and brussel sprouts, for example) cause immediate, unsightly tarnishing that needs immediate removal—always wash a silver salt container after use. However, silver and silver plate flatware should generally be given an occasional polish and otherwise washed and dried by hand. If the pieces are used regularly, this will keep them clean for a good while. Gilt pieces should be polished very seldom to preserve their soft-looking finish, which would otherwise wear down to the plain silver beneath. Never place pieces of flatware individually in a compartmented, upright-drying basket since they will scratch against each other. For the same reason, if you must put your silverware in a dishwasher, fill each compartment with a "handful" of pieces and then add no

*A well-struck, legible set of hallmarks (above), for Newcastle, England, 1870, which are an asset to value. Care must be taken not to soften their clarity by overpolishing.*

more to it. Dishwasher detergent may attack and dull the surface of silver articles. Bone-handled knives should not be immersed in water at all, since this will weaken the adhesive and loosen the blades.

Silver cleaning dips are preferable to abrasive silver polishes for solid silver flatware, since they extract the discoloring chemicals (mostly sulfur compounds) instead of rubbing away the discolored metal. Dips are what they say they are; never leave silverware standing in them as this will cause a "tide" mark. The dips work electrolytically and so must never be used for plated silverware; the direction of the electrical circuit set up by the existence of the base metal core results in the progressive stripping of the silver plate rather than the extraction of the tarnishing impurities in the plated layer.

## THE RESTORER'S BRIEF

The combination of myriad light scratches and repeated polishing give silver a desirable, gently patinated sheen, but deep scratches need to be dealt with by a silversmith to maintain value. On plated silverware, planishing and replating are necessary. Ask the silversmith to hammer or straighten dents and bent prongs; they will need to be heated and annealed (plunged in cold water) to restore the tensile strength of the area. If the prongs of a fork have worn unevenly, it is better to leave it alone, and accept

that they reduce the value of the set, rather than have them trimmed evenly, which gives them a truncated, out-of-proportion appearance. Seek immediate repair of cracks and tears, involving silver-soldering, heating, and annealing, to avoid further deterioration. Antique silver-handled knives (1740-1830) are normally made of resin-filled, thin sheet metal, which is very prone to tears and cannot be repaired. Only the better-quality, rarer knives with cast handles are repairable. Antique gilt dessert services ideally should not be regilded.

*Original gilding, as on the dessert knife (left), which wears easily, should be preserved as much as possible, by gentle washing and only very rare use of cleaner.*

# A SILVER COFFEE POT

COFFEE POTS COME UNDER THE HEADING OF USEFUL WARES, BUT WHILE MOST HAVE WORN WELL, OTHERS WITH THINNER METAL ARE NOT AS STRONG, AND MAY NOW BE BEYOND REPAIR.

Coffee, tea, and chocolate pots are closely related serving vessels made in a very similar way. Methods of construction vary from casting to fabricating of cut sheet-metal which is fused at the join in the case of a cylindrical piece, or by joints in the case of a faceted shape. While cast pieces are generally very sturdy, those made of sheet metal vary greatly from heavy to flimsily thin gauges, and wear and problems are proportionate. Handles are made of ivory or carved wood: commonly ebony or fruitwoods such as pearwood, and occasionally boxwood.

SILVER WINE EWER, BY JOSEPH AND ALBERT SAVORY, 1852; *the intricately detailed, cast and applied decoration, and hand engraving would be diminished by overpolishing.*

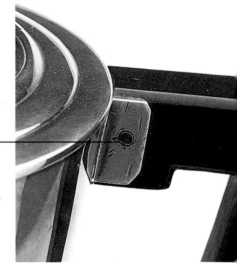

***Hinges:*** *May weaken and fail in time, in which event repair is vital to maintain value, but this must be done by a restorer.*

***Joints:*** *Where separately shaped, flat sheet metal sections have been joined together, the soldered joins could spring apart, or on thinner silver, may split (as there is little metal for the solder to grip onto); either will devalue the item drastically and should be resoldered with silver solder. Old repairs in lead-based or low-temperature solder eat into the surrounding silver and should be replaced with silver solder.*

**Finials:** *May be of ebony, fruitwood, or ivory, all of which may crack over time. If they are so damaged they are no longer usable for opening the lid, or if lost, finials should be replaced in keeping with the original style.*

TIFFANY COFFEE POT, UNITED STATES, C.1900; *the thickness of the metal and quality of craftsmanship ensure a long life.*

**Bruises:** *Occur either to the body or the cover and are an occupational hazard for coffee pots, especially if the metal is thin. If corrected by a professional silversmith who specializes in restoration, both value and strength will be maintained. Slight dents on thicker metal are probably not worth worrying about.*

**Handles:** *Here made of ebony, but may be of fruitwood, usually pear, or ivory; all tend to crack and fracture in time, especially in dry conditions, and for safety need replacing rather than glueing. The sinuous shape of wood handles means they have crossgrain at some point in their profile, which tends to split. Some 1800s handles are of silver with heat-insulating, ivory or wooden spacers at the junction with the body of the pot; these may have cracked due to drying out, leaving the handle loose and unsafe to use.*

**Foot:** *May have become distorted from being dropped or put down too heavily. A specialist smith should be asked to repair this in order to maintain practical and investment value.*

## TRENDS IN DRINKING

Coffee, tea, and chocolate were being imported into Europe by the mid 1600s and as they were expensive luxuries, there was soon a demand for silver vessels to serve them in. By 1700, the pots were being made principally in tapered, cylindrical, or faceted form, all with domed covers. As they were made from heavy-gauge silver, they are very sturdy, and many have survived in good condition. Rococo-style wares made in the 1740s to 1760s, are typically of slightly thinner metal more suitable for the embossing that characterizes the style. The raised decorative highlights of these pieces commonly lose their sharp definition through extensive polishing. Unworn examples are valued at a premium.

In the Neoclassical period of 1770–1800, which was typified by bright-cut decoration (whose appeal arises from the contrasting reflections of light from the faceted-line engraving), structural problems are common. This is because this period made great use of thinly rolled sheet silver, which means that few pieces remain in good condition. They are commonly found with patches to strengthen weakened parts, resoldered joints, and repaired hinges. Bright-cut engraving, once worn, loses most of its appeal, and either cannot be or is very difficult to refresh successfully. The early 1800s—the Regency period in England, Empire in continental Europe, and Federal in the United States, saw an upsurge in casting in the manufacture of tea and coffee pots, resulting in strongly made wares. Other, cheaper pieces continued to be made in thinner sheet metal, which in time develops structural problems because the weight of metal was not suited to the encrusted decoration that was popular at the time. The late 1800s saw the adoption of die-stamped decoration, and as with later pieces, especially from the 20th century which were made by spinning, their durability rests in the thickness of metal employed.

*Each silver part of the George II circular tea kettle stand with lamp burner (above) should be hallmarked, and if the hallmarks do not match, parts have been replaced, which will reduce the value of the whole set.*

## GENERAL CARE

Constant washing is better than frequent cleaning with a silver polish, however mild, particularly for embossed or engraved pots, in order to preserve the decoration. Always rinse to remove smears or soap residues, and dry the pot with a soft cloth. Clean with a commercial silver cleaner annually, or more frequently only if still discolored after washing; foams are less abrasive than powders or pastes and easier to use, especially on embossed or intricate pieces. Take care not to let any polish come in contact with wooden or ivory handles, or other metals. To remove interior tannin stains, fill the pot with a solution of one part washing soda crystals to six parts water.

## THE RESTORER'S BRIEF

Dents in the body of the pot or a distorted foot will reduce the value of an object and should be corrected; do not attempt to push them back yourself since this could weaken the metal. Extensive repairs need to be followed by heating and annealing to restore the tensile strength necessary if a piece is to be used. If this leaves a "firemark," ask the restorer to disguise it by a light silver-plating. Hinges, handles, and insulating spacers must all be repaired if they are failing.

*A reinforcing silver L-shaped piece has been soldered underneath the handle of a cream jug that had been split at the join (right).*

## IDENTIFYING SILVER

Sterling silver is a term that originated in England to distinguish it from silver plate or lower grade alloys. It was part of a very organized British silver hallmarking system which developed as a form of consumer protection. By means of stamped marks, usually on the base of silverware, not only can the quality of silver be established, but also the maker, date, and town of assay (where it was authenticated). Continental European countries also operated systems of control marking, such as the French "poinçons" and the Russian marks, which guaranteed quality and showed town of assay, but only indicated a general period of manufacture. In the United States, silver, unlike plate or lower grade alloys, is usually marked "sterling." Some manufacturers merely marked their wares with catalog or pattern numbers, although Tiffany and Gorham, for example, always marked their pieces meticulously.

To interpret British hallmarks, you need to refer to a standard reference work which tabulates the cycles of date marks for each of the assay offices.

British silver over a small weight must, by law, be marked with a series of punches showing the silver standard, town of assay, date of manufacture, the duty mark when appropriate, and the maker's mark. These official marks were and still are stamped at the "hall" of the assay office or craft guild responsible for guaranteeing the purity of precious metal wares.

Sterling silver, the standard current for most of the controlled period of English silversmithing, was set in the year 1238 at a purity of 925 parts per 1,000 (92.5 percent) and is marked with a lion passant. However, to curtail the illegal practice in the late 1600s of clipping metal from the edges of coins (that were also then made of sterling silver), the standard of domestic silver was raised, for a short period (1697–1720)to 958 parts per 1,000 (95.8 percent). But silversmiths and the general public complained the new higher standard resulted in

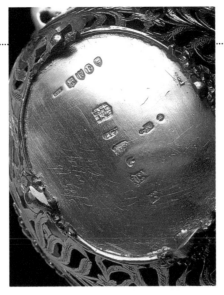

*Even silver imported into England had to bear a hallmark from an English assay office (above), together with, from 1842, the letter F.*

an alloy that was too soft, so in 1720 the sterling standard was reinstated, while coinage was given a milled edge to prevent clipping.

After 1720 the production of Britannia silver, as the higher percentage silver is known (from the seated figure of Britannia instead of the lion passant mark), was optional, and is sometimes used in commemorative ware.

The annual date letter was introduced in 1463, the letters running in successive alphabetic cycles in Court script, Gothic, or Roman upper- or lower-case styles, at first in complete cycles and later with a slightly curtailed alphabet in 20-year cycles, so any individual letter appears on a consistent year every other decade. In 1784 worked silver was taxed and a mark of the sovereign's head in profile introduced to show that duty had been paid. The duty was repealed in 1890, and the mark was discontinued, but has been used intermittently, such as in coronation and jubilee years.

English assay offices were, and some still are, in the cities of London, Birmingham, Exeter, Newcastle, Norwich, Sheffield, and York.

### London 1558

London's leopard's head assay mark     date mark     lion passant

### America

Alvin corporation

# THE CANDELABRA

S HEFFIELD PLATE PROVIDED A CHEAPER ALTERNATIVE TO EARLIER SHEET METAL AND CAST SILVER. BUT IN ADDITION TO THE INHERENT STRUCTURAL PROBLEMS OF CANDELABRA AND CANDLESTICKS, WAS THE PROBLEM OF THE THIN LAYER OF SILVER WEARING THROUGH.

**Fabrication joints:** *In sheffield plate, joints like those between the pan and pipe of a nozzle are susceptible to failure over time; immediate resoldering is desirable to avoid further deterioration of the adjoining surfaces. Splits in a sheet silver or silver plate loaded candlestick may only be repaired with lead-based solder, but this, over time, will cause the surrounding area to deteriorate.*

ROCOCO FOUR SCONCE CANDELABRA, *with more elaborate detail than was possible on a sheffield plate item.*

**Decoration:** *Border decoration of pre-made, thinly cast, or die-stamped silver with a lead solder filling was applied to the main piece and tends to puncture or tear away. The odd repair can be effective but it is not viable to buy an item in such condition, and the owner would be advised to live with the imperfections.*

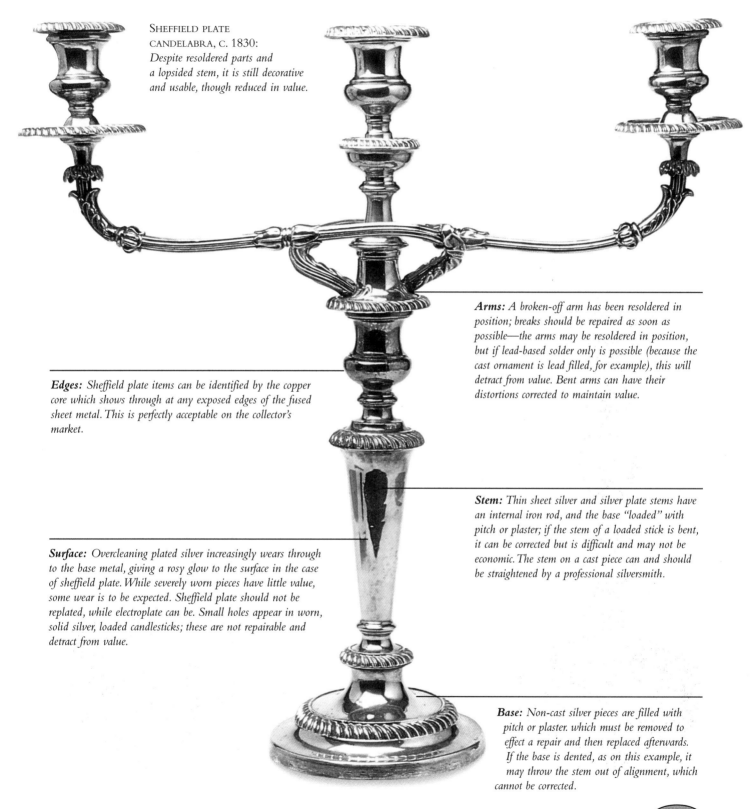

SHEFFIELD PLATE
CANDELABRA, C. 1830:
*Despite resoldered parts and
a lopsided stem, it is still
decorative and usable, though reduced in value.*

**Arms:** *A broken-off arm has been resoldered in position; breaks should be repaired as soon as possible—the arms may be resoldered in position, but if lead-based solder only is possible (because the cast ornament is lead filled, for example), this will detract from value. Bent arms can have their distortions corrected to maintain value.*

**Edges:** *Sheffield plate items can be identified by the copper core which shows through at any exposed edges of the fused sheet metal. This is perfectly acceptable on the collector's market.*

**Stem:** *Thin sheet silver and silver plate stems have an internal iron rod, and the base "loaded" with pitch or plaster; if the stem of a loaded stick is bent, it can be corrected but is difficult and may not be economic. The stem on a cast piece can and should be straightened by a professional silversmith.*

**Surface:** *Overcleaning plated silver increasingly wears through to the base metal, giving a rosy glow to the surface in the case of sheffield plate. While severely worn pieces have little value, some wear is to be expected. Sheffield plate should not be replated, while electroplate can be. Small holes appear in worn, solid silver, loaded candlesticks; these are not repairable and detract from value.*

**Base:** *Non-cast silver pieces are filled with pitch or plaster. which must be removed to effect a repair and then replaced afterwards. If the base is dented, as on this example, it may throw the stem out of alignment, which cannot be corrected.*

## LIGHTING THE WAY

Silver candlesticks for household use survive from around the 1660s, after prolonged political unrest throughout Europe had ceased. Very few branched candelabra survive from before the 1760s. At first, candlesticks were made of sheet metal of reasonable thickness and were sturdy enough for some to have survived, but by about 1675 cast sticks were the vogue. These were particularly strong and long-lived. The principal feature to watch for signs of wear is the increased use of chased decoration through the 1700s. This is particularly relevant to the Rococo period of 1740s and 1760s; pieces with worn highlights from overcleaning sell at a distinct disadvantage. Such overcleaning has had far more disastrous results on examples from the succeeding Neoclassical period of 1770-1800, when thin sheet metal was extensively used. Candlesticks and candelabra shafts of this period are flimsily made and had to be strengthened with an iron rod up the stem, while the base was filled with pitch or plaster with a piece of green baize or felt cloth on the underside. Many of these "loaded" pieces have numerous small holes from repeated cleaning, which devalue a piece considerably as restoration is not viable. Once the stem has become bent, this too, is virtually impossible to correct. The slender, attenuated lines of Neoclassical style meant that the branches of solid silver-stemmed candelabra often had to be of silver plated metal to be strong enough to support the cantilevered nozzles weighed down by candles. Before the invention of electroplating in 1840, these would have been of old sheffield plate. English Regency, continental Empire, and American Federal period pieces from the early 1800s saw a return to sturdy cast construction, but for economy's sake, loaded pieces continued to be made throughout the 1800s.

*The heavy gauge of this early 19th-century candlestick (left) means that it is sturdy and self-supporting, needing no internal filling or "loading" to bolster its structure, and any distortion from use can be corrected or repaired.*

## GENERAL CARE

(For care and restoration of plated silver, see following pages). Avoid overcleaning all silver articles—an annual polish should be adequate. Use silver cleaning foam when cleaning any piece of silver that is not a piece of flatware; if some silver polishes are not removed properly, they may in time cause oxidizing, which in serious cases could lead to the silver disintegrating. Cast candlesticks should be washed regularly in a mild detergent solution before the point of tarnishing is reached, but do not allow liquid to seep into hollow sections; wipe these with a damp cloth, and after a rinsing wipe, use an electric hairdryer to blow all crevices dry. Intricate or hollow

*The underside of a cast candlestick (right) shows the screw-fitting plug of the stem in the center. It is important not to let water or cleaning fluids dribble into the hollow stem during cleaning as they may lodge there and cause deterioration.*

*The annual cleaning of solid silver (above) with a commercial cleaner, applied with a sponge and polished with a soft dust cloth.*

articles should not be immersed in silver cleaning dips, as any vestiges of cleaner that are not rinsed away in the interior could, by combining with sulfur from the atmosphere, cause blackening tarnish. Never immerse loaded candlesticks in water; simply wipe regularly with a damp cloth and dry thoroughly.

Use nondrip candles so you do not have a wax cleaning problem, and never let the candles burn to less than an inch (25 mm) of the sconce. The sconces take most of any wax deposit, and if they can be removed, should be washed regularly in hot water to remove the wax. Protective glass candle rings can be placed on the sconces. Obstinate wax deposits can be eased off gently with a thin wood skewer wrapped in cotton wool soaked in hot water.

Dismantle a candelabra before moving it, and to store, wrap the individual pieces separately in acid-free tissue to minimize tarnishing.

## THE RESTORER'S BRIEF

Antique cast candlesticks usually need little restoration other than straightening out bent stems or distorted bases of dropped pieces. Worn chasing on a good-quality candlestick can be refreshed, but you must be sure of the capabilities of the craftsman you entrust a piece to, and the ethics of such "improving" are questionable in any case.

Loaded candlesticks and candelabra once worn or distorted really have to be accepted as they are since very little is economically worth doing on them, or even possible. The metal skin of filled or loaded silver and silver plate candlesticks and candelabra is often so thin that it would fall apart on attempting to remove the pitch or plaster filling to effect any repairs such as removing dents or straightening the stem.

Care must be taken to check on the state of any silver plating: old sheffield plate should never be replated electroplate may be replated, but if it is an antique piece, it must be done sympathetically and then polished to regain an aged patina. This work is more appropriately done by a reputable restorer than a silversmith dealing with modern silver.

*The top of one candlestick broke from its plaster-loaded base after being dropped. Unskilled attempts at sticking the parts together has resulted in stretching and tearing of the thin silver skin. This is worth having repaired because it is one of a pair. On its own, though, it might only have scrap value.*

# SHEFFIELD PLATE

SHEFFIELD PLATE SATISFIED THE GROWING DEMAND FOR A CHEAPER ALTERNATIVE TO SILVER IN THE 1700S, BUT THE IMPRESSIVE SURFACE FINISH WAS ALL TOO SHORTLIVED.

In the 1740s, Thomas Bolsover of Sheffield, England, produced heat-fused sheet metal with a thin silver layer overlaying copper that could then be fashioned into all kinds of household articles. By the 1760s, the silver covering was applied to both sides of the copper, but it proved difficult to conceal the copper at the edges once the piece was constructed. Although increasingly sophisticated methods were devised, as a result of wear, copper edges now characteristically show on most sheffield plate items. The silver used in old sheffield plate was of 92.5 percent sterling standard which gives it a visual edge over the brighter, pure silver of electroplate.

Early sheffield plate was simply shaped and pierced, and suited to straightforward, pre-1800, Neoclassical designs. But then came a fashion for heavily ornamented, cast silver, and sheffield plate was adorned with thin-cast or die-stamped, solid silver motifs, back-filled with lead solder, and fused into place. This left a legacy of punctured or lifted decoration with jagged edges revealing an unpolishable solder core, and very expensive repair costs.

The production of old sheffield plate was killed off by the introduction of electroplating in the 1840s.

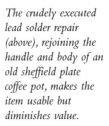

*The crudely executed lead solder repair (above), rejoining the handle and body of an old sheffield plate coffee pot, makes the item usable but diminishes value.*

## GENERAL CARE

Repeated polishing in the past has usually exposed the underlying base metals of sheffield plate. Treat it in much the same way as silver: Polish only once a year, and wash simple pieces frequently in mild, soapy water, before tarnishing sets in. Take extra care not to overclean areas here the copper core is showing through. Do not immerse ornamented pieces in water, as the water may seep into the lead solder core of the applied decoration and hasten deterioration. Instead, use a cloth dampened in a mild detergent solution and blow dry thoroughly with a hair dryer.

## THE RESTORER'S BRIEF

The characteristic, rosy sheen of sheffield plate is worth preserving, so never have it electroplated, which would produce a layer of the wrong medium—pure as opposed to sterling silver—and reduce value. In recent years, a commercial sheffield plate cleaner has been marketed which claims to restore appearance, but the effect is short-lived, and if the cleaner is not continually reapplied, the appearance quickly reverts. Constructional failure is common with worn pieces of sheffield plate. Lifted or torn areas of applied decoration may be resoldered, but once the damage has occurred, the tendency is for it to creep to an adjacent area. Extensive areas of lifting may have distorted and will not be economical to repair; each case must be considered on its merits.

*The engraved initials on the c. 1790 salver (right) have exposed the copper beneath the sheffield plate surface.*

# ELECTROPLATE

T HE INTRODUCTION OF ELECTROPLATING
MADE MORE INTRICATELY SHAPED AND
DECORATED ITEMS POSSIBLE, BUT THE PROCESS
OFTEN CONCEALED POORLY MADE CORES.

The vast production of old sheffield plate in central England
was terminated within a very few years of the patenting of
electroplating in 1840 by George Elkington of Birmingham,
England. The great advantage of this new process was that
pieces could be cast and completely assembled in base metal
and then plated, rather than shaped from the fused copper
and silver "sandwich" of sheffield plate. Electroplating covered
any soldered joins, so they no longer needed concealing as a
separate process. Unfortunately, shoddy workmanship could
also be concealed, rendering many inferior articles not worth
repairing today. Additionally, the deposited layer of silver
could be very thin, further aiding the relative cheapness of
the finished article and reducing its useful life.

The longer the immersion in the electrolytic bath, the
thicker the layer of silver that is deposited, so that better
quality pieces are sometimes stamped with the words
"double" or "triple." Some articles were sectionally plated:
areas likely to receive heavy wear were exposed in the bath
for longer while the other areas were blanked off with wax.
Toward the close of the 1800s, nickel was found to be the
ideal core metal, leading to electroplated nickel-silver
(commonly known by the initials it is marked with: EPNS).

## GENERAL CARE AND
## RESTORATION

Electrolytically deposited silver is 100 percent pure and so
tarnishes more easily than sterling silver and, therefore, needs
polishing more frequently, which inevitably leads to quicker
wear. Frequent washing in mild soap is even more important
than with solid silver, followed by rinsing and thorough
drying with a soft cloth. Never immerse silver plate in silver
cleaning dips, as the direction of the electrolytic current set
up by the presence of the base metal core will strip the silver
layer, not clean it. However, expense allowing, there is no

*The electroplating process was soon picked up by European and
American manufacturers, as in this 1930s American cocktail shaker.*

reason not to replate electroplate, provided an antique piece is
then repolished to an acceptable patina. Such restoration is
best entrusted to a restorer rather than a modern silversmith
who may produce a workmanlike but unsympathetic finish.

# PRECIOUS JEWELRY COLLECTION

**B**ECAUSE OF THE INTRINSIC VALUE OF THE MATERIALS USED IN PRECIOUS JEWELRY, THE INTRICATE WORKMANSHIP, AND BECAUSE IT IS WORN, MAINTENANCE IS ESSENTIAL FOR BOTH VALUE AND SECURITY.

The precious nature of jewelry is not defined purely by the cost, quality, or rarity of its materials. Precious and nonprecious materials can be combined in the same piece, as with 18th-century pastes set in silver. Design and technical expertise are of paramount importance, and other factors: a convincing provenance, an historical association, the design or model for the piece, the jeweler's signature engraved on it, or its original case, will greatly enhance value, and such evidence should be as carefully preserved as the jewelry itself. Any restoration work should strictly adhere to the original; deviations from this will diminish the piece's value as an example of the jeweler's work, and inexpert workmanship will undermine its status as an antique.

PENDANT, 1880s, *with step-cut amethyst and claw-set diamonds in 18 carat gold.*

**Metals:** *Platinum is the hardest metal, and does not tarnish. Gold and silver are lustrous and non corrosive, though silver tarnishes. Both are alloyed with other metals to increase hardness, which results in variations of color and strength, and it is not advisable to carry out repairs unless the colors can be matched accurately.*

**Clasps:** *Most are fairly simple mechanisms, and if broken or faulty should be replaced immediately. Expensive pieces are often secured by a box snap clasp—a small box into which a flat tongue is inserted and released by depressing a thumbpiece—which will continue to be effective if handled with care. A clasp which is hidden within the overall design, has been elaborately worked, gem-set, or has a complicated mechanism, should be handled by a jeweler familiar with such work, and restored sympathetically.*

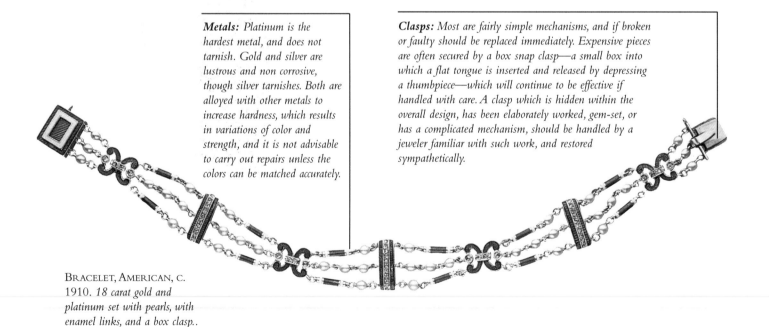

BRACELET, AMERICAN, C. 1910. *18 carat gold and platinum set with pearls, with enamel links, and a box clasp..*

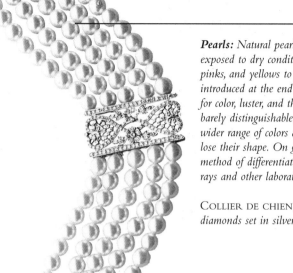

**Pearls:** *Natural pearls can crack and lose their luster if exposed to dry conditions. Their colors range through whites, pinks, and yellows to grays and blacks. Cultured pearls were introduced at the end of the 1800s, and the best of them—for color, luster, and the thickness of their nacreous skin—are barely distinguishable from natural ones. They come in a wider range of colors and are often harder and less likely to lose their shape. On good quality examples, the only certain method of differentiating between the two is by means of X-rays and other laboratory tests.*

COLLIER DE CHIEN, *early 1900s. Strung pearls, with diamonds set in silver and backed with gold.*

ROSE GOLD AND PLATINUM RING WITH RUBIES AND DIAMONDS, 1940s. *The stones appear to be solidly embedded in the metal but the settings are open-backed, which enhances lucidity but reduces protection.*

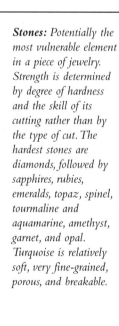

**Stones:** *Potentially the most vulnerable element in a piece of jewelry. Strength is determined by degree of hardness and the skill of its cutting rather than by the type of cut. The hardest stones are diamonds, followed by sapphires, rubies, emeralds, topaz, spinel, tourmaline and aquamarine, amethyst, garnet, and opal. Turquoise is relatively soft, very fine-grained, porous, and breakable.*

JABOT PIN, C. 1925, *carved jade bust mounted in platinum with pavé diamonds.*

## TRADITIONAL TECHNIQUES

The construction of jewelry has changed little throughout its history. An 8th-century Greek bronze fibula (brooch or clasp) employs the same attachment principles of pin and catch as a present-day brooch, while most earring suspension fittings are timeless. Items of precious jewelry have always been adapted to suit changing fashions: parures (matching sets) are dispersed, pendants become brooches, and stones are recut and reset. The results can be worth little more than the value of their constituent parts, but a skilful adaptation can have value in its new form.

Until the 1800s, gems were generally mounted in protective box settings or high collets with a minimum of surface exposure. The open setting gained popularity during the 1850s, and by the century's end, many stones were left unbacked and secured by claws, bringing lightness to the design but an increased vulnerability. From about 1900, the strength of platinum has been widely exploited, enabling settings to be so fine that the stones appear almost unsupported. Nineteenth-century industrialization brought revolutionary changes to jewelry production. Gold and stones from India and South Africa were plentiful and inexpensive. Quantities of cheap machine-made jewelry poured out of the factories in centers such as Birmingham, England, Pforzheim, Germany, and Providence, Rhode Island, well into the 20th century. Though this mass-production broadened the jewelry-owning public, design quality and technical standards suffered. Much of the work from Birmingham, England was

*The floral brooch (above) converts into earrings. Silver settings such as this were considered a more attractive backing for diamonds, and were sometimes backed with gold to avoid skin irritation.*

*If any garnets or pearls on this memorial brooch were to be replaced, they would have to be matched closely to maintain value. The reverse (below) shows the close-fitting case which protects the painted miniature from moisture and dust. The pin and catch clasp style has been used since ancient times.*

rather flimsy stamped gold, silver, and plated versions of fashionable prototypes, and popular "novelty" brooches and pins in the form of names, hearts, horseshoes, or wishbones.

From about the middle of the century some of the major jewelry houses and prominent artist-jewelers such as François Désiré Froment-Meurice (1837–1913) in Paris, the Castellani family in London, Fortunato Pio (1793–1865), Alessandro (1824-1883), and Augusto (1829–1914), and Tiffany & Co. in New York (founded 1834), began to engrave signatures or monograms onto their jewelry. But most jewelry remains unmarked because of its scale and fragility; marking punches can undermine and distort the metal. However, any marks which sustain a provenance should be carefully retained.

## GENERAL CARE

Store items of jewelry separately, ideally in individual bags or boxes lined with acid-free tissue; gems and metals housed together can cause abrasions and chipping, and chains and other materials can become entangled. The luster of pearls is enhanced by wearing them—as described by Carol Ann Duffy (1955– ) in her poem *Warming her Pearls* (c. 1987):

*"Next to my own skin, her pearls. My mistress*
*Bids me wear them, warm them, until evening..."*

They should be re-strung regularly, with nylon or silk string, and knotted between pearls to minimize loss should the string break. Occasional cleaning by an expert is advisable.

Remove rings, bracelets, or heavy necklaces while bathing or doing housework; rings slip off and soap and dirt can settle around stones and clog delicate settings. Knocking against hard surfaces may chip gemstones and scratch or tear metal. To remove oxidization, burnish metals with a lint-free jeweler's cloth. Stones and metals can be cleaned in lukewarm water with a non-chemical detergent added, using a soft toothbrush or paintbrush and cotton swabs. Rinse in clean water, drain on absorbent paper, and dry carefully.

## THE RESTORER'S BRIEF

Do not attempt to repair antique jewelry yourself. Complex repairs, or work on multiskilled pieces which may involve metalwork, enameling, and gemsetting, for example, restoration should be handled by a specialist in those areas. Any material changes to an item of precious jewelry may affect its value, and should be noted. Radical alterations, such as the removal of a pendant or shortening a chain, can destroy the balance of a design.

Discuss with a specialist, the risks involved in replacement of stones, enamel, and metal components, to ensure that any work undertaken will not interfere with the integrity of the design, and compromise its value.

To safeguard jewelry bought mainly for investment, damaged or missing stones should be replaced with their nearest equivalent in color, cut, and weight. If you are primarily concerned with aesthetics, you could replace with a less expensive stone of comparable color, such as a garnet instead of ruby, or with a synthetic gem, although the value of your jewelry will diminish accordingly. Always ensure that the cut of a replacement conforms with the style of the piece; it would be inappropriate to replace a smooth, uncut cabochon, for instance, with a modern 58-facet brilliant cut. Synthetic

*The author scrutinizes jewelry carefully before buying, with a 10x magnifying glass. It is possible to spot the thin nacreous skin of inferior cultured pearls this way. Close examination can also help establish whether a metal is solid or plated, and signs of poor restoration such as hairline cracks or clumsy soldering.*

stones can so closely resemble natural ones in both physical properties and appearance, that detection is possible only with a fiber-optic probe. A synthetic should be sold to you as such. Gem dealers and restorers should also disclose such deceptive treatments as fissure-filling fractures in stones with resins and glass, or enhancing color and refractivity by impregnation with oils.

Armed with this knowledge, their clients can then make an informed choice.

Re-enameling should be placed only in the hands of a craftsman who is fully conversant with period techniques and pigments. Poor, ill-conceived patching of damaged parts of enamel and 'cold' enameling can destroy the appearance and value of a piece.

# COSTUME JEWELRY COLLECTION

COSTUME JEWELRY WAS MADE TO CATCH THE PASSING FASHION, RATHER THAN TO ENDURE, AND, LIKE OTHER JEWELRY MADE FROM NONPRECIOUS MATERIALS, IS OFTEN MORE FRAGILE THAN ITS PRECIOUS COUNTERPARTS.

Costume jewelry is a 20th-century term born of designs created to accessorize a particular outfit or fashion, but jewelry has been made since the earliest civilizations from alternatives to precious gemstones and metals, sometimes to deliberately imitate its valuable counterparts, sometimes to explore the decorative value of a particular material such as wood, shell, or a readily available metal or gemstone. The resulting pieces are, up to a point, as strong or as weak as the material they are made of, and as always it is essential to know what this is for wise care. The technology and craftmanship involved in its manufacture also play an important role in an item's lasting value and durability.

**Metal:** *Look closely at clasps and exposed edges of silver and gold jewelry to check whether it is plated. Polishing removes gold or silver plate; it is better to leave the authentic patina. Shiny surfaces are suspect and may detract from value if due to overpolishing. If the plated surface of a simple item of jewelry has completely worn away, it can be recoated, but check that the right period color can be achieved. It is not worth unmounting a piece of jewelry set with stones in order to replate the metal.*

**Verre églomisé:** *the gilded decoration on the eglomis bracelet (right) is applied to the glass surface, and protected with a layer of varnish or metal foil; it is extremely fragile.*

HASKELL NECKLACE *with faux pearls and plated antique Russian gold.*

**Clasps and clips:** *Check regularly and repair immediately, especially if you wear your jewelry. Keep a stock of spares picked up from flea markets to serve as replacements in keeping with the original design. Broken clasps on base metals can be resoldered and replated, but those on white metal alloys can not.*

EGLOMISÉ BRACELET, *1830s, with safety chain.*

**Pearls and beads:** *Imitation pearls may have a pearlized lacquer made from fishscale essence covering a glass or mother-of-pearl bead. Inspection of the thread helps identify the thickness of the skin. In any event, imitation pearls are to be treated with the greatest delicacy; the coating wears or chips off all too easily. Top-quality faux baroque pearls are characteristic of jewelry such as the necklace by the American designer Miriam Haskell (left) but it is difficult to find matching modern replacements. Glass beads can be heavy and may chip or crack with one swing against a resistant surface.*

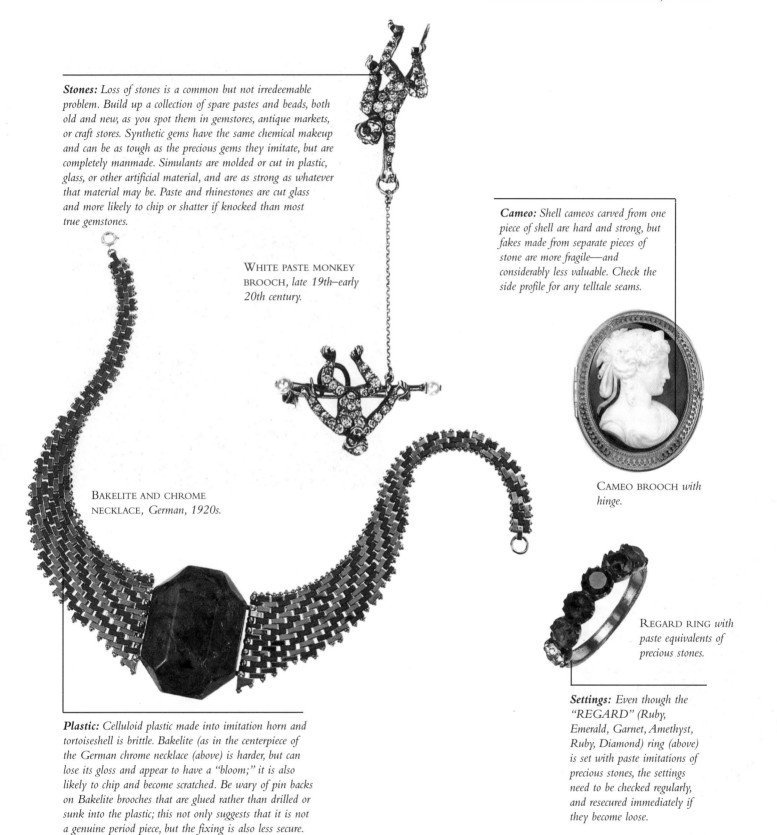

**Stones:** *Loss of stones is a common but not irredeemable problem. Build up a collection of spare pastes and beads, both old and new, as you spot them in gemstores, antique markets, or craft stores. Synthetic gems have the same chemical makeup and can be as tough as the precious gems they imitate, but are completely manmade. Simulants are molded or cut in plastic, glass, or other artificial material, and are as strong as whatever that material may be. Paste and rhinestones are cut glass and more likely to chip or shatter if knocked than most true gemstones.*

WHITE PASTE MONKEY BROOCH, *late 19th–early 20th century.*

**Cameo:** *Shell cameos carved from one piece of shell are hard and strong, but fakes made from separate pieces of stone are more fragile—and considerably less valuable. Check the side profile for any telltale seams.*

CAMEO BROOCH *with hinge.*

BAKELITE AND CHROME NECKLACE, *German, 1920s.*

REGARD RING *with paste equivalents of precious stones.*

**Plastic:** *Celluloid plastic made into imitation horn and tortoiseshell is brittle. Bakelite (as in the centerpiece of the German chrome necklace (above) is harder, but can lose its gloss and appear to have a "bloom;" it is also likely to chip and become scratched. Be wary of pin backs on Bakelite brooches that are glued rather than drilled or sunk into the plastic; this not only suggests that it is not a genuine period piece, but the fixing is also less secure.*

**Settings:** *Even though the "REGARD" (Ruby, Emerald, Garnet, Amethyst, Ruby, Diamond) ring (above) is set with paste imitations of precious stones, the settings need to be checked regularly, and resecured immediately if they become loose.*

# TECHNOLOGICAL IMPROVEMENTS

In the ancient civilizations of Mesopotamia and Egypt, cheap jewelry was made out of glass and other readily available materials alongside precious jewelry. The earliest imitation jewelry available for today's collector dates from the 1700s, when the skilled gemcutters of Bohemia (now the Czech Republic) began to produce high-quality imitation stones. They used the lead glass invented by English glassmaker George Ravenscroft, which was tougher and denser than ordinary glass, making it easier to cut and facet; it was also clear, took color well, and had a better sparkle. The fashion for paste—as the glass gemstones became known—reached its peak in France where Georges Frédéric Stras explored the full potential of the glass gems. They were usually mounted in gold and/or silver, but sometimes in gilt metal. Some stones were foiled-backed with paper-thin sheets of metal such as silver or copper to increase fire and depth of color. The metals react to damp in the atmosphere and will tarnish and corrode, so the mounts in which they were set were pinched tight to make them airtight. The best-quality and most durable examples of paste have stones sealed within smooth-backed gold or silver cups. Inexpert foiling is identifiable by a crumpled or flaked appearance and discoloration.

Costume jewelry, as distinct from antique paste, is often made of base metals such as brass or copper, which will tarnish, or pinchbeck. An alloy of zinc and copper introduced in the 1720s that resembled gold, pinchbeck occasionally shows a little verdigris which is easily removed with a warm soapy water solution. Later in the century, the process of fusing a thin film of silver onto a base metal produced Sheffield plate, a low-cost alternative to solid

*The pinchbeck and gilt metal parure, c. 1825 (above) does not tarnish but does sometimes show a little green verdigris which is easily removed with a cotton swab dipped in warm, soapy water, and squeezed out well. Make sure each item is completely dry after cleaning.*

*French jet, as in the c. 1910 necklace (left), is a very hard glass. It can be distinguished from real jet—a form of fossilized coal—by its colder touch and tiny air bubbles which are sometimes visible. It is more likely to chip and shatter than real jet.*

silver. In Providence, Rhode Island, the same technique was adapted in the early 1800s to produce gold-filled or rolled gold and a mass of cheap jewelry. Both, especially soft gold, are subject to wear, although electroplating, introduced in the 1840s, produced thicker and more durable plated metals.

Some nonprecious materials were recognized in their own right rather than as cheap alternatives; cut steel, with its sharp-cut gunmetal glitter became fashionable in the late 18th century but had gone out of fashion by c.1850. It is also extremely tough. Jet, a very hard form of black fossilized brown coal, was cut into mourning jewelry in the 1800s; it is more resistant to shattering than its imitation, French jet, which is in fact glass. The ultimate in cheap, versatile materials, from the late 19th century, was plastic. Celluloid plastic, a mix of fiber, camphor, nitric acid, and sulfuric acid, developed in the United States in 1863, was dyed to imitate tortoiseshell and horn and molded into costume jewelry, dressing table sets, and buttons; but it was brittle and inflammable. More successful was Bakelite, which could be cut, molded, drilled, and chiseled, and was fashioned into a mass of jewelry in the 1920s and 30s, but can lose its gloss and crack with age.

## GENERAL CARE

If you wear your jewelry, regularly check settings, links, and fastenings, and always put it on after dressing (to avoid catching on threads) and making up, since cosmetics, hair spray and perfume can corrode the delicate finishes on plated jewelry, faux pearls, jet and other beads. Never wash pieces in water which could dissolve adhesive, tarnish metal, discolor paste, and shrink or rot the string on a beaded necklace. Paste should be cleaned with a dry jeweler's powder, though you can wipe individual stones with a cotton swab (bud) just moistened with a drop of window-cleaning liquid, as long as no liquid seeps into the setting.

Never use proprietory cleaners on metal mounts, as the plating could wear or flake off. Metal can be revitalized with a light dust from a jeweler's cloth, but a patina is invariably desirable except on deliberately bright rhodium pieces, and these do not tarnish.

*How **not** to store your jewelry (above), as hard gems and metals can scratch softer materials, and chains become tangled. Instead, store separately in boxes or cloth pochettes, or wrap in acid-free tissue.*

## THE RESTORER'S BRIEF

The decision to restore or replace is very much an individual one. If you wear your jewelry, it is important from both aesthetic and security points of view for it to be intact, so restore, replace, and enjoy. But if you collect for investment only, think twice, for other collectors might devalue from restored pieces.

Some jewelers will not repair costume jewelry, and indeed, they may not have the requisite experience for the most delicate material, and plated and base metals, for example, react differently from precious metals. So check, especially if soldering is involved. Ask for a necklace to be restrung on cotton necklace thread, rather than nylon or steel. Even though these are apparently stronger, they do tend to stretch or bend out of shape, and string of course, can be knotted between each bead if the design allows, so that in the event of a break, you do not lose all the beads.

Simple gold and silver plated items can be replated, but if stones have to be removed it may not be worthwhile.

The most common problem with paste jewelry is loss of gems; ask a restorer for advice on where to find period substitutes, but do build up your own supply of odd pieces from antique stores and markets.

*Before having costume jewelry repaired, check that the jeweler has experience in the specific materials which are often more delicate than their precious equivalents.*

# THE COIN COLLECTION

THE VALUE OF A COIN CAN PLUMMET AS A RESULT OF OVERZEALOUS CLEANING. SOMETIMES COINS LOOK AS THOUGH THEY HAVE FINE SURFACE DETAIL, BUT ALL THE DETAIL IS PRESERVED IN THE CORROSION, AND REMOVING THIS COULD BE FATAL.

## THE FABRIC OF A COIN

Because coins have been mass-produced since ancient times, and hoardes are still occasionally discovered, specimens from the civilizations of Asia Minor, Greece, and Rome can still be found on the collectors' market. In Asia Minor, c. 600 B.C., coins were made of electrum, a natural alloy of gold and silver. Other early coins were made of bronze, an alloy of copper and tin, a durable copper and tin alloy, or even—in ancient Britain and Greece—of iron. Of the wide spectrum of metals and metal alloys used through the centuries, all, apart from pure gold, tarnish or corrode as a result of exposure to the atmosphere.

From c. 630 B.C., coins began to be stamped and engraved, and it is the preservation of such markings that has such an effect on value. Even a mint coin, which has never been in circulation, can vary in brightness, clarity of design, and degree of surface marking—but may be worth more than ten times its used version.

**OBVERSE OF 1858 COPPER PENNY:** *A smooth brownish or greenish patina on copper and bronze is acceptable and desirable, but if green verdigris is allowed to develop into the bright green powdery spots of "bronze disease," this must be halted by a conservator if the coin is to survive, and humidity levels lowered in the storage unit, possibly using silica gel crystals.*

**BRITISH HALF CROWN, 1712. SILVER.** *A smooth, black or bluish patina on silver is acceptable, even desirable, as long as the surface decoration is not obliterated. Silver coins alloyed with copper tend to lose their copper components in burial, which leaves a very rich silver surface, but extreme fragility. For this reason, never try to straighten a bent coin, as it may break.*

**FRENCH FRANC:** *A patina like this can add to a coin's aesthetic and actual value, as long as the design and any lettering shows through.*

**COLOMBIAN GOLD PESO, 19TH CENTURY:** *Pure gold does not tarnish, but it is very soft metal and wears easily. If it is alloyed with other metals such as nickel or silver, tarnishing will occur.*

**OBVERSE OF BRASS TOKEN OF THE HUDSON'S BAY COMPANY,** *valued at one beaver pelt. The quality of the original workmanship in the striking (or minting) of the coin, such as clarity of detail, is important, as it often provides a clue to the history of the coin.*

## GENERAL CARE

Hold a coin at the edges between thumb and index finger; avoid direct contact on the face or obverse as the salts from your skin accelerate discoloration and tarnishing.

Coins need to be stored so that they are protected from any moisture or pollution in the environment and from knocking or rubbing against each other. A custom-made coin cabinet in air-dried mahogany, rosewood, or walnut equipped with slim drawers and cutout slots or divisions for the coins, is attractive, and allows easy access and display, but is expensive. Certain highly resinous woods, such as oak, pine, or cedar, and manufactured fiber board made from compressed wood, are particularly acidic and will induce a chemical reaction and tarnishing. Lay each coin on acid-free felt or paper, and place small bags of moisture-absorbing silica gel crystals in the drawers. These can be dried out in an oven set at a low temperature and reused.

Alternatives are metal containers, glass stacking systems, or coin albums or windows—as long as they are made with chemically inert plastic.

Commercial brass or silver cleaning polishes, and denture cleaners are all abrasive and must never be used on valuable coins and medals as they could irreparably damage the surface. Surface dirt and grease should come off in warm water with a touch of mild detergent added. Always use a brush with soft bristles of a natural—never an artificial—fiber, a pure cotton cloth, or a cotton swab, and rinse and dry thoroughly. Lightly wipe but never rub the relief areas, so that tarnish remains in the crevices to emphasize the design. A cotton swab dampened with petroleum spirit should help remove black tarnish on silver. Finally, to add a protective surface, apply a thin coating of paraffin wax using a soft-bristled brush.

## TERMS OF QUALITY

*For the collector, the condition of a coin is the most significant aspect, especially with regard to examples produced over the last two centuries. A scale of qualitative terms has been devised to describe condition. Coins described as "fair, good, medium, or poor" are the lowest ratings.*

**FDC** *(fleur de coin) Perfect*
**Unc** *(uncirculated) Mint condition (although the quality may still vary)*
**XF** *(extra fine) or* **EF** *(extremely fine) Minimal wear probably only visible under magnification*
**VF** *(very fine) Light wear visible to the naked eye*
**F** *(fine) Obvious wear but all essential design and elements distinct*
**VG** *(very good) Worn and usually only valuable if rare*

*The closefitting drawers and doors of a traditional coin cabinet (above) keep out the three major enemies of coins, especially excavated examples: dust, moisture, and atmospheric pollution.*

## CONSERVATOR'S BRIEF

Coins are conserved rather than restored, and if in any doubt as to whether tarnishing or verdigris should be removed, a conservator should be consulted. The condition of excavated coins varies according to the ground environment from which they came, and is always potentially unstable. So it is worth asking advice even as far as what is apparently only surface dirt is concerned.

If the item is so discolored that it is impossible to distinguish or identify the design, it is likely to need highly skilled cleaning. Corrosion can be removed by chemical solutions or by using extremely delicate chisels and scalpels under magnification, but either method can be traumatic, and the possible outcomes should be discussed with the conservator in advance.

It is worth asking for a protective dilute lacquer coating to be applied to a conserved coin—just enough to protect it from further degradation, but not make it unnaturally shiny.

Thin strands of natural fiber, fine weaving and stitching, and often intricate patterns and colors, make textiles among the most delicate and difficult of antiques to preserve. They attract insects, quickly acquire mold in damp conditions, and embrittle and fade in light. Unlike works of art on paper—a similar, fiber-based organic medium—they are not automatically framed and sealed in a protective frame. But this may be essential for the preservation of old and precious textiles, even if they were originally designed for practical use. If your decision is to walk on your carpet, or wear your period gloves, you must do so in the knowledge that the pleasure will be a relatively transitory one, for their life will inevitably be shortened as a result.

# TEXTILES

# A PILE CARPET

**_Weft threads:_** _Usually straight on machine-made carpets and uneven on handwoven rugs._

R ECOGNIZING THE DIFFERENT TECHNIQUES, MATERIALS, AND DYES USED IN THE MAKING OF A PILE CARPET WILL HELP YOU DETERMINE ITS LASTING VALUE, AS WELL AS ITS ORIGINS.

Before you mourn the bald patches and frayed edges a pile carpet has acquired in its lifetime, you can assess how well it was made in the first place; for this will have a bearing on its durability as well as its value.

Few examples survive from before the 18th century—and these are often only fragments—bearing witness to the vulnerability of a carpet's natural fibers to damp and mold, insect attack, to breakdown and fading from light, and above all, to the ravages of wear. Before you decide to use your carpet, not only do you need to assess its provenance and value, its quality and condition, but to consider whether a rug designed for slippered feet in marble halls should be subjected to heavy modern household wear.

**_Design:_** _Motifs and symbolism, colors, materials, and textures are all indicators of a carpet's origins and whether it is handwoven or machine-made, both of which may have a bearing on quality and durability. Modern, machine-woven examples tend to have regular patterns—and uniform quality; they are a different breed altogether and should not be compared.with handwoven textiles. Handwoven rugs are freer in style, and variable in quality. Tribal rugs tend to have a lower knot count than those produced in village workshops, but can still be of high quality._

**_Selvage or side cords:_** _In a handmade carpet the side cords are an extension of the whole piece, and oversewn between the warps; if the oversewing wears and the side cords are exposed, immediate restoration is necessary. Machine-made carpets are often woven in narrow lengths and sewn together to complete the pattern. The edges therefore do not normally have a separate binding, but seams should be checked and resewn when necessary._

A 16TH-CENTURY PERSIAN CARPET—_so rare, precious, and delicate that it should be on display rather than used._

**_Pile:_** _Check closely for bare patches; they may have been disguised with paint. The denser the pile, the more difficult it is to pull out the pile from the front unless there is damage to the weft and warp threads. On the looser pile of many machine-made carpets, tufts are less secure. Worn patches on valuable rugs should be stabilized by a conservator and the removal of original material avoided._

*Ends and fringes: On handmade rugs, these are an integral part of the whole piece and if they become worn or unraveled, pile and border designs will be lost if they are not restored quickly, or the warp ends "stopped" by blanket stitching to help prevent unraveling.*

*Main body of the carpet: A carpet that is worn evenly will lose less value than if there is a single, very obvious, worn patch. A large, prominent stain against a plain background would devalue, but a small stain disguised by the pattern, or which could be hidden by furniture, would have little effect. Some stains, such as dog's urine, are virtually impossible to remove. All should be treated by an expert.*

## KEY TO CARPET KNOTS

*Symmetrical, Turkish or Ghiordes knot, common in geometric designs, and often seen on tribal rugs. Yarn is wound around two adjacent warps.*

*Equally durable is the asymmetrical, Persian or Senneh knot, generally used for curvilinear designs. The yarn is wrapped obliquely around two adjacent warps.*

*The Jufti or false knot produces coarser, less hardwearing carpets, as one piece of yarn is wrapped around four warp threads, resulting in a lighter density weave. This is the symmetrical version.*

*Asymmetrical version of the Jufti or false knot, used for curvilinear designs. Jufti knots are quick to weave and have been used on 17th-century Persian rugs and 20th-century rugs from eastern Iran.*

*The Spanish knot—only really used in Spain—is loose, as the yarn goes around a single alternate warp (which is visible between the knots). This gives a smooth finish to the diagonal lines, while horizontal and vertical lines are slightly stepped.*

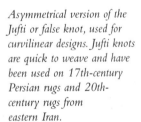

123

*1930s copy of a traditional Savonnerie design (right) retains the luxuriant quality with which the French factory near Paris has always been associated. Savonnerie first pioneered European—as distinct from Orientally inspired—designs in the 17th century.*

*The easily transportable loom (below) used by nomadic tribes of Central Asia produces small, narrow rugs which tend to be slightly uneven in shape and width. Pile rugs, unlike flatweaves, are always woven in one piece.*

## IT'S ALL IN THE PILE

The techniques used for pile carpets today are fundamentally the same as those established by the great weaving traditions of Turkey and Iran that flourished in the 16th century. They were picked up by the leading European factories of Savonnerie and Aubusson in France, and Axminster and Wilton in England during the 18th and 19th centuries.

Pile carpets are made from tufts of yarn knotted onto a warp and kept in place by the weft. The warp and weft form the ground weave, usually of cotton—which keeps its shape well—or jute. On some old and nomadic carpets, wool has been used for the warp and weft as well as the pile, but it is not as strong. The main key to quality—and value—is the

*Look at the underside of a pile carpet to see how densely knotted it is. To identify whether the knotting is symmetrical or asymmetrical, fold the pile horizontally along the weft and examine a row. A magnifying glass helps.*

goat wool. Delicate silk rugs were not made for heavy use; those with a silk warp and weft may split in the foundation weave across the warp.

Natural dyes from vegetable, organic, or animal sources were traditionally used, and varied in stability according to the skill of the dyer and the mordants used. Aniline dyes introduced in the 1850s were cheaper, easier, and produced brighter colors, but faded easily and led to fiber breakdown. From the 1920s, synthetic chrome dyes offered good quality and permanence of color.

density of knots; the more there are within a given area, the less likely the carpet is to flex or for the pile to flatten, and the stronger it will be, since only a small part of each tuft is exposed to wear. A fine 18th-century Persian carpet may have several hundred knots to the square inch; an inferior example could have as few as 12 knots per square inch. Indian and Chinese carpets tend to have a thicker, higher pile than the close-cut Central Asian examples.

Sheep's wool is the most common and hardwearing yarn used, although its durability varies according to the type of sheep, climate, and pasture. Some nomadic tribes use camel or

*Custom-made fabric strips (right) can be sewn along the sides of a rug to reinforce it, add weight to prevent curling, and help keep the rug from slipping on the floor.*

*From the early 1900s, rugs were often chemically treated and repainted to suit the taste of different Western markets, such as the 1930s "painted Sarouk" (below), but the process shortens the life of the fibers.*

*Where threads have become separated, a carpet restorer or conservator can introduce a new length of yarn, usually finer than the original, which runs along the broken thread. Equally, a new weft thread can be woven in, recreating the foundation weave.*

*To replace a fringe, yarn is looped through the weft threads and secured where it will be hidden by the pile. The ends are then trimmed to an even length.*

# THE FLATWEAVE RUG

MOST FLATWEAVES ARE REVERSIBLE, WHICH MEANS THAT WEAR CAN BE SHARED BETWEEN BOTH SIDES, BUT EQUALLY, ANY REPAIR WILL SHOW ON BOTH SIDES.

Flatweave textiles are a woven web of warp and weft threads with no knots and no pile, and have been made for thousands of years, predating pile carpets. Traditionally, they have been woven by tribal and nomadic communities for their own needs—notably in Central Asia, India, and the Americas—using wool from domestic animals. Only if there was any surplus was it sold commercially. Before transposing flatweave rugs to a modern home, it is worth bearing in mind that they were designed for a completely different lifestyle: to insulate and decorate the walls or doors of tents, and as blankets. Even floor coverings were not designed to be walked on in anything but stocking feet, certainly never with outdoor shoes.

AYDIN KILIM: *An example of a good-quality flatweave, tightly woven throughout; a slightly fuzzy appearance is a sign of badly spun yarn.*

*Selvage: The lengthwise edges where the weft threads loop around the warp may become misshapen or wear away, and should be overcast to strengthened them. The cords often break because they curl or bend over the edge of an underlay that has been cut too small.*

*Fringe: The fringe is usually an extension of the warp threads that are the framework of a flatweave textile. They need to be knotted and or braided to prevent the entire rug from unraveling. If they become worn, or catch and break, they must be repaired immediately. Overcasting at this point may indicate previous repair or a preventive measure; neither will detract if sensitively done.*

*Slits: These are a feature of kilims which are made using the slit-tapestry weave technique. They occur where the weft of a particular color is discontinued and a new color introduced. Slits do not make a kilim weaker than any other flatweave, but they can become caught, and if this happens, strain is put upon the surrounding weft threads.*

*Dhurries (right), from India, Pakistan, and Tibet, are usually of cotton, and tend to be heavier and duller in color than other flatweaves. Some are coarse, tough weaves for floor and bedcoverings; others are finer decorative weaves for festive occasions.*

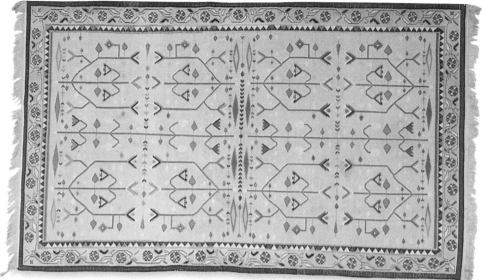

**Seams:** *The join between two or more pieces which have been made on a narrow loom, for example. Check that they are secure to guard against future tearing or distortion.*

## CHANGING COLOR

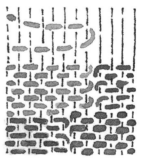

*The slit tapestry weave technique used on kilims (above), showing a change of color in the weft threads.*

*Slits at color changes can be avoided by dovetailing (above), in which different colored wefts are returned around the same warp.*

## TRIBAL TRADITIONS

The construction and quality of flatweave rugs vary according to where they are, or have been, made. Unlike pile carpets, in which the wefts travel across the full width of the textile, in flatweaves, the wefts may travel across and back over only a few warps as they form the pattern, and this results in a less rigid construction. Flatweaves are also less yarn-intensive and quicker to weave, so are generally not only less expensive, but not as resistant to wear as pile carpets. They are also lightweight and usually reversible. The weft threads are woven into the warp and because they are usually finer and more loosely spun, each row can be compacted tightly against the last so that the warp is concealed by solid color and pattern. Sumak flatweaves of the Caucasus and eastern Anatolia have a more rigid construction as the wefts not only cross the full width of the weaving, but are taken back and forward to create a particular surface texture which appears like a diagonal stitch.

As with pile rugs, flatweaves made by tribal communities tend to show inconsistencies in the weave tension due to the constant dismantling and setting up of the loom in transit; but they are more likely to be colored with natural dyes, and carefully graded wool from local resources. Quality may be more variable in village workshops, where larger rugs are woven on permanent looms, because wool and dyes are bought in cheaply. Flatweaves from commerical workshops are very much geared to the colors and patterns required by the Western market.

Whatever the age of a flatweave, the way to judge quality—and durability—is by look and feel. Some tribes use coarse grades of wool for the warp threads, others cotton or jute; all have to be good, strong quality to withstand the high tension on the loom. Sheep's wool is the most common—and reliable—weaving yarn, and invariably carefully graded in nomadic communities; but even this varies in texture and strength according to the breed of sheep, local climate, type of pasture, and the use for which the textile is designed.

Natural dyes—from local resources such as henna, bark, fruit peel, and plants—were traditionally used until the 19th century. The first chemical dyes used from the 1860s were unstable, but were superseded in the 20th century by more reliable chrome dyes. The natural dyes tend to be more subtle in color; their lasting power depends on the skill of the dyer.

## GENERAL CARPET CARE

Always place a precious rug or carpet where it will not be worn by constant or heavy traffic, away from dampness and any potential danger spots such as within range of sparks from an open fire. Turn it around from time to time so that overall exposure to use, light, and heat is even. Place protective cups or small circles of wood beneath furniture legs and castors, especially in the case of a pile carpet, to prevent the pile or weave from being crushed. Take advantage of the reversibility of many flatweaves and share the wear between the two sides to extend their life. If necessary, close the curtains during the day when the room is not in use, for once colors have faded they cannot be restored. Bear in mind that insect damage is more likely where there is no circulation of air, such as beneath furniture, where the carpet is undisturbed.

Never nail or glue a rug to the floor, or glue anything to it if it is to be hung. Ask a carpet restorer to advise you on the safest way of hanging and on the best means of support. A wall-hung textile should be backed with linen and hung on a wall that is flat and free from moisture, and not facing a window. It should be hung with the warp running vertically to take the strain, as the wefts tend to stretch and distort.

*Nonslip underlay should extend beyond the main woven area of a rug to support fringe ends and selvage; it also protects from dust and any roughness in the floor surface.*

*Compare the bad, amateur repair (left), which is obvious, ugly, and weak, and the barely visible yet reliable repair (right) in which colors, pattern, and textures have been carefully matched.*

Lightly vacuum rugs and carpets regularly to keep dust, mites, and moths at bay. Dust and dirt have an abrasive effect, so vacuum the top regularly and the undersurface every six months. Use a very soft brush, or a cylinder vacuum cleaner on low power with a piece of net secured over the nozzle so that fringes are not caught. On a pile carpet, work in the direction of the pile. Never use an upright vacuum cleaner since the revolving brushes can be brutal. Turn the carpet upside down on the floor and tamp (pat) the reverse gently but firmly with the flat of the hand or a fly swatter. This will loosen a surprising amount of gritty dirt, and not harm the carpet if it is kept flat. Blot any spillages immediately before they soak in; avoid rubbing, which disrupts the pile. Serious stains should be treated by a restorer.

To store, always roll rather than fold a carpet, interleaving with acid-free tissue paper, and with a pile carpet, with the pile uppermost to minimize crushing. Inspect regularly. Do not apply any chemical insect repellent.

## THE RESTORER'S BRIEF

Repairs on antique or valuable carpets should always be done professionally, and sooner rather than later to prevent further deterioration, especially if they are in use. As a general rule, invisible repairs that have been well executed do not affect the value of a carpet or rug, whereas poor ones such as patches glued over a hole will. In fact, a good reweave of a small area that has been torn, moth-eaten, or unevenly worn would increase value, whereas to take out part of a rug so that an area of loss no longer shows would devalue it.

Carpets and rugs in constant use should be professionally cleaned from time to time. Severe stains should be tackled by a professional restorer and may not always be successfully removed.

Ask the restorer to match stitches, materials, and dyes in keeping with the original; this is especially important with flatweaves. Pile carpets can be repiled only if the wefts and warps are strong enough to support it, and these may need to be rewoven first. Have worn kilim ends or side cords repaired promptly.

*Once the selvage had given way, a hole soon developed on the flatweave (above). A matching wool thread was run round the hole to about $1/2$ inch (1 cm) into the surrounding undamaged area.*

*The warp threads were reconstructed with strong cotton replacements run across the hole.*

*Carefully matched wool threads were woven in and out of the replacement warp and packed down tightly against each other to recreate the original weft.*

# AN EMBROIDERED SAMPLER

SAMPLERS, OR "EXAMPLERS," WERE TRADITIONALLY A MEANS OF PRACTICING NEEDLEWORK TECHNIQUES, BUT GRADUALLY THEY WERE MADE TO BE DECORATIVE. AN UNFRAMED SAMPLER IS EASIER TO EXAMINE BUT HAS ALSO BEEN EXPOSED TO THE ENVIRONMENT.

In the 1500s, samplers provided a record of different stitches, motifs, border patterns, and other designs used on costume or ecclesiastical garments. The stitches were placed, in no particular order, on linen that was loose-woven enough for the techniques to be clearly seen. By the 1600s samplers evolved into sewing exercises for children, and stitches were more formally arranged on long, narrow strips of linen, often featuring verses or improving texts. These are now rare and highly valued. Threads were linen or silk in naturally dyed colors, with the occasional use of metal threads, and in favorable environmental conditions have kept their colors remarkably well. Square samplers were a feature of the 18th century, and were still usually worked, following patterns from books, on a fine linen ground. Such grounds have proved susceptible to marked fiber degradation, and if wet cleaned, can disintegrate. Very delicate examples on satin, fine glazed muslin, or fine wool, are more susceptible to damage from light than coarser fabrics. Fine wool, easily mistaken for fine linen, is particularly prone to insect infestation.

By the 1800s, samplers were produced in huge numbers, especially with the introduction of printed kits—which often used cheaper materials—and lost their individuality. Chemically dyed threads from the 1860s proved unstable, particularly the blacks and greens.

## GENERAL CARE OF NEEDLEWORKED TEXTILES

Old and delicate needlework should be professionally mounted and framed, or larger, stronger pieces can be hung (see p.135). Whether hung, framed, or in use, textiles should be kept out of direct sunlight, and away from dampness and pollution such as smoke, which they all too readily absorb.

Remove surface dust from unframed textiles regularly but gently, using a soft-bristled sable brush. Stronger fabrics can be vacuumed with a cylinder vacuum cleaner on low power, with a fine net over the nozzle to prevent loose threads or beads from being caught. Ask an expert for guidance, if in doubt. Before putting textiles into storage, make sure they are clean, as stains can eat away at fabrics and attract insect pests. Go to a conservator rather than a cleaner, as modern cleaning fluids can savage delicate textiles and dyes. Roll the textile, with the patterned, beaded, or worked side uppermost, loosely around a tube covered with acid-free tissue, interleaving with the tissue as you go. Contact with highly acidic materials such as lowgrade wood composites or paperboard accelerates deterioration. Place the textile in a cloth bag (not plastic, as condensation may form) or acid-free box. If the textile is folded, fill out the folds generously with acid-free tissue to minimize creasing and strain on the fabric, and interleave with tissue.

Check regularly for signs of insect attack. When taking out of storage, do not force folds out. They should be gently eased out by a conservator.

*Stains on fine, embroidered materials are difficult to remove, especially where there is stitching from which the color might run. A conservator tests for color, surface stability, and to identify the stain to establish whether solvents can be safely applied.*

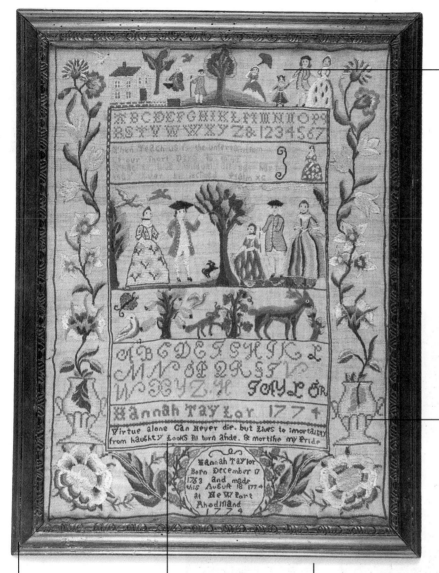

**Background:** *Yellowing caused by fiber degradation can be improved. Check for fiber distortion caused by tension or shrinkage, or if the sampler has been nailed to a stretcher. A conservator can reinforce weak or torn areas from the back with acid-free card covered in a washed cotton or linen onto which the sampler is sewn.*

**Stains:** *Needles and pins from a sewing box, nails where the sampler has been attached to a stretcher, or metal threads may have corroded and stained the fabric. The cause of the corrosion must be removed— if this does not involve cutting some of the fabric away—and the stains treated to prevent their spreading and rotting the fabric.*

**Stitching:** *Because of their fineness, and weakened by the dyeing process, embroidery yarns degrade quickly, especially if not protected by a frame. Whole areas of stitching may have disappeared, and can not be restored. Look at the bottom of the frame for fiber particles—a sign that silk threads are disintegrating. Faded or muted colors do detract from value, but nothing can be done to restore them.*

**Frame:** *If a sampler is in its original frame and on its original stretcher, it should be kept intact if it is not threatening future stability. Otherwise, have remounted, using acid-free materials, in a sealed, glazed frame, to keep out insects, dusts, and pollution.*

**Fold lines:** *If samplers have been repeatedly folded and packed away in a sewing box, fold lines with stressed and stretched fibers weaker than the surrounding fabric will have occurred and can sometimes be restored by an expert.*

**Backing:** *Sometimes samplers were mounted on stretchers or a piece of rough wood, sometimes faced with paper. If any of these materials is split or highly acidic, have them replaced with acid-free materials, but check for any labels and dates before discarding.*

AMERICAN 18TH-CENTURY SAMPLER *worked by 11-year-old Hannah Taylor, preserved in a sealed frame.*

# CANVAS AND BEADWORK

LOOSE-WOVEN LINEN CANVAS, EMBROIDERED WITH SILK OR WOOL THREADS, WAS RELATIVELY STRONG, BUT EMBELLISHMENT WITH INCOMPATIBLE MATERIALS SUCH AS METAL OR GLASS COULD HAVE SEVERE REPERCUSSIONS ON THE LONGTERM SURVIVAL OF AN EMBROIDERY.

A linen or cotton warp and weft that was often completely concealed by embroidery to create a dense, colorful, patterned fabric combined reasonable strength and decorative appeal. From medieval times, it provided a practical and versatile means of covering upholstery, for bed and wall

*If this beadwork bag (above) continues to be used to any great extent, the continual flexing of the lightweight textile will weaken the securing threads. On some bags, the beads are woven into the textile rather than embroidered on top.*

**Beads:** *Missing or broken beads should only be replaced if authentic alternatives are available; if not, the affected area can be reworked in matching embroidery thread. A clouded surface on glass beads indicates irreversible glass disease—leading to crazing and crumbling—which is accelerated by damp. The process can be slowed by keeping the piece in a dry environment, but this could cause embrittlement of the textile. Slight discoloration or tarnish on metal beads or threads is not serious, unless corrosion has set in, which could stain and rot the textile.*

**Color:** *Differences in color tone may be due to dirt or dust, which are relatively easy to put right, but if fading is the cause, this is costly to put right and will not regain value. Better to live with imperfections.*

**Backing fabric:** *If chemical reaction from disintegrating glass or metal beads has stained, embrittled, or rotted the canvas, this should be stabilized immediately. Tension in the stitching can also weaken the backing. Sometimes the backing is incompatible, as with a beaded chiffon dress or bag, A supporting fabric can be applied, but useful days are over. Check the reverse for weaknesses and repairs; newer, stronger threads could strain the original materials.*

**Embroidery:** *Have lost stitching promptly replaced with matching yarns; a single length of thread is used for whole sections of the same color, and one break will threaten the whole section. Embroidery should not reach the edge of the canvas, but many pieces have been cut to fit frames or upholstery, which can result in loss of stitches and fraying. The edges can be secured by blanket stitching.*

EMBROIDERED PANEL, LATE 1800s, on plain canvas, with glass and metal beads.

hangings as well as bell-pulls, purses, belts and waistcoats. Many canvas work designs were inspired by hanging tapestries—which are woven, not embroidered. (Canvas work is often wrongly referred to as "tapestry," which can cause confusion if discussing the subject with a conservator.) The stitches—mainly cross stitch, gros point, and petit point (tent stitch)—are simple, but only as strong as the thread that was used.

In the 19th century, there was a fashion for leaving an unembroidered canvas border around a main design (which incorporated pile stitches to accentuate the three-dimensional effect). The warp and weft of the bare area were wrapped in colored silk before the canvas was woven. The silk wrapping faded quickly, and is now sometimes only visible with a magnifying glass.

Crewel work, first popular in the 17th century, was revived in the late 1800s. The ground fabric, traditionally a substantial linen-cotton mix, was worked in a limited palette of colors in wool yarn. Today's collector needs to check the reverse to make sure that old embroidery has not been reapplied to a new ground.

*A textile conservator uses yarns that closely match in texture, type, strength, and color to secure the braiding on a textile.*

## Adding sparkle

Glass and metal beadwork added three-dimensional sparkle to all forms of embroidery, reaching a height of popularity in the 1850s, for items such as footstools, firescreens, and purses,, but also introduced the fragility of glass, the corrosion of metal and the problems of combining hard and soft materials.

Beads were exported from Germany to Europe and America from c. 1810. Later came printed, squared, paper embroidery patterns to make "Berlin woolwork," which sometimes incorporated beads, and from the 1860s, was sold with yarns colored with brash, unstable aniline dyes.

Even 20th-century needlework, with later, colorfast dyes, should be cleaned by a specialist. The open weave of most canvases is stiffened by gum arabic which would be removed by washing. Distortion during the embroidery process (the diagonal tent stitch results in a canvas shaped like a parallelogram) is rectified by pinning the canvas square over a damp cloth; the gum arabic softens, enabling the distortion to be corrected, but resets on drying.

*Fitting embroidery over a stool (left) immediately puts strain on the exposed canvas; use gradually leads to the stitched surface wearing away, exposing the underlying canvas, which in turn, splits. A conservator can support the reverse to strengthen and stablilize the embroidery. Upholstery pieces should be supported on linen slightly larger than the canvas, and the edges used to tension the embroidery.*

# A PATCHWORK COVERLET

P ATCHWORK MADE PRACTICAL USE OF LEFTOVER MATERIALS, BUT THEREIN LIES MUCH OF ITS WEAKNESS, AS THE RECYCLED FABRICS MAY ALREADY HAVE BEEN WORN AND FADED, OR OF DIFFERENT AGES OR WEIGHTS, AND COULD LITERALLY TEAR EACH OTHER APART.

Patchworks have long provided an economical alternative to woven textiles. The strength of an individual patchwork or quilt depends on the materials used, their condition, how they have been cut and joined together, and on the overall construction of the finished piece. The Amish sect in America, for example traditionally made coverlets like the one featured from leftovers from dressmaking and any scraps of material that came to hand. The items were fairly rough and ready, intended for everyday use rather than for decoration, but were firmly handstitched in strong cotton and generally well made. Subsequent heavy use, however, has meant that authentic 19th-century examples tend to be heavily worn.

The printed cotton chintz that was popular in 18th-century applied patchworks held its color well; so when the original patchwork wore out, motifs were recycled—cut out and applied to a white cotton ground. This technique known as "broderie Perse," was popular in England and America from the 1780s to the 1830s. While recently reconstituted patchworks are generally not desirable, broderie Perse has become a collectors' item in its own right, and because of the compatibility of the original cotton chintz and the later cotton ground—they are also reasonably sturdy.

Quilting—notably in 19th-century American piece patchworks, and whole cloth quilts from the northeast of England and Provence, France—adds constructional strength, since the top surface is attached to a backing fabric, often with a layer of batting (wadding) between, and the whole secured with an all-over network of stitching. If a patchwork is joined only to a backing fabric at the edges, there is much more movement and stress. Design, too, has a bearing on strength; a patchwork made with pieces cut on the bias, or diagonal, is not as strong as one made with segments cut with the weave.

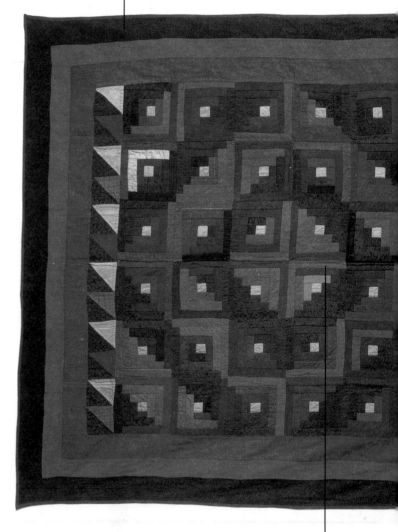

*Fabric:* The coverlet featured incorporates both cotton and wool, which, depending on the quality of each, could be of different strengths and pull against each other. In some patchworks, vulnerable velvets, silks, or worn or faded fabrics meet strong cottons, so always check for tearing at these points.

*Folds:* Crease marks where the fabric has been folded—in a "hope chest" for a bride-to-be, for example—strain the fabric, and should be eased out by a conservator.

*This 1865 American quilt is pieced (patchwork) and appliquéd. On some quilts, embroidery and appliqué work may not necessarily be contemporary with the original—clues may be in the period fabrics used and hand or machine sewing. Depending on when these were applied, value may not be affected, but check to make sure they are not covering up repairs or weaknesses.*

In the 1860s, mass-production of silk and bright new chemical dyes heralded a fashion for silk patchworks, but the dyes were not always stable, and the silk more susceptible to fraying than cotton. For general care see, p.131.

Fragments of unfinished patchworks are sometimes found with the templates still in place. Unless they are causing the fabric to deteriorate—because they are made from highly acidic paper stock, for example—it may be wise to leave them in place. They will have become an integral part of the structure of the piece, and contribute to its character and interest, especially if any printed templates give clues as to origin or date. Such a piece could be mounted in a double-sided boxed frame.

**Seams:** *Check carefully for signs of broken or weakened thread. Professional resewing is advisable to prevent further deterioration. On unquilted pieces that are joined to a backing fabric at the edges only, or examples with bias-cut patches, seams within the main field are likely to be strained.*

**Patches:** *Examine the pattern as a whole for replacement patches that look out of place and would detract from value. The occasional worn patch is not serious; it can be reinforced from behind, or protected by net, or both, but should certainly not be replaced.*

AMISH PIECED AND QUILTED COVERLET, 1880.
*The quilts were very much made for household use, and examples in good condition are rare and expensive.*

# THE RESTORER'S BRIEF

Seek expert advice if you want to use a textile or for the best means of display. Old, rare, or delicate textiles should only be hung in a safe, clean, dry environment away from direct heat or light. Small items, like the sampler, can be mounted in a sealed frame. Double-sided boxed frames mean both sides of a piece can be seen beneath clear plexiglass (Perspex) sheets, and it is protected from ultraviolet light .

Always have antique textiles cleaned by an expert who will identify fabrics, threads, and dyes used, and treat accordingly, to prevent dyes from running, shrinkage, and distortion.

A hole, a seriously weakened area, or even a whole piece can be reinforced from the back with a compatible fabric dyed to match, or a protective web of net stitched to the upper surface. Loose threads can and should be secured to prevent further deterioration, but to have an area darned or patched with new materials would not only devalue, but might be unethical. Serious degradation of fabrics and threads can not generally be reversed, only stabilized, carefully handled, and preserved in a controlled environment.

## HANGING A TEXTILE

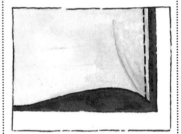

*Backing fabric protects from dust; the bottom left open so air circulates.*

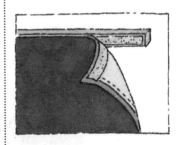

*Velcro tape is sewn onto washed, undyed webbing tape slightly wider than the Velcro. Sew the tape to the textile and backing fabric.*
*The receiving Velcro is stapled to a wood batten which is screwed to a wall. As Velcro increases in acidity after 15-20 years, it should be replaced.*

# FASHION ACCESSORIES

**A**S FASHION ITEMS, ACCESSORIES ARE EPHEMERAL, AND WERE NOT NECESSARILY MADE TO LAST.

Fashion accessories are constantly opened and closed, put on and taken off, and worn, used, or carried in potentially damaging environments, from wet, windy weather or bleaching sunshine to rooms filled with cigarette smoke, food and drink. These are all danger points to bear in mind if you opt to continue using your stylish Dior handbag or suede opera gloves. Repair on delicate materials that were designed to last only as long as the passing fashion, may be impossible.

An enormous range of materials has been used for fashion accessories, and often, many different materials are combined in one item. The leather sole of a shoe, for example, may need completely different care from its velvet upper and rhinestone buckle. Another factor to take into account before you force your way into a turn-of-the-century glove or shoe, is that modern hands and feet are considerably larger than those of your fashion-conscious predecessors.

*Leather: Ranges from cowhide to chicken skin and suede, so seek expert advice on how to keep it supple. It absorbs stains, which are difficult to remove, and is susceptible to mold if exposed to dampness. In water, leather stretches and loses its natural oiliness and should only be surface cleaned by an expert. The tanning process may have incorporated elements—such as alum salts for white kid—that wash out in water, causing the hide to revert to its natural color.*

SUEDE GLOVES, *1950s.*

*Gloves: Apart from the particular vulnerabilities of the materials used—such as cotton, silk, lace, or leather—staining and stretching are the most likely problems. Whether stains should be removed—they could contribute to the history of the gloves—the methods used and chances of success depend on the material, but to avoid shrinkage or further damage, should be referred to an expert. 19th-century gloves are usually too small to fit the modern hand. Seam allowances are minimal, leaving no leeway if the seam bursts. They can be resewn by an expert if the surrounding material is not torn, but should not then be worn.*

CHARLES JOURDAN SHOES, 1970S, *in satin with a rhinestone trim.*

**Rhinestone or diamanté:** *Check the foil backing, which is prone to flaking. Avoid exposure to water. Loose stones should be secured, and missing ones replaced in keeping (see pp. 114-117).*

**Satin:** *Highly susceptible to damage from harsher materials such as a leather lining or decorative features. Fraying and tears are difficult to restore because of the sheen. Water stains cause movement of the dye or staining from supporting materials. These and other stains may be "chased" with a fine, damp brush, but only with extreme caution. Never attempt to recolor satin.*

**Shoes:** *Each element in a shoe needs to be treated independently, from the fine materials of the uppers, often with embroidered or paste decoration, to soles of leather, rubber, wood, or plastic. Toes, heels, and seams are most vulnerable. Check for corrosion stains from metal used to reinforce an arch or a heel, for example. Once rubber has dried out and cracked, or become slightly tacky to the touch, it cannot be restored, so keep in a stable, environment with low humidity. Maintain shape by stuffing shoes with acid-free tissue, storing them in acid-free boxes.*

EMBROIDERED SATIN CLUTCH
BAG, *French 1940s.*

**Lining:** *Tends to gather dirt from cosmetics and other items. It is often of a delicate material, easily torn by sharp objects such as keys. Relining should be avoided, especially if it bears a label; better to ask a restorer to stabilize the existing lining, and not use the bag.*

**Handbags:** *Clutch bags especially are likely to have accumulated oil from the skin through handling. Cleaning must be expertly done according to the type of stain and the different materials that may be used in any one bag. Handles and straps that have given way at their fixing points, as well as fasteners, clasps, and zippers should be repaired in keeping. If left unmended, they could further damage the adjacenmt materials.*

DANCE RETICULE, *France, 1920s, celluloid set with paste.*

**Plastic:** *Early plastics, such as the celluloid of the late 1800s, become friable and occasionally sticky. Later Bakelite is stronger but loses its luster and may crack. All plastics embrittle and discolor eventually if exposed to strong light. Store in a sealed bag of aluminized polypropylene film to stabilize. Do not wrap in any material that could stick to the plastic—including acid-free tissue.*

**Fringes:** *All applied decoration, but especially fringes, are prone to being snagged, unraveled, or torn off. They can be repaired by careful stitching or sympathetic replacement, but at considerable expense, though value will probably be enhanced.*

**Hats:** *Fading, distortion, or other problems arising from exposure to weather can sometimes be reversed. Torn or loose trimmings should be secured to prevent further deterioration. The interior may be stained with grease, perspiration, or cosmetics, which in turn attract and absorb dirt. If staining is unsightly, cleaning by a specialized restorer is worth considering. A torn lining should not be replaced, especially if it bears a designer label, but tears can be stabilized by a conservator. Regularly shake out gently, or blow with a hairdryer set on low to prevent buildup of dust. Never leave hatpins in as they leave rust marks and holes. Store hats in acid-free boxes large enough not to crease or crush brim, crown, or trimmings. Check regularly for signs of insect attack; if mothballs are used, do not let them touch the hat.*

VELVET HAT, *1950s, French.*

**Feathers:** *Feathers attract dust and insects, and restorers disagree about how to clean them, so keep them as clean as possible. Regularly shake them or blow with hairdryer set on cool. Experts can reset broken quills and barbs, and revive the shape of, and dye ostrich feathers. While replacements for some feathers can be found, others are from endangered or extinct species; it is worth keeping a lookout for spares at antique stores and markets. Store feathers in an acid-free box large enough not to crush them.*

**Velvet:** *Crushed pile can be refreshed by steaming over a special pinned velvet board, or face to face with another piece of velvet, but if tufts fall out, nothing can be done.*

PARASOL, *cotton on metal frame, 1910–1920.*

**Umbrellas and parasols:** *The main area of stress is the fabric—where it is stretched across the ribs, the crease lines from when it is folded, and from repeated opening and closing. Exposure to sun and light eventually weakens the fabric, and weatherproofing such as waxing, oiling, or varnishing eventually cracks, exposing the underlying textile. Tears and splits particularly along seams, are virtually impossible to repair but can be strengthened. To re-cover an umbrella or parasol will make it usable but would considerably diminish its value as an antique. From the collector's view it is better to retain the original material even if it is damaged.*

*Check the joints of the ribs, which may have collapsed; these should be repaired, and look for signs of rusting on metal ribs. Rust may leach into and rot the nearby fabric. The weakest parts of the stick are where it joins the handle at the bottom and the ribs at the top. Broken wood sticks can be repaired, using the correct wood—a simple splint may be all that is necessary—and bent metal can be straightened.*

To use clocks or precision instruments, or even to keep them working, inevitably and inexorably wears them down. Periodical maintenance will keep timepieces functioning properly and help stave off the aging process, and the preservative surfaces applied to precision instruments can be renewed.

Clocks and precision instruments marry function and aesthetic appeal, resulting in a sometimes sensitive combination of materials: the different metals in a movement or mechanism... the enamel, painted, or glass dial... gilded ornament fixed onto a wooden case or mount. Such complexity of construction may call upon several distinct disciplines as far as maintenance and restoration are concerned.

# Clocks & precision instruments

# THE GRANDFATHER CLOCK

THE "GRANDFATHER" CLOCK, AN EARLY PENDULUM CLOCK, WAS ONE OF THE FIRST TIMEKEEPING DEVICES TO KEEP RELIABLE TIME, AND WAS A FINE ITEM OF FURNITURE IN ITS OWN RIGHT, BECOMING A SHOWPIECE FOR CABINETMAKING PROWESS.

The grandfather or tallcase (longcase) clock is a weight-driven pendulum clock, and like all pendulum clocks, whether bracket, mantel, or wall, only keeps time and operates properly if it is kept stationary when going, and should not be moved with the pendulum swinging freely or severe damage may be incurred. Tallcase clocks are weight-driven, bracket and mantel clocks spring-driven, wall clocks can be either; both methods are equally robust.

**Hinges:** *These should wrap around the inner edge of the door and the trunk frame. Wrong hinges should be replaced to be in keeping with the original design.*

**The trunk door:** *The carcass is constructed with a horizontally grained crosspiece attached to the end of the main long-grain board to stop it from bowing. Signs of movement or even tearing in the veneer here are to be expected and accepted. Only if either the crosspiece or the veneer is loose is action needed; reveneering would detract from the value.*

**Sides:** *Bowing from front to back can be accepted, but movement outward from the door leaves an unsightly gap and, more seriously, can prevent the door lock from engaging, as in the detail above right; correction can be costly.*

**Plinth:** *Many of these clocks stood on damp, stone floors that were swilled down with water, leading to rot in the base. The veneer may have been replaced or the carcass on which it was laid rebuilt; either would detract.*

TALLCASE CLOCK, ENGLISH, 1680s, *in burl (burr) walnut veneer on an oak carcass is a fine item of furniture as well as a classic timekeeper.*

**Feet:** *Tallcase clocks before 1680 commonly stood on bun feet, which were often substituted later by a baseboard (skirting). Restoration of bun feet is desirable. Copies can be made to order by a reputable restorer.*

**Veneers:** Seek advice on whether the veneer is original, allowing for repairs. In the late 1800s, many plain burl (burr) walnut cases were embellished with marquetry to improve their value. On marquetry clocks question whether any marquetry is not original. New marquetry on a rebuilt plinth can be accepted where it has been replaced because of loss due to stress, for example at the top and bottom of the trunk door.

**Hood:** The most vulnerable part of the case, as it is subject to rough handling when taken on and off, leading to the breaking off of the lower molding that masks the junction with the trunk. All the moldings on the hood and main case are cut in cross-grain which is prone to cracking and curling, leading to lifting and losses; extensive losses or replacement devalues the clock, though a good restorer can refit or replace moldings.

**Dial:** Should not be regilded, but the silvered finish of the chapter (hour) ring should be renewed every 60 years or so. The spandrel ornaments—the cherubs—are only screwfixed from behind so should periodically be checked to see that they are held fast.

BAVARIAN TALLCASE CLOCK, MID 1700s, *in painted and gilded pinewood. The swirling Rococo decoration is very likely to chip, and gilding lost from the sculpted edges; both would need to be restored to maintain value.*

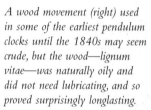

*The movement and dial (left) are held in place only by gravity on the "seatboard" under the movement, resting on the sawn-off upper ends of the case sides. With the dial at the front making the movement front-heavy, beware of its dropping forward when the weights are removed.*

*A wood movement (right) used in some of the earliest pendulum clocks until the 1840s may seem crude, but the wood—lignum vitae—was naturally oily and did not need lubricating, and so proved surprisingly longlasting.*

## SWINGING STYLE

The tallcase or longcase clock developed rapidly following the invention of the pendulum in 1657, and over the next 100 years hardly altered—except in mechanical and decorative details—so that comments on care remain true through all periods. Early pendulums were susceptible to changes in temperature: heat caused the pendulums to lengthen fractionally and beat more slowly, and cold made them beat more quickly. From the 1720s, temperature compensation devices counterbalanced the different rates of expansion of the various metals within the pendulum, and the nickel-steel "Invar" pendulum introduced in the early 1900s was completely resistant to temperature changes.

The movement of the floorstanding grandfather clock—dial, long pendulum, and two driving weights—is housed in a wooden case consisting of the trunk and the hood which slides on top of it. The method of construction dictates the problems encountered in caring for the case. Clocks made of solid or sawn oak or pine are comparatively stable. But many fine tallcase clocks have an oak or pine carcass with a more

expensive and delicate decorative veneer or marquetry finish, and over the years stresses appear between the two, especially along the joint lines of the carcass. These surface finishes include plain veneers of ebony (1660-75), ebonized pearwood (1670-90), burl or straight grain walnut (1670-1760 and 1840-70), mahogany (1750-1900), satinwood (1780-1800 and 1890-1910), and rosewood (1810-1860), which are all comparatively stable. More decorative and fragile are marquetry (1670-1715), and japanning or lacquer (1710-1760) which tend to chip or flake.

## GENERAL CARE

The most common error in handling tallcase clocks is to move them still assembled. To function at all, a pendulum must be suspended from a rigidly fixed fulcrum within the clock, and therein lies the secret to pendulum clock care: this rigidity must be maintained.

Because they are top heavy and could topple over, screw a tallcase clock to the wall. Before moving—even if only by a few feet—tallcases must be taken down into their constituent parts, otherwise serious damage can occur to either the case or the movement, as the separate parts are held together only by gravity and will shift in relation to one another. Let the weights run down completely before unhooking them, otherwise, the lines on which they hang tend to unravel from the barrels they are coiled around and become caught up in the wheels of the movement. A clockmaker would be needed to untangle the resulting muddle. Take care not to let the movement fall on you when taking apart or assembling the clock, as the dial corners are very heavy. Have someone else

hold the movement steady while the weights are not in place.

Take particular care of the thin flexible suspension spring at the top of the pendulum; if this becomes kinked, it affects the pendulum's action and can cause it to stop altogether, and a replacement will have to be fitted by a clockmaker.

If the clock is being moved far or shipped, tape the pendulum to a plank of wood, or invert it and suspend it upside down in the trunk by firmly tying the heavy "bob" (in use hanging at the base) through the holes in the backboard. Make sure hood and trunk are packed separately and that the

*The French tallcase regulator (below) shows the multi-rod "gridiron" pendulum, a temperature compensation device that regulates the movement of the pendulum.*

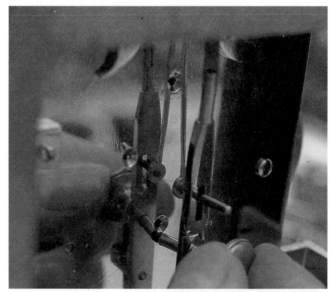

*Before moving a pendulum clock, the pendulum has to be completely removed or locked as in the mantel clock (above), which shows locking using a special securing nut found on some designs.*

*To set the hands to the correct time, gently push the minute hand by its tip (right) to avoid catching the hour hand with your finger.*

weights are secured from damaging either. Pack the movement face down in a container deep enough to ensure that the delicate, rocking crutchpiece (with which the pendulum engages) is not subject to any pressure.

Always wind up the striking side before the going side. It should be impossible to overwind the movement; simply turn the key to the point of resistance. Never use an ill-fitting key. If you are going to be away when the next winding is due, stop the clock to prevent the escapement from being damaged on winding down, as the wheel stops turning but

the pendulum continues swinging a while. Only turn the hands clockwise, never backward. When pushing the hands to reset the time, stop at each hour to allow the strike to count out the full number.

Do not attempt to improve silvering on a "metal-mounted" dial with silver cleaning preparations as this removes the protective layer of lacquer. Treat the case itself as though it were a piece of furniture, but dust marquetry surfaces with a soft-bristled brush rather than a dustcloth which may catch.

---

## THE RESTORER'S BRIEF

When buying an antique clock, check that it has been serviced and carries a mechanical guarantee; if necessary, have the movement checked by a clockmaker and overhauled. Have your tallcase clocks serviced about every ten years, because wear increases rapidly as the oil in the movement becomes viscous and picks up dirt, rendering it an abrasive rather than the lubricant it is intended to be, and the pivot bearings wear down, leaving the gears to mesh inefficiently. Basic overhauling includes bushing and redrilling of the pivot bearings, and reoiling, reassembly, testing, and timing.

For the case, use a cabinetmaker or restorer who specializes in clock cases rather than a general furniture restorer, since there are small differences in detail of treatment. Splitting joints in the case must be repaired immediately, as their failure may bring the whole clock crashing down. A clock that has undergone extensive restoration or wholesale replacement of its moldings is devalued compared to one that has been patched only. Loose moldings can be refixed at home with a reversible glue. Crossgrain cut moldings that have cracked and curled up must be eased back and glued in position by a restorer before they snap off and are lost. Stress fractures in the veneers at the joints of the carcass are a question of degree. In

severe cases the veneer has to be cut away before the joint is realigned and glued and replacement veneer cut back in. If the joint is stable, the gap can be filled and the veneer pieced back together or at worst a new section cut in. With other areas of the case, an unattended cracked and raised piece of veneer is easily caught, so it must be reglued, possibly by the owner, using reversible wood glue.

### The dial

The silvered finish on the dial rings of so-called "metal mounted" dials is achieved by rubbing silver nitrate powder onto a cleaned brass surface. Silvering must be lacquered immediately to stop it from tarnishing, but this is not everlasting and should be periodically renewed. The process of resilvering involves sanding the engraved surface, wearing away a little of the definition each time it is renewed, so it is better to resist the process as long as possible. With the exception of tallcase regulators—which are grained

vertically—sanding and silvering should always be done by hand in small circular motions, rather than on a spinning machine which produces a concentric graining, with a sheen like that of a compact disk.

Painted dials, made of tinplate painted in enamel colors and lightly fired, develop a network of fine cracks (crazing), white areas discolor, and decorative details fade. Be sure that the restorer does not erase the crackelure or bleach the white areas since this would destroy the period look of the dial and seriously reduce the value of the clock.

*A view into the top of a bracket clock movement (below) showing the crown-shaped verge escape wheel of a verge escapement. Verge escapements were commonly replaced by anchor escapements in the 19th century, but an original or reconverted verge is much more desirable.*

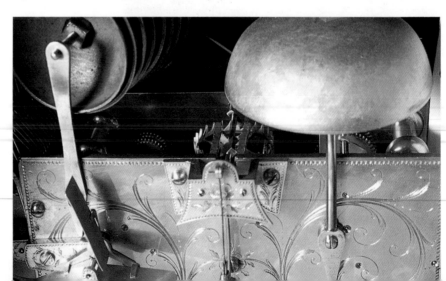

# BRACKET CLOCKS

Bracket clocks are the spring-driven counterparts to the weight-driven tallcase clocks, like miniaturized versions of the hood and movement, but constructed as fully assembled units. They can be transported whole if kept upright, but the pendulum must be removed if no clip or screw clamp is present to secure it. To do this, wedge the ticking crutchpiece with a piece of folded paper between it and the backplate; otherwise, the hands will revolve rapidly and the strike or chime will be set off while the clock is in transit.

Do not be tempted to pick up the clock by the carrying handle unless you want to be left holding only the handle and the immediate piece of wood it was bolted to, while the remainder has fallen to the ground. There are no screwed joints in clock cases, and the glue is now, at 100 to 300 years old, dried out and brittle. So always place your hands underneath it and never carry it by what was originally the carrying handle.

To start up a bracket clock, set it in position, wind it, and set the time, and only then grasp the case on each side and, firmly but gently, raise one side and put it down again, which will set the pendulum swinging.

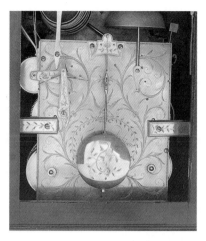

*Bracket clock (left) with ebonized veneer, of the 1770s. The dial is covered in velvet, which will need replacing periodically.*

*The backplate (above) shows a pendulum of anchor proportions; a verge pendulum usually has a smaller "bob."*

## False finishes

Throughout the period bracket clocks were made (1660–1900), ebonizing remained just as popular a finish as more colorful show-woods such as walnut or mahogany. Since 1950 some ebonized clocks have been unscrupulously bleached to remove the black staining of their fruitwood veneer, a process which reveals the color of the fruitwood, but which appears contrived and unsatisfactory. If you are buying, such clocks should be avoided. Reebonizing is possible, but unless the clock is by one of the best makers, it will not add to the value of your clock; you will simply have the satisfaction of knowing it is correct. Marquetry bracket clock cases are extremely rare, whereas japanning (or lacquer) is frequently encountered.

## Conversion dilemmas

Bracket clocks need to be overhauled more often than tallcase clocks, every five to eight years.

Many bracket clocks were originally fitted with peripheral functions such as calendar works or a quarter repeat. Traditionally, if one of these functions stopped working, it was removed to avoid the expense of repair. The rebuilding of a quarter-repeating train is desirable, but expensive, and only worth doing for valuable clocks.

In the 1800s many older bracket clocks were converted from a verge to the supposedly more efficient anchor escapement. This devalues a clock by some 25 percent, but to convert it back costs about $4,000 (£2,500), which will still leave it worth about 10 percent less than it would be with the original verge, so the clock needs to be worth more than $16,000 (£10,000) for this to make economic sense.

# THE MANTEL CLOCK

MANTEL CLOCKS, THE MOST HIGHLY DECORATIVE OF ALL CLOCKS, ARE OFTEN REGARDED SIMPLY AS ORNAMENTAL OBJECTS THAT INCIDENTALLY TELL THE TIME. THEIR OWNERS ARE LESS CONCERNED WHEN THEY FAIL MECHANICALLY THAN THEY WOULD BE WITH OTHER CLOCKS.

Mantel clocks were first developed around 1735 in France during the reign of King Louis XV when it became fashionable to add a deep ledge or shelf at the top of mantelpieces wide enough to take a clock. This was the period of the Rococo style, famed for its playful fancifulness. Even more so than the bracketed wall clocks from which they developed, the cases of mantel clocks rapidly became increasingly decorative, incorporating a movement and dial into every other contemporary decorative art medium, and embracing a variety of materials, including enamel, ormolu, bronze, wood veneer, ceramics, and marble. Following fast on the French lead, mantel clocks startedto be made elsewhere in Europe, except in England where the genre did not catch on until the 1760s, and the clocks tended to be more sober in style and slightly sturdier than their Continental counterparts. In the 1800s mantel clocks were made in huge quantities, in revivalist or eclectic styles.

## GENERAL CARE

It is ironic that the most natural place to site a mantel clock, on the shelf from which it derives its name, is inadvisable if it is over a working fireplace. Heat rising from the fire propels dirt onto the case and into the movement, especially when, as so often with French mantel clocks, the movement is not sealed from the open air. Fluctuations in temperature as the fire burns and goes out leads to erratic timekeeping because of the slight expansion and contraction of the metal, which causes changes in the pendulum's length. Bear in mind when cleaning that the different materials react in different ways. Avoid the use of water or of commercial furniture, metal, or glass polish, as these may seep into crevices and react with materials other than the ones they are intended for. In most cases, cleaning should be restricted to dusting with a soft-bristled brush (a cloth may catch on the mounts), and anything more serious should be undertaken by a restorer. Before moving a mantel clock always take off the pendulum and use a piece of folded paper to wedge the ticking crutchpiece connected to it.

## THE RESTORER'S BRIEF

In both the 1700s and 1800s, the majority of mantel clocks employed simple hour or half-hour striking circular movements of standardized dimensions ready-made to be fitted by the casemaker, who then sold the finished piece. There is generally little about them to surprise a clockmaker today, and being spring driven, they should, like bracket clocks (p.145), be overhauled every five to eight years. Occasionally a mantel clock formed only the superstructure of a larger composition containing a musical mechanism in the base playing on a gallery of bells or a run of barrel organ pipes. These mechanisms have frequently undergone a hard life and may need extensive and expensive repair. If the musical mechanism has been removed completely, leaving a vacant space, replacement is rarely economic.

*After the clock has been wound, place the clock in position and set to time. To set the pendulum swinging, gently lift and put back down, one side of the clock (right).*

**Gold-plating:** *It is imperative to preserve the original gilding if possible. Before embarking on any restoration or regilding, have the mounts merely washed in mild soap to reveal the true state of the gilding.*

**Mounts:** *These have integral pins at their backs that are held by plaster in drilled holes in the marble body. Any that work loose must be re-fixed immediately for fear of their being lost.*

**Enamel dial:** *Susceptible to chipping, particularly around the winding holes, or to hairline cracks if subject to stressing. Such damage can be repaired by a professional restorer, but as soft or "cold" enamel will be used, the result will be detectable to the experienced eye.*

**Marble carcass:** *Likely to become chipped along any edge or corner, or to fracture if subject to comparatively minor stressing, since the movement represents a heavy center of gravity within the case.*

**Feet:** *The feet also are set by plaster in drilled holes in the base of the marble, and frequently work loose. They must be fixed promptly; otherwise they are likely to be lost, or worse, the force of a loose foot falling off may crack the marble carcass.*

LOUIS XVI MANTEL CLOCK, 1780s. *The ornamental mounts are highly decorative but detach easily and must then be refixed promptly to prevent loss and devaluation.*

# THE WALL CLOCK

Any type of clock can be slightly adapted at the point of manufacture to hang on the wall. Because they have to resist the force of gravity, wall clocks are generally sturdily built.

Although some French wall clocks may represent the ultimate in decorative refinement, most examples are more utilitarian and relatively trouble-free in terms of constructional and mechanical defects. Wall clocks are generally pendulum controlled, but may be either weight or spring driven; both mechanisms are equally robust. They were made in all periods and only differ from other contemporary clock forms, such as tallcases, bracket, and mantel clocks, in being wall mounted.

American wall clocks stand apart from their European counterparts because they were mass-produced. They were initially made entirely of wood, including the wheels of the movement, somewhat in the tradition of Black Forest clocks from Germany. With the stepping up of brass production in the 1820s, Connecticut clockmakers started to use metal for their movements—which surprisingly proved less durable than their wooden counterparts. With the introduction of rolled brass in 1837, mass-production with movements (both plates and wheels) entirely stamped out of brass really accelerated. These workaday clocks were designed to be cheap yet long-lasting, requiring very little maintenance, and they are some of the easiest clocks for an amateur to service. They are mostly driven by weights suspended just inside the edges of the case, their lines passing over pulleys in the top of the case and back down to the movement.

***Dial:*** *The painted tinplate may chip or become scratched, but can be retouched in keeping with the original by a specialist dial restorer.*

## GENERAL CARE

Most English and German wall clocks are weight driven and are either cased movements with the driving weights hanging free, or fully cased and resembling truncated tallcase clocks. Treat both types as though they were tallcase clocks (p.140). French makers in Paris preferred spring-driven movements for their increasingly fantastic cases, which need the same approach to care as mantel clocks (p.146). Provincial French wall clocks, on the other hand, are generally of the free-hanging weight variety and more like tallcase clocks. The 1800s saw numerous spring-driven, wood-cased circular wall clocks known as dial clocks. These utilitarian clocks were intended for such public places as offices, schools, rail stations, and inns, as well as less grand household settings like kitchens. Treat them in the same way as English bracket clocks (p.145).

To start a wall clock, make sure it is hanging level and give the pendulum a swing with the fingertips.

AMERICAN PILLARED SHELF CLOCK, 1860s: *The movement is incredibly sturdy and longlasting; it is the case and dial that are likely to need restoration.*

**Movement:** *Rarely needs more than cleaning off of the old oil and reoiling. Replacement parts cannibalized from another similar clock are cheaper than having them made to order. The lines on which the weights are suspended should be checked and replaced if necessary.*

**Veneers:** *These are typically very thin and susceptible to lifting and cracking. Any loose sections must be stabilized without delay, though if the area affected is small this can be done by the owner, using reversible wood glue. A piece of loose veneer has been taped temporarily into place (above) to avoid loss.*

**Gilding:** *Gilding is laid on gesso, and is worth having restored by a specialist if severely worn.*

**Glazed doors:** *On this example, both were originally decorated with transfer prints; the one immediately below the dial is in reasonable condition, but the lower one has been replaced with an embroidery that should again be replaced with a proper transfer.*

**Case structure:** *As the weights hang within the case, make sure that the case itself is sound, with no loose structural joints.*

149

# THE CARRIAGE CLOCK

CARRIAGE CLOCKS ARE PORTABLE AND MECHANICALLY ROBUST. ALTHOUGH THEY CAN TAKE A CERTAIN AMOUNT OF JOLTING, SEVERE KNOCKS WILL CAUSE DAMAGE TO THE MECHANISM, CASE, OR DECORATION, OR TO ALL THREE.

Carriage clocks are mechanically tough enough to perform well as traveling clocks, but there are fragile elements in their construction and decoration. This is particularly so for later decorative examples which were always intended more as home-bound timepieces, and it must also be borne in mind that after 100 or more years of use, the movement may be worn and therefore suitable only for sedentary use.

Although some are enameled or made of silver, most carriage clock cases are of gold-plated brass and formed like a four-poster bed with a solid base to which the movement, viewable through the glass panels to the top and all four sides, is secured.

## THE PORTABLE TRAVELING CLOCK

The first carriage clock was made in 1796 by France's greatest-ever clock and watchmaker, A. L. Breguet (1717–1823), and was taken by Napoleon to Egypt in 1798 as a campaign clock. This established the type as hardwearing and practical, and it was no coincidence that production and popularity increased in tandem with the spread of the railroads from the 1830s. Production faltered in the First World War and did not continue beyond the 1920s. Carriage clocks were manufactured mainly in France, but some were also made in England, Austria, and Switzerland.

Breguet's first carriage clock reveals a breakthrough in design: he placed the escapement and balance horizontally on a small platform across the top of the plates of the movement. Previously, traveling clocks had the escapement integral to the movement with the balance wheel mounted vertically on the backplate; Breguet's change of plane resulted in better shockproofing and timekeeping.

Dials of carriage clocks are commonly of white enamel, which is prone to developing hairline cracks in the surface

*Panels:* Porcelain or enameled panels may be chipped or cracked from overtightening of the case or if the clock is knocked. Repairs can be effected, but will detract in comparison to panels in mint condition. More common are clocks with glass panels, sometimes beveled, on all four sides. If these are broken, they should be replaced since they will let in dirt and dust.

FRENCH CARRIAGE CLOCK, *gold-plated on engraved brass, c. 1860: the porcelain paneling is less common than glass, and if in perfect condition commands a premium.*

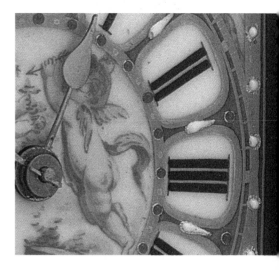

The enameled porcelain decoration (above) was fired, and then the gilt border applied. Finally, pearl-like porcelain beads were glued on; these tend to fall off and need replacing with modern copies to maintain value.

**Scratches:** Scratches to the case foot or top are difficult to disguise and so detract if they are obvious. Minor scratches can be removed though some metal is lost.

**Gold-plating:** Gold-plating on the case has commonly been worn away by unnecessary polishing, leaving bare brass. If so, the case will need re-gilding, but the result is never as desirable as original gilding in good condition and will fetch a lower price. Original gilding in good condition has a semi-matte and very finely granular finish; modern gilding is often either too bright and not of the right color.

**Foot:** May be distorted if the clock has been dropped, and complete correction is generally not possible.

*Good quality carriage clocks were provided with leather-covered wood carrying cases (above), but after 100 years and more, these are rarely in good condition; if they are, of course, the value increases.*

tarnishes. The correct approach is to breathe on the case and buff the misted area with a soft dusting cloth. Fly-blow and general dirt on porcelain and enamel side panels may be removed with a barely damp cloth.

As with other types of clock, never move the hands backward to set the time. However, on carriage clocks, it is possible to move the hands on "through" the hour without stopping to allow each hour to be struck out in full—as long as 12 o' clock is allowed to strike in full before moving on to the time required. Always wind the striking side first, before the spring that drives the hands, and do both before setting the time. To start the clock if it does not do so of its own accord, grasp it in one hand across the underside and give it a firm but gentle horizontal circular twist from side to side.

and chips at the corners. Some clocks dating from around 1900 have opaque glass dials, erroneously known as "opaline," which are also easily cracked. Some highgrade French clocks and many English ones have dials of engine-turned silver or florally engraved gilt brass. These are sturdy, but look carefully at silver examples, which may have unsightly scratches from poor handling when the clock has been taken apart. Perhaps the most decorative—but fragile—dials are of colored porcelain or champlevé enamel, often accompanied by side panels en suite.

## GENERAL CARE

Never bring liquids into contact with carriage clocks. Cleaning agents may seep between the case and its panels into the movement, clogging it up and stopping it from going. But more serious still, and the most commonly perpetrated error has been to over-polish their cases which causes the wearing away of the lacquered surface and the gold plating. The more these are polished, the more they are eroded and the quicker the brass of the case is exposed and

*Overpolishing of the pierced gilt on this miniature French carriage clock, c. 1890s (above), would diminish the value considerably, and it would be worth having it regilded if necessary.*

# THE RESTORER'S BRIEF

Carriage clocks must be given a general overhaul by a clockmaker on acquisition and then at least every ten years.

In the 1960s and 70s there was a vogue for substituting a new, Swiss, platform escapement for the original, because it was cheaper than repair and because timekeeping was better than even a repaired original. Since then, for aesthetic reasons, there has been a reaction against them; an original platform, or a reconditioned one of the old pattern, is now much more desirable—and is often a requirement to pass the vetting process at many antique shows. However, the supply of previously discarded platforms held by clockmakers is by now virtually exhausted. Eventually, new platforms will have to be accepted if they are already fitted in antique carriage clocks, unless a manufacturer revives the old pattern.

Cracked glass panels let in dirt and should be replaced; this has no detrimental effect on originality or value. However, repairs to porcelain and enamel panels or dials—while desirable in their own right—will always be detectable to the expert eye and reduce value according to their extent. Enamel is repaired using "cold enamels" or resins with pigments added, this makes it impossible to match the translucency of the original material. Repaired cracks in porcelain tend to show when the panels are held to reflect the light. Cracks in opaline dials can be disguised by bleaching out dirt, or more severe ones can sometimes be repaired with resins. Porcelain and enamel repairs must be carried out by specialists in those fields, but via a clockmaker since the clock has disassembled to remove the panels.

Many carriage clock porcelain panels immitated 1700s Sèvres "jeweled" decoration. These diminutive ceramic beads were glued on and by now may have partly flown. Replacement is advisable, but it is difficult to obtain an exact match; if only a few are missing, it may be expedient to have those remaining spaced out evenly.

Ask the restorer's advice on regilding: how much can it match the original finish; what will the finished color be like? Modern gilding differs enormously from what was achieved in the 1800s, but with carriage clocks, unlike, for example an ormolu mount, can benefit from regilding if much of the original has been lost and if it is done sympathetically.

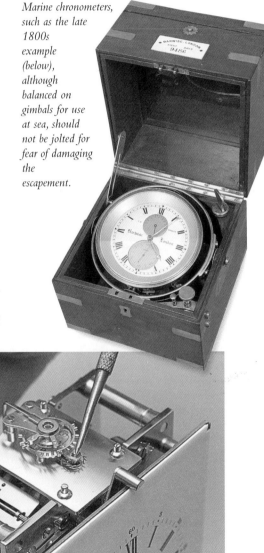

*Marine chronometers, such as the late 1800s example (below), although balanced on gimbals for use at sea, should not be jolted for fear of damaging the escapement.*

*Old and modern platforms are noticeably different from each other. Old platforms are usually silvered, and often have two bridges at right angles (below left); modern versions (below right) are gilt and have a single, curved Y-shaped bridge.*

# THE POCKET WATCH

POCKET WATCHES ARE MORE NUMEROUS THAN ANY FORM OF TIMEPIECE EXCEPT FOR WRISTWATCHES. THEY ARE GENERALLY RELIABLE AND GIVE LONG SERVICE, YET IT IS RELATIVELY EASY TO DAMAGE THEM SEVERELY, SOMETIMES IRREPARABLY.

The pocket watch was not so much invented, as a reduction in size of the portable spring clock; its ultimate development has been the wristwatch. As an intensely personal item, it has frequently been dressed up as a luxury object—furnished with a precious metal case, exquisitely and decoratively engraved, enameled, or set with gemstones—and as it has been drawn in and out of pockets, gradually but inevitably, it shows signs of wear.

**Engraved initials or family crests:** *Personalized engraving on this sort of case cover is a drag on the value of an estate pocket watch. If the engraving is not too deep, it may be erased, which will go some way to restoring market value. Purely decorative engraving, especially the comparatively shallow, engine-turned process, wears with use and is difficult or prohibitively expensive to refresh.*

**Winding and hand-set stem ratchet:** *Usually the first mechanical part to exhibit extensive wear. Repair must be carried out promptly to prevent further damage to the movement and will not affect the value.*

**Balance staff:** *The escapement's balance staff is the watch's most fragile mechanical part and likely to fracture if jolted severely. As most pocket watches are obsolescent, replacements have to be made to order, which may well be more expensive than the value of the watch.*

**Case covers and band:** *Subject to bruising or dents from knocks. These may generally be repaired, though dents to the band are particularly difficult to remove; if they are erased completely, value can be restored.*

AMERICAN 1920s HALF HUNTER POCKET WATCH: *a mass-produced design of high quality and durability.*

154

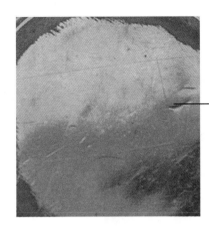

**Scratches:** *Deep scratches on the case covers can be lightly abraded out with a fine stone, and bruises planished out to improve appearance, but the processes leave slight depressions, which will detract.*

**Winding button:** *Composed of a thick layer of precious metal (gold or silver) over a brass core. A worn winder with the core exposed reduces value, but restoration is not economical. Substitution of the part from another watch that is otherwise beyond repair is the most feasible option.*

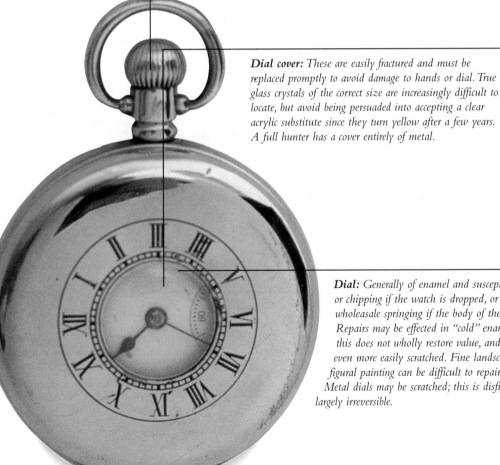

**Dial cover:** *These are easily fractured and must be replaced promptly to avoid damage to hands or dial. True glass crystals of the correct size are increasingly difficult to locate, but avoid being persuaded into accepting a clear acrylic substitute since they turn yellow after a few years. A full hunter has a cover entirely of metal.*

**Dial:** *Generally of enamel and susceptible to cracking or chipping if the watch is dropped, or even wholesale springing if the body of the case is flexed. Repairs may be effected in "cold" enamel or resin, but this does not wholly restore value, and the surface is even more easily scratched. Fine landscape, scenic, or figural painting can be difficult to repaint in keeping. Metal dials may be scratched; this is disfiguring and largely irreversible.*

*This silver-cased, early verge watch, c. 1660, is not a practical timekeeper as it predates the introduction of the balance spring, so it is unlikely to be used. It will therefore need no regular maintenance—unlike a watch that is constantly used.*

## VARIATIONS IN STYLE

While some American watches are set with one or more well-spaced, comparatively large diamonds within star pattern engraving, gemsetting on European watch cases commonly consists of closely set small stones that occasionally work loose because of the necessary lightness of the metal claws holding them in such proximity. These can be replaced, but at some expense.

The movements of earlier watches hinge forward, dial first, from their cases, which necessitates opening the front crystal and pulling up a small catch with a thumbnail. This is an awkward process for those not practiced in the art and sometimes results in cracking the enamel dial or crystal by pressing too hard when closing the watch. Later watches with keyless winding have access to the movement through hinged double-backed or double-bottomed cases—a much easier arrangement. Keyless stem-winding from a knurled button in the pendant was taken up in Swiss watches from about 1860, in America by c. 1870, and in England from c. 1880. The combined winding and handsetting functions of a

modern wristwatch's button stem are not necessarily found in early examples of keyless stem winding on pocket watches. Frequently, either a lever by the edge of the dial must moved sideways, or a small button in the case band near the pendant must be kept depressed, to engage the pendant with the hand setting mechanism.

## GENERAL CARE

Do not wind a watch that has not been run for two years or more. First have it cleaned and overhauled. Seek advice from a clockmaker, and if necessary write down the instructions, on how to open your watch, wind it, and set it to time to guard against damaging it, as there are many different arrangements for these functions. Preferably, use a fingernail to open the case, as knives may damage the opening flange and may slide and scratch the inner surface of the cover as it opens. As with other timepieces, only wind the hands forward when setting the time. Never wind a watch that is very cold, as this may cause the mainspring to fracture.

*The enamel on white metal, 1930s purse watch (above) was designed to be kept in a purse or pocketbook, but with constant use, the enamel is likely to have chipped.*

*Chipped enamel, as in this 1820s buckle watch (above) should be repaired using "cold" enamel (which is not fired). This will be detectable to the experienced eye, but is preferable to leaving the chip unchecked.*

## ROLLED GOLD WATCHES

*American watch manufacturers concentrated on mass-producing watch movements for sale as cheaply as possible. To further this aim of reaching a mass market worldwide, the rolled gold case was developed. Heavily gold-plated brass cases in good condition, may, at first sight, resemble solid gold cases. However, they are much stiffer on opening and closing, and their secret is revealed by the lack of hallmarks or gold warranty markings inside, replaced by an inscription to the effect that the case is guaranteed to last so many years. The wording differs according to where the case was made; in America: "Guaranteed to wear 10 years"; in England: "Guaranteed to be made of two plates of gold with plate of composition in between and to wear a minimum of 20 years."*

AMERICAN ROLLED GOLD POCKET *watch, c. 1900, showing the warranty marks.*

*It is important to hold a watch firmly when rewinding. The author holds the repeating watch (left) steady in one hand, then pulls the repeating slide with his thumb.*

## THE RESTORER'S BRIEF

Have a pocket watch overhauled every four to six years, so that the oil does not become viscous and cease to act as a lubricant. Ask the restorer to clean the dial gently, to retouch any faded numerals on metal dials, and repair chips (see above left). Hairline cracks in enamel dials cannot safely be bleached as the peroxide used oxidizes the copper support. If the numerals are clear, the dial is best left alone. Bruises in the covers and band of solid gold and silver cases should be repaired, and the exterior and interior surfaces gently polished to remove scratches.

# BAROMETERS

**B**AROMETERS USED TO BE A VITAL TOOL IN FARMING, SHIPPING, AND OTHER PROFESSIONS THAT WERE DEPENDENT ON THE STATE OF THE WEATHER.

The glass tube mercury barometer was invented by Evangelista Torricelli in Italy in the 1640s to measure height, and developed for domestic use as a weather indicator in the late 1600s in England. However, because of the Venetian glassmaking tradition, barometer production became almost the exclusive preserve of immigrant Italian makers, both in Europe and America. Mercury barometers divide into the more reliable column (or stick) and wheel (or banjo) types, both with the potentially explosive combination of dense, heavy mercury in a fragile glass tube.

On stick barometers, the reading is taken directly from the top of the mercury visible in the glass tube. On wheel barometers, which were made in increasing numbers from around 1780 and were the more numerous type during the 1800s, the reading registers on a circular dial. The hand is driven by a pulley wheel (driven by a cord ending in a counterbalanced weight resting on the rising and falling mercury), which may stick, and the barometer may need tapping so that it self-adjusts.

**Casework:** *Usually a "mixed media" combination of metal, wood, and glass; check for staining and warping where different materials meet.*

**Internal glass tube:** *Shattering must be avoided at all costs because of the danger of the mercury spilling. Can be replaced in keeping to maintain value.*

**Register plates:** *May be silvered or of ivory. If the silvering has degraded to an unacceptable level, or if stained by previously spilled mercury, these should be resilvered. Ivory register plates cannot be cleaned of mercury staining.*

**Stick barometers** *like this English 1860s example (left), must be hung absolutely upright to operate correctly.*

**Hand:** *May stick and the case may need tapping for the pulley operating it to self-adjust.*

MERCURY WHEEL BAROMETER, c. 1840. *This is the most common type of mercury barometer, but it is less accurate than a stick barometer.*

## GENERAL CARE

All barometers must be adjusted for the altitude at which they are being used. This involves the manual adjustment of the level of mercury in the tube to compensate for the decrease in atmospheric pressure at increasing altitudes. The method of doing this varies according to the type of barometer; your restorer should be able to advise. Mercury barometers must be hung absolutely vertically to read correctly.

Dust lightly to clean; rubbing may cause the mercury to surge. Avoid using cleaning liquids or water that may seep behind the glass and discolor the register plates or dial. Surging of the mercury up the glass tube of a column barometer while moving may shatter the tube and must be avoided. Mercury is highly poisonous, and the human body cannot rid itself of any it has absorbed, either through the skin or digested, or inhaled as vapor.

A special permit from an airline is required to carry a mercury-filled barometer by air, and a professional freight packer should be used. It is preferable to have the mercury removed for shipping and have the tube professionally refilled on arrival, but an enclosed-cistern column barometer can be moved complete with mercury. Again, avoiding any jerky movements, very gradually tilt the barometer at an angle to cause the mercury to rise to the very top of the tube, and then as long as it is kept at an angle just short of horizontal, it can be hand carried. Wheel barometers should be professionally "corked" and then transported upright.

## ANEROID BAROMETER

*Aneroid barometers were invented by the Frenchman, Lucien Vidie in 1843. They work on the principle of the expansion and contraction of a metallic vacuum canister registering on a circular dial via a rack and pinion mechanism. Compact and relatively strong, readily portable, and free of poisonous mercury, the aneroid rendered the mercury barometer virtually obsolete. Cases are commonly sturdy and circular, made of gilt brass (which, like carriage-clock cases, should not be polished as this will remove the gilt), or of turned wood, often embellished with carving, which should be treated like a piece of furniture. Pocket aneroids often have a fitted leather case. Aneroids need only very occasional servicing, involving cleaning, then rack-and-pinion gearing and regulating the registering of the hands. A punctured or ruptured vacuum canister would have to be repaired to make the instrument function at all.*

1890s ANEROID BAROMETER *with carved mahogany surround: a sturdy barometer that demands no special treatment.*

---

## THE RESTORER'S BRIEF

Despite its wood carcass, work on a mercury barometer is best carried out by a barometer specialist because of the special skills required to remove and refit the mercury-filled glass tube. The tube needs to be correctly filled with mercury to register accurately; ask the restorer to explain how you can adjust it

*Unlike mercury barometers, which need special care before moving or storage, aneroid barometers (left) just need to be wrapped in acid-free tissue, bubble-wrap and paper board.*

for different altitudes. Even though it is out of sight, the long door in the backboard of a wheel barometer must fit properly and be hung on smoothly functioning hinges, so that pressure is not placed on the tube and fracture when it is being opened or shut.

The register plates calibrated with the barometric scale should be re-silvered, either if the silvering has degraded to an unacceptable level, or if they have been stained by previously spilled mercury. Ivory register plates cannot be cleared of mercury staining.

## OTHER PRECISION INSTRUMENTS

*Pocket-sized magnetic compasses (above) were made throughout the 1700s and into the 1800s in gilded metal or wood cases, and enamel or painted card disks. Although portable, dropping them would cause irreparable damage.*

Like barometers, scientific instruments are constructed in combinations of metals, woods, and glass, with appropriate protective finishes, some with cases of pasteboard (*carton pierre* in French) or leather. From the mid 1700s, brass was used for the main body of instruments because of its strength; it also proved durable over many years' repeated use for geared or sliding pieces such as the focusing of telescopes and microscopes. To preserve them and guard them against pitting, the brass surfaces were gilded from the 1500s to early 1700s, and until the mid 1800s or later they were lacquered; from then on they were either lacquered or nickel-plated.

Many surveying and navigational instruments, such as theodolites and levels, sextants and octants, primarily involve measuring, and so exhibit calibrated scales. These are often engraved on an inlaid silver band, which was soft and easy to engrave accurately, but requires lacquering to prevent tarnishing.

The lenses on early examples of optical instruments such as pre-1750 telescopes and microscopes were permanently fixed and cannot be extracted for cleaning; later pieces unscrew to give access for cleaning. Some types of microscopes or surveying instruments have sets of alternative lenses and other accessories. These are stored in the fitted wooden case originally furnished with the piece, and if the box is missing or the accessories depleted, the value of the whole is cut up to 75 percent. Dirty lenses are detrimental, but in instruments where they are fixed will just have to be accepted as devaluing the piece; those that unscrew can be cleaned by a professional or knowledgable amateur. Scratched lenses detract but should not be replaced as that would reduce value even more.

Cases and their metal fixtures should be lightly dusted or wiped with a damp cloth occasionally, not cleaned with either metal, wood, or glass polishes, which could seep into or damage neighboring materials.

## THE RESTORER'S BRIEF

Ask a restorer to fix wooden cases to prevent their disintegration, to reglue loose joints with animal glue, and mend or replace broken hinges and locks in keeping. Leather cases are less durable, but their survival is less important as they were usually merely basic containers and rarely housed accessories. From a European standpoint, it is preferable to retain an original gilded, lacquered, or oxidized finish, even if it is partly worn or degraded. However, the preference in the United States can be for a much brighter look, achieved by cleaning, polishing, and relacquering. It follows, therefore, that instruments subjected to the American treatment will suffer in value if resold on the European market.

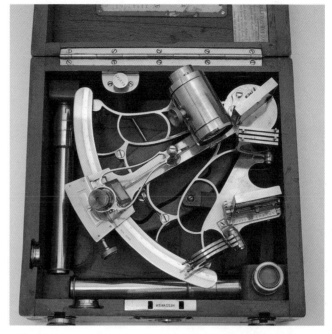

*Although it may be tempting to display the late 19th-century sextant separately from its mahogany fitted case, the case must be preserved as well, as it would dramatically increase the value of the whole piece. The sextant is of brass with a silver scale.*

*The original finish on this lacquered brass, 1890s binocular microscope (left) and its oxidized stand, should be preserved as much as possible for the European market, but in the United States, a restored, brighter look is acceptable.*

## GLOBAL CONCERNS

**Globes are constructed with printed paper "gores" or segments pasted over a composition core, which are lacquered to prolong their life. However, the lacquer is not everlasting and the core may split or the gores otherwise become damaged by flaking or scratching. Internal ruptures must be repaired first before loose sections of gore are refixed and missing segments replaced— these days using photocopies of the originals. Worn lacquer must be renewed to preserve the gores.**

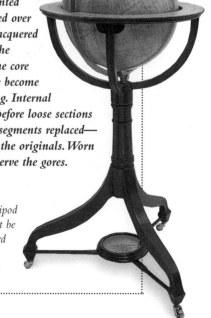

*Celestial globe with a mahogany tripod stand, 1868 (right). The globe must be rotated carefully in its stand to guard against scuffing the lacquer coating which protects the printed segments.*

161

Toys were not made to be precious antiques for adults, they were created for children to play with—and if they have been used for their original purpose, will carry honorable signs of love and wear.

Many toys—such as exquisite, but fragile dolls, or model cars and trains with their delicate, small-scale mechanisms—though designed for children, were not always strong enough to withstand hard play. But even if they are now only suitable for display, there is still much to enjoy, for in their construction and design, they reflect much of the artistry, invention, and craftsmanship of their age.

# TOYS &dolls

# TEDDY BEARS

EVEN THOUGH THEY ARE NOW FAVORITE AND HIGHLY PRICED COLLECTIBLES FOR AN ADULT MARKET, TEDDY BEARS WERE DESIGNED FOR CHILDREN TO PLAY WITH AND OFTEN LOOK VERY MUCH LOVED AND WORN. BUT THIS CAN CONTRIBUTE TO THEIR CHARM AND CHARACTER.

The most valuable bears are those of good pedigree—good-quality toys usually made by one of the top manufacturers—and in good condition. However, one can safely assume that a teddy bear will not have been cared for with the delicacy with which one would handle a porcelain figure. Many of the most appealing bears have worn fur or a missing eye or nose, and such defects can be an essential part of their character. It is important to prevent further damage or deterioration, by repairing a split seam to prevent the stuffing from falling out, or replacing moth damaged pads. Beyond this it is a matter of personal taste and judgment. One way of checking a teddy bear's state of health is to hold it up to your nose and smell it. Warning signals are a smell of damp or decay, or even of strong cleaning fluid, all of which should deter you from buying.

*Fur:* Natural mohair plush was traditionally used, but cotton plush, burlap (hessian), and synthetic plush are also common. Worn patches can be re-covered using similar materials, but might destroy the character of the bear. Tears and splits in the cloth or fabric can be mended but should be done professionally.

*Ears:* Can become unstitched and sometimes lost. If one ear is lost, it is wiser to leave well alone, especially on a valuable bear.

*Joints:* Cardboard disks strengthen the joints at neck, shoulder, and hips. Check at the joints for splits or thinness of cloth, especially the arms and legs, where the material may have rubbed against the inner cardboard disks.

Look for labels such as this on the foot of the big Chad Valley bear in the main picture; loss would reduce value.

*Pads:* Should be of felt, leather, or cloth; most have long stitches representing claws in the same thread and color as that used for the nose. These can be replaced by similar, but modern materials. Most old teddy bears have moth damage to their pads.

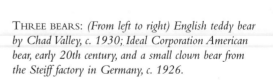

THREE BEARS: *(From left to right) English teddy bear by Chad Valley, c. 1930; Ideal Corporation American bear, early 20th century, and a small clown bear from the Steiff factory in Germany, c. 1926.*

**Eyes:** May be "boot button," glass, or plastic, and attached by stitching, spikes, or glue. Check the back of the neck to see if there is a small knot—a sign of stitched eyes—which is the most secure method.

**Nose and mouth:** Most are stitched in black or brown thread, depending on the color of the bear; the designs vary according to manufacturer, and if restored should follow the correct design. Chips in very early sealing-wax snouts or a rubber-like composite called gutta percha can be filled; the job is best left to a professional restorer who will know the most suitable materials to use, although the earliest Steiff bear's sealing-wax nose cannot easily be replaced. Plastic noses were sometimes used from the 1950s.

**Stuffing:** Ascertain the stuffing material by giving the bear a gentle squeeze: excelsior, a fiber made from strands of wood fiber, "crunches"; kapok feels soft; and foam is bouncy. It is important to know for care and restoration.

**Seams:** Check all seams for splits that can be easily repaired with strong cotton thread. Do not be alarmed by a handstitched chest seam; many bears were finished this way, and restoration should follow suit.

*Two white plush Steiff teddy bears dating from c. 1905 and 1908 (left), one without the all-important button in its ear. The bright, silvery Steiff metal button (right) was used 1952-1970. Earlier Steiff buttons have usually aged to dull pewter.*

difference in texture by rubbing it with your fingers.

The first bears, especially those made by Steiff, have black "boot button" eyes (so called because they were exactly like the buttons found on leather boots of the time), round and black with a ring on the back to secure with thread. Glass eyes were also used, and those which were secured by strong stitching have survived well. Some were attached by wire spikes (which are dangerous for young children); others were

## BEAR DEVELOPMENT

The earliest teddy bears date from c. 1903, and are highly sought. Generally, the ones most likely to be of lasting quality, skilled workmanship, and made with good materials are those from the leading makers such as the German companies Steiff, Bing, and Hermann. English makers include Merrythought, Pedigree, and Chad Valley, and in the United States, the Ideal Novelty Toy Corporation, Knickerbocker, and Strauss. Many of these companies also made stuffed toys and fabric dolls.

The earliest teddy bears have fur of mohair plush, a soft and durable natural fiber that was produced in blond, beige, gold, or cinnamon, and trimmed to different lengths known as long plush, short plush, and bristle plush. Mohair is still made today so can be used for repairing old teddy bears.

In the late 1940s and 50s, synthetic plush became more popular. It differs from natural plush in much the same way that wool fabric differs from synthetic—you can feel the

*A rare cinnamon plush clockwork teddy bear made by the German manufacturer, Bing, c. 1914, with a maker's metal disk under its left arm. When activated, the ball rotates and the bear moves forward.*

glued on and tend to be lost easily as the glue dries out. The best-quality bears had stitched eyes. The majority of bears have snout (nose) and mouth stitched in black thread, and some manufacturers have specific patterns of nose stitching.

Early German teddy bears were filled and stuffed with "excelsior," fine strands of wood, twisted into skeins. This has sometimes been broken down through play—especially if the bear is held by the upper arms—into a sawdustlike consistency. English makers used kapok, a natural fibrous material like cotton fluff (cotton wool), to stuff the body and excelsior in the head. From the 1960s bears were filled with synthetic, washable stuffing.

## GENERAL CARE

Teddy bears—or indeed any fabric toy—should be kept in a dry, dust-free place, away from direct sunlight, and handled gently. If the fur is dirty, it can be brushed with a soft toothbrush and then wiped with a clean cloth dipped in a warm soap solution, working the foam only into the fur. Wipe off the soap suds with a damp clean cloth so that the fur does not become sticky, and leave the bear to dry in a warm place. Do not use a hair dryer, which can make the fur brittle. If necessary, repeat the washing process.

To store a bear, wrap it in acid-free tissue paper and place in a cardboard box; inspect it regularly for moth damage and dampness.

*A typical gold plush bear from the 1950s, showing glass eyes that are stitched to hold them firm, and black-stitched nose and mouth.*

## THE RESTORER'S BRIEF

The ideal collectible bear is one in good condition. However, if restoration is done sympathetically—you do not want your 1910 Steiff bear to end up looking like a 1998 copy—the bear will look attractive and live longer. Before considering any restoration, it is worth finding out as much as you can about the designs and methods of the bear's maker, so any restoration can be in keeping with the original construction and materials. For example, stitched mouths and noses should be in the original pattern; some are horizontally stitched, some vertical; others have a long dropped stitch at each end of the nose stitching. Generally, the fur should be left as it is, even if it is worn. Patching can be done, but matching is hard and can look clumsy. Stuffing, however, can revive a sagging bear, and modern materials can be used. If the chest seam was hand stitched, it should be repeated once the new stuffing is in place. Eyes can be replaced by authentic-looking modern reproductions and secured by stitching; spikes are too dangerous and glue does not last. If pads are missing, they can be replaced with similar felt fabric, which is easily available, and stitched neatly in place with thread, but check you are not covering a maker's label; if so, leave a gap in the stitching so it can be seen, or remove it and restitch it to the new pad.

# DOLLS

THE MOST VALUABLE PART OF AN ANTIQUE BISQUE OR WAX DOLL IS THE HEAD; IF IT IS IN GOOD CONDITION, THE DOLL AS A WHOLE WILL MAINTAIN SIGNIFICANT VALUE, EVEN IF HAIR, CLOTHES, OR OTHER PARTS OF THE BODY ARE MISSING OR DAMAGED.

It is hard to imagine a doll with a fragile porcelain or wax head being given to a child to play with today. Modern children are used to indestructable toys which can be thrown on the floor and picked up unharmed. Dolls of the 1700s were often made of wood, which was not very cuddly, but at least it was durable. Perhaps the designers of the 19th and early 20th centuries—from when the most highly sought collectors' dolls date—did not intend their dolls to be played with, or perhaps children of those times did not play with their toys in the same way; they were, after all, dressed as small adults—and expected to behave as adults.

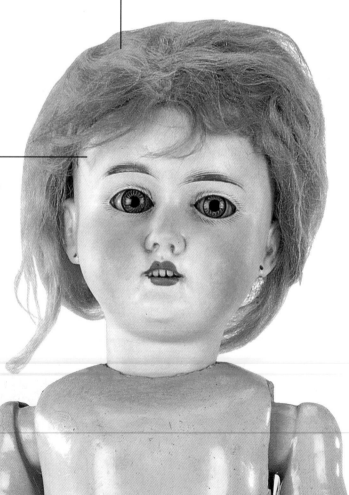

*Hair:* Mohair or real hair is used to cover a cardboard pate, which in turn covers the head cavity. In most cases the wig and pate can be removed to allow inspection for damage. The head itself is the most valuable part of the doll. If the hair is in poor condition, it is not too serious; a replacement wig will enhance appearance and not have much effect on the value of the doll.

*Head:* The most vulnerable and the most valuable part of the doll. A bisque head is hollow and made of fine china, so it is easily chipped, cracked, or broken. Cracks and chips can be successfully restored to give a good appearance. However, any repair to the head greatly diminishes the value of the doll. Look out for the maker's initials and mold number on the back of the head; each maker produced many head molds, each identified by a number. Some molds are very rare—and valuable—while others were made in their thousands.

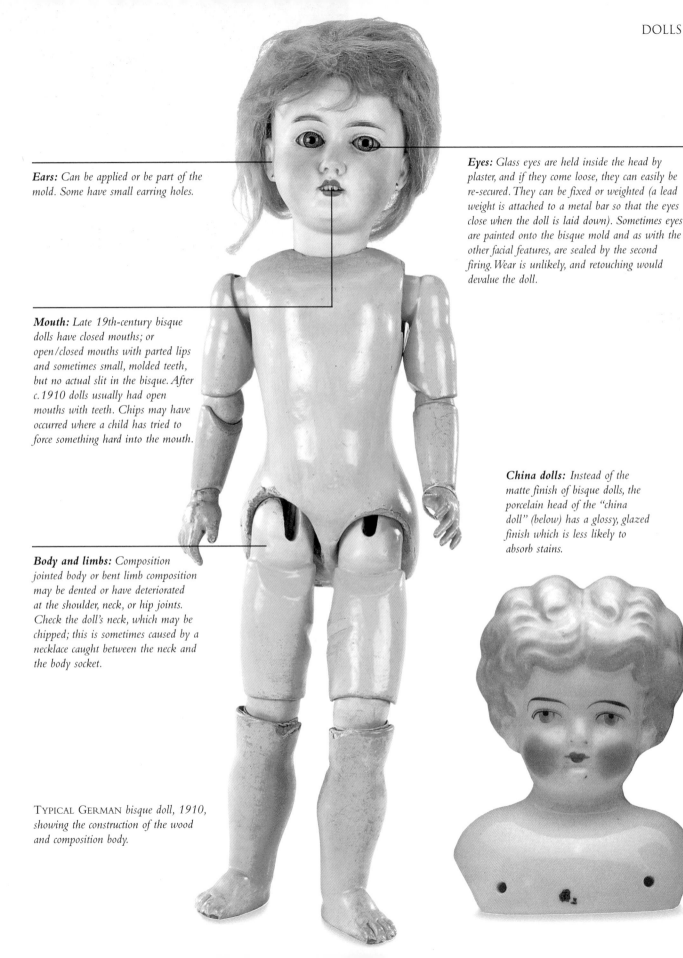

**Eyes:** *Glass eyes are held inside the head by plaster, and if they come loose, they can easily be re-secured. They can be fixed or weighted (a lead weight is attached to a metal bar so that the eyes close when the doll is laid down). Sometimes eyes are painted onto the bisque mold and as with the other facial features, are sealed by the second firing. Wear is unlikely, and retouching would devalue the doll.*

**Ears:** *Can be applied or be part of the mold. Some have small earring holes.*

**Mouth:** *Late 19th-century bisque dolls have closed mouths; or open/closed mouths with parted lips and sometimes small, molded teeth, but no actual slit in the bisque. After c.1910 dolls usually had open mouths with teeth. Chips may have occurred where a child has tried to force something hard into the mouth.*

**China dolls:** *Instead of the matte finish of bisque dolls, the porcelain head of the "china doll" (below) has a glossy, glazed finish which is less likely to absorb stains.*

**Body and limbs:** *Composition jointed body or bent limb composition may be dented or have deteriorated at the shoulder, neck, or hip joints. Check the doll's neck, which may be chipped; this is sometimes caused by a necklace caught between the neck and the body socket.*

TYPICAL GERMAN *bisque doll, 1910, showing the construction of the wood and composition body.*

## DOLLS FOR PLAY AND DISPLAY

Bisque dolls are by far the largest category of antique dolls. Dolls with bisque porcelain heads were produced in France and Germany from the mid 1800s, the best-quality and most expensive dolls by French makers such as Jumeau, Bru, and Steiner. From the early 1900s, the quality of German dolls dramatically improved. Very few bisque dolls were made in the United States or Great Britain.

Bisque is unglazed porcelain. The porcelain clay was poured or pressed into molds to give the doll its characteristic features, and then fired. The delicate painted features were added and fixed by a second firing. This produced a perfect, matte finish complexion. Like any porcelain, bisque is thin and brittle. Because of the fragile nature of the head, many bisque dolls were kept away from children except on Sundays and holidays, when they were brought out to be admired, so earning the nickname of "Sunday Dolls."

Dolls' bodies can be made of various materials; the most common, from the late 19th century, was a toughened form of papier mâché known as composition. This was covered by a thin layer of gesso and then painted to give a realistic finish; surface cracks can occur, and the composition itself can become dented. One of the most famous dolls from the American Ideal Novelty Toy Corporation in the 1930s was "Shirley Temple," whose composition face has since tended to craze. Nothing can be done about this, and the condition is generally accepted by collectors.

From the second half of the 1800s,

*A German bisque doll by Kammer & Reinhardt/Simon & Halbig, c. 1914. The mold number is 128, an uncommon one, which pushes the value up.*

*A poured wax doll (right) made in England c. 1880, in its original whitework underclothes. The head, shoulders, lower arms, and legs are wax, the body is cloth.*

*Hard plastic dolls by Madame Alexander often represented famous people or fictional characters of the 1930s to 1950s, including Louisa M. Alcott's* Little Women *(above), and Scarlett O'Hara from* Gone with the Wind. *The plastic is much tougher than previous materials and, unless exposed to extreme conditions, is unlikely to discolor or crack.*

bodies were made from fine kid in white or pink or cloth. These can tear or split at the seams; repair will detract from the doll's value to some extent, but should be done to prevent further deterioration. The American company Izannah Walker made dolls with painted stockinette-covered heads in the late 1800s. As with any cloth doll, they are vulnerable to dampness, which causes mold and makes fillings become hard and lumpy.

In the late 1800s wax dolls were made in England by Montinari, Pierotti, Chas. Marsh, and others. They are very susceptible to changes in temperature, and unless they are kept at an even temperature and in a controlled environment, they may crack.

### Fine features

The eyes of bisque dolls were usually made of glass, either in a fixed position or weighted with a small piece of lead inside the head cavity so the eyes close when the doll is laid down. Some early French dolls from the late 1800s had spiral glass eyes known as "paperweight eyes" because they resembled the paperweights of the period. Mouths were open or closed, or even "open/closed," which means that the mouth appears to be open but there is no actual opening in the bisque. Wigs, usually of mohair or sometimes of real hair, were fixed onto a pate with animal glue, which in turn covered the head cavity. The head is hollow, and the wig and pate cover the crown. The pate is usually shaped cardboard, but cork pates were used for early French dolls, and plaster pates were used on dolls made by the German manufacturer J.D. Kestner.

Original or contemporary clothes can greatly enhance the value of any doll, especially if they are in good condition, though it is possible to re-dress the doll in the correct style following old patterns.

*A French Bru Bébé doll, c. 1880, with a bisque head and lower arms, and black kid body. Kid or cloth bodies are problematic to clean; you could try a commercial fine-leather cleaner, but test it first on a small, inconspicuous area, or have the doll cleaned professionally by a restorer. If the body is split or torn, it can be stitched, or small areas neatly patched.*

## GENERAL CARE

The face of a bisque doll can be cleaned by dipping a cotton swab (bud), into warm, soapy water and gently cleaning away the dirt, finishing with a clean, damp cloth. Brush the wig with a small brush, but be especially careful with mohair which can become brittle. If the pate has become detached, use reversible wood glue or animal glue (as was used originally). One way to check for cracks or restoration is to shine a powerful light into the head cavity, so it is important that the pate can be removed in the future which would not be possible if modern nonreversible glues were used.

Composition is water-soluble, so clean it with a slightly damp cloth.

Clothes can be washed by hand if they are cotton; silk and satin are more delicate and tend to split with age. Splits can be reinforced to prevent them from getting worse and improve the appearance, but if the fabric is weakened with age, this can create vulnerable areas around the repair.

Display the doll securely, in a cabinet, either on a doll stand obtainable at doll fairs or through advertisements in doll magazines, or more attractively on a doll-sized chair, in a buggy, or on a baby's highchair. If the doll is to be stored, wrap it in acid-free tissue paper, and protect the head with bubble wrap; place it face down in a cardboard box to avoid any strain of the plaster holding the eyes in place, and inspect regularly for signs of insect attack or mold.

## THE RESTORER'S BRIEF

Damage to the head can reduce the value by half; even though it can be almost invisibly restored. Hairline cracks are best left alone; chips and breaks should be treated by a restorer.

Wigs are often damaged, or even cut by the doll's young owner, but they can be replaced with realistic synthetic hair on a stretchy net base. The restorer should stick this in place lightly so it can be removed. The old wig should be kept—it is part of the doll's history.

Glass eyes can become detached, and it is relatively simple—and therefore not too expensive—for a restorer to reattach them. Ask the restorer if it is

possible to replace missing eyes with authentic old glass eyes, though these are expensive and difficult to find. Good plastic copies can be obtained, but still look inferior.

Broken or missing teeth can be replaced, either with the originals if they can be found inside the head, or with modern reproductions—which should not affect overall value.

If the doll is jointed at the knees, hip, wrist, elbow, and shoulder, it is held together with elastic cord. This loses its strength over the years and can be replaced. This is best left to a restorer with the right materials and technique, as stringing too tightly can put a strain of the neck and joints of the doll.

*The Martha Chase cloth doll (right), made in America, c. 1920, has a stockinette head with features and hair painted on with oils. Unless in very poor condition, dolls like this should be left alone, and any cleaning or restoration only done by an expert.*

# THE ROCKING HORSE

**Ears:** *The tips of the ears are often broken. They can be replaced but it is acceptable to leave them since they add charm and character to an old horse.*

**M**OST OF THE PROBLEMS AFFECTING ROCKING HORSES COME FROM THEIR BEING SO MUCH LOVED—AND USED—THAT PAINTWORK BECOMES KNOCKED AND CHIPPED AND THE TACK WORN.

Because of their size and weight, rocking horses are not outdoor toys and have generally lived in a stable indoor environment. Damage therefore tends to be overall play wear from generations of young owners rather than from dirt and damp. As they were passed down from one generation to the next, they were often inexpertly retouched and repainted. If this is the case, it is invariably worth seeking a restorer's advice on repainting from scratch. The main decisions as far as restoration is concerned, however, will rest on whether the horse is for show or for use, in which case the riders' security must be taken into account.

**Eyes:** *Usually made of glass and glued into the head. The eye socket is sometimes painted red to give a fiery look to the eye. Lost or broken eyes can be replaced with similar glass ones.*

**Base:** *Wooden bow rockers were very strong, but over the years they can split or break. Pedestal bases are most vulnerable on the upright supports, and should be checked regularly for safety reasons.*

**Tack:** *The saddle and bridle are made of leather, often with silk rosettes on the browband. Leathercloth or Rexenne, an imitation leather, was also used. The reins and stirrup leathers can split and break; new ones can be bought, which will enhance the appearance and make the horse safer but will not add to value. A saddler would be the best person to repair the saddle, although this could be expensive.*

**Mane and tail:** *Traditionally made from horsehair, and in many cases clipped or cut by their young owners. The mane is attached to a tape and nailed to the neck; the tail is fixed with glue into the rump of the horse. If the tail becomes detached, children often stuff small objects into the cavity: retrieving them can be amusing and interesting. New horsehair manes and tails can easily be purchased, and nylon is a good, and cheaper, substitute.*

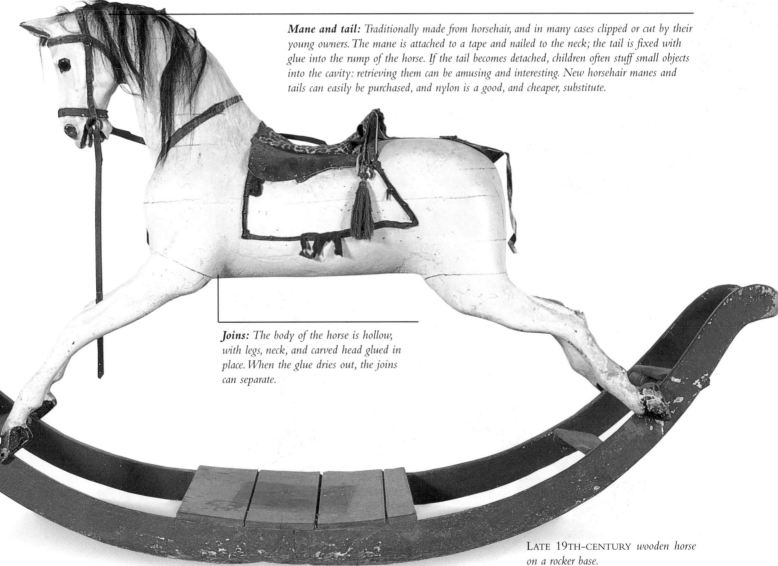

**Joins:** *The body of the horse is hollow, with legs, neck, and carved head glued in place. When the glue dries out, the joins can separate.*

LATE 19TH-CENTURY *wooden horse on a rocker base.*

## ROCKING VARIATIONS

Early rocking horses, or hobby horses, from the 1600s are rarely seen outside museums, and have planked, enclosed, sides, shaped like a cradle, with a seat and carved head. More commonly seen are the rocking horses from the late 19th and early 20th centuries, with outstretched galloping legs mounted on wooden bow rockers or trestle base. These were the traditional rocking horses with splendid carved heads, arched necks, and dapple gray finish. British horses usually have a hollow construction, made up in sections, but in the United States, they were often solid wood—and known as "shooflies" or " hobby horses."

Some were covered in real pony skin, which looks authentic but tends to dry out and split along the seams, and is difficult to repair. The ponyskin versions have two bases—a pull-along platform with four small metal wheels, which fits neatly into the second, rocker, base. Cloth-covered horses were also produced, and more recently fur-fabric covered ones, bur they do not have the style or romance of a wooden horse, or its value. Also collected are wooden fairground horses, which are made in the same way as rocking horses and should be treated similarly, and velocipedes—wooden horses on tricycle bases, with pedals that cause the horse to move up and down.

*The hide-covered German horse (above) can be removed from its rocker base and used as a pull-along horse. Hide tends to dry and split especially along the seams, which is difficult to repair.*

*American horse by an early 19th-century maker in the British style (left), from the Rocking Horse Gallery, Virginia. Many such horses were carved from solid wood, and were very heavy.*

## GENERAL CARE

Rocking horses were, of course, made for children and not as collectors' items. We can also assume that they will have been used, and will continue to be used. If children are going to play with the horse, basic care is necessary. Check that the bolts holding the horse to the base are safe, that the wooden joints are not parting or becoming loose, and that the leather straps are kept supple with saddle soap and leather preserver, just as the tack used by a real horse should be. The mane and tail can be detached, washed in a mild soapy solution, rinsed well, and left to dry away from direct heat, before being refitted. Do not place the horse close to a radiator or other direct heat as this dries the leather, wood, and glue, causing the glued sections to loosen. General wear from use is acceptable, but loss of original finish through knocks and cracks can affect value. While it is inconceivable to have a rocking horse and not let a child ride it, put a small child on a valuable horse only under adult supervision.

If your horse is to be used rather than preserved as a valuable collector's item, and deterioration not too extreme, you can do some restoration work yourself (see below), but always use reversible materials.

*A horse for small children—it is only just over 2¹/₂ feet (76 cm) high on a 9 x 8 inch (23 x 20 cm) platform. It was made in France in 1913 and is covered in brown velvet.*

## THE RESTORER'S BRIEF

If the horse is to be used and has been repainted as it passed from one family to another, then much can be done at home to improve its appearance, but do consult an expert first. Go to a saddler for repairs to harness and saddle. Remove the horse from its base. If the gesso (the chalky layer beneath the paintwork) is only slightly damaged, clean with a damp cloth and fill any cracks with a plaster-based filler. If it is badly worn, rub it down carefully. This is a good time to check for woodworm. Rub with fine sandpaper before applying an undercoat and gloss top coat, using good quality wood

paint. A valuable antique rocking horse should only be professionally restored or retouched—if at all. Its dapple-gray finish may have mellowed to a much prized creamy ocher color. Minor damage—such as a chipped ear—should be left, as it can add character. If eyes need replacing, ask for glass rather than plastic replacements. Any restoration should be retain as many of the original features as possible.

*The dapple effect is applied when the topcoat is completely dry. Using a sponge, dab dark gray or black paint around a small, circular template. Practice first on a piece of paper and look at illustrations of a similar horse for positioning.*

# MECHANICAL TOYS

Mechanical toys can be hand-operated, keywound clockwork, or have an electrical mechanism. The mechanisms will in time give trouble, and access to them is often not easy without damaging the outside of the toy.

Mechanical toys are usually constructed with a geared mechanism concealed within an outer casing. This may take the miniaturized form of a familiar moving object, such as a train, a doll, or a character from real life. Most will have been well used by their original, demanding owners, and continued use may well destroy the mechanisms—leaving it alone is generally the best policy for future survival. The exterior materials and finishes are not particularly durable either; great care is needed to preserve them, given the rough handling they generally received when new—the results of which are likely to be quite obvious.

Traditional Russian hopping and chirping bird; *the chirp comes from tiny paper bellows, the edges of which may tear, and the chirp is lost.*

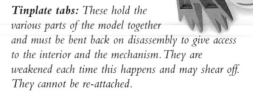

**Wind-up mechanism:** *This is not necessarily very difficult to repair, but gaining access may damage the exterior of the toy or the tabs. The mechanisms are not very sturdily built, so the substitution of a broken spring with stronger one may strain the mechanism and cause further damage, perhaps to the gears.*

**Paint finishes:** *Commonly chipped from original play, and do fade in bright light . If in acceptably used condition, leave well alone: restored paintwork, however skilfully done (and this should always be done by an expert), will reduce value.*

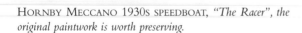

Hornby Meccano 1930s speedboat, *"The Racer", the original paintwork is worth preserving.*

**Tinplate tabs:** *These hold the various parts of the model together and must be bent back on disassembly to give access to the interior and the mechanism. They are weakened each time this happens and may shear off. They cannot be re-attached.*

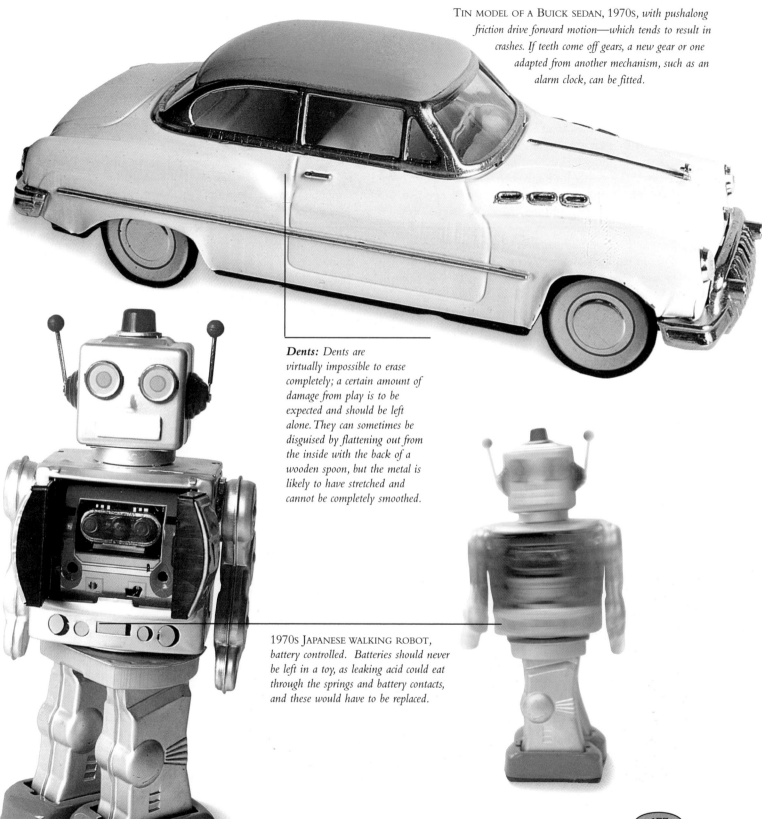

TIN MODEL OF A BUICK SEDAN, 1970S, *with pushalong friction drive forward motion—which tends to result in crashes. If teeth come off gears, a new gear or one adapted from another mechanism, such as an alarm clock, can be fitted.*

**Dents:** *Dents are virtually impossible to erase completely; a certain amount of damage from play is to be expected and should be left alone. They can sometimes be disguised by flattening out from the inside with the back of a wooden spoon, but the metal is likely to have stretched and cannot be completely smoothed.*

1970S JAPANESE WALKING ROBOT, *battery controlled. Batteries should never be left in a toy, as leaking acid could eat through the springs and battery contacts, and these would have to be replaced.*

177

## MECHANICAL REVOLUTIONS

Individually made, gold, enameled, and jewel-set automaton miniature animals and musical snuffboxes were made around 1800 in Switzerland. These are rare, extremely delicate, and fragile, but were aimed at an adult market and normally handled with great care. Production of mechanical metal, usually tinplate, toys for children started in the mid 1800s. The first major center for production was the German town of Nuremberg. Mechanical toys broadly divide into two categories: whimsical performing figures or animals, mainly made in France, and transportation vehicles.

Nonmechanical trains had been made from the 1830s, but significant numbers of wind-up or steam-driven toy trains were not produced until the second half of the 1800s. These were originally composed of a soft lead alloy, but the resulting casting, although superior to pure lead, was still heavy and relatively brittle, rendering the toys susceptible to damage, and models were only generalized types rather than accurate representations.

From about 1915, a new diecast alloy known as "mazak," based on zinc, was introduced. It was lighter and harder and allowed accurate modeling, but because of the impurities in it, does in time become brittle and crack. This tendency is increased by humidity and leads to eventual virtual disintegration.

In the closing years of the century, model railways were made in sufficient quantities at a low enough price to make them accessible to a wide market. Standard gauges (widths) of track were adopted by all manufacturers, meaning that new

toy companies were able to join the great expansion, using diecast bodies. Electrically driven trains were first made around 1880 in Germany, 1890 in the United States, and from around 1900 in England. The most famous American model train makes are Ives, Lionel, and American Flyer; German ones Marklin, Schoenner, Carette, and Bing; and in England, Bassett-Lowke, and Hornby.

Diecast model automobiles were introduced about 1910 in France and the United States and followed a similar evolution to trains. Since the early 1960s, greater realism was achieved by the introduction of opening doors, hoods, and trunks, although these weakened the structure, while the similarly inspired addition of rubber tires, aluminum wheel hubs, and clear plastic windows increased the number of parts that could be lost or broken.

## GENERAL CARE

The main problems for collectors of toys are atmospheric: sunlight fades paintwork, and humidity hastens the natural degradation of the tinplate or diecast alloy: never keep metal toys in a kitchen or bathroom. If possible, display in a glazed cabinet that also affords some protection from dust and fly-blow, perhaps using sachets of silica gel to control humidity. Avoid cabinets made of oak, the acids in which engender lead rot and diecast decay. On metal toys avoid using cleaning solutions, which may wear away the painted decoration, and never use soap and water, as this rusts tinplate and speeds decay in diecasts; instead, dust with a soft brush or for stubborn stains wipe with a soft cloth impregnated with

*The main dangers to mechanical diecast toys, like this early 1900s example (left) are atmospheric: sunlight fades paintwork and humidity brings degradation of the tinplate or diecast metal structure.*

*Original packaging should be handled as little as possible and wrapped in acid-free tissue, as it will add greatly to value.*

machine oil. If the interior is easily accessible, you can remove rust with a soft wire brush or steel-wool, and oil lightly. Lightly oil moving parts, but wipe off any excess oil afterward. Remember the tabs that hold the separate body components of tinplate toys together weaken every time they are bent, and once broken cannot be repaired.

Many mechanical toys are too valuable to use. If you do want to make one work, only wind it up a little to reduce the risk of snapping the spring.

Steam engines should never fired up, as the heat of the burner scorches the painted decoration and any residual water in the boiler leads to corrosion.

## FIGURAL AUTOMATA

*Mechanized dolls were originally made of metal in the clockmaking towns of Augsburg and Nuremberg, southern Germany, during the 1600s. The art spread to Switzerland in the later 1700s and France in the 1800s, incorporating fragile materials such as bisque, enamel, and delicate textiles. Simple and comparatively cheap automata in perishable materials aimed at the children's market continued to be made in Nuremberg until the 1920s. Luxury products of exquisite quality for adults were concentrated in France, around Paris, in the late 1800s and very early 1900s. Specialized workers made costumes and accessories, while the mechanism was often sourced in Switzerland, and the heads in Germany. However, the materials are highly perishable, and many are now in very poor condition. Attitudes to restoration vary from market to market; the United States likes total restoration, even full recostuming, whereas in Europe the taste is more for repair and stabilization.*

*Smoking monkey, c. 1860, made by Gustave Vichy.*

## THE RESTORER'S BRIEF

Definite conventions have been formulated regarding the processes and materials for the restoration of toys. As a result, restoration, especially to paintwork, is often best left alone. A mechanical toy with restored paintwork is always worth less than one in acceptably used condition. Tinplate once rusted on the

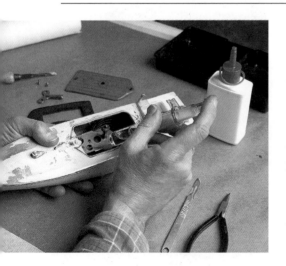

*The amateur owner can lubricate the moving parts of a mechanism with light engine oil, as long as the mechanism is not very delicate, and excess oil is wiped off.*

outer surface is unrestorable. What you can and should do is ask a restorer to make any repair as the delicate mechanisms. Any replacement parts should be compatible in strength with the original mechanism to avoid stress and possible gear damage. If rot has attacked diecast toys, plugging the holes with polymers or resinous compounds will make no difference; the condition is irreversible. To prevent further decay, keep the object in a dry environment.

A FRAME FOCUSES THE EYE ONTO ITS CONTENTS; IT CAN BE HIGHLY ORNAMENTAL, EXISTING SIMPLY TO ENHANCE WHATEVER IT IS SURROUNDING. BUT FRAMES CAN ALSO SERVE A VITAL PROTECTIVE FUNCTION: THEY DISGUISE THE STRETCHER THAT MAINTAINS THE SHAPE OF AN OIL PAINTING…AND HOLD THE MOUNT AND GLAZING THAT ARE THE FIRST LINE OF DEFENSE A WORK OF ART ON PAPER HAS AGAINST THE OUTSIDE WORLD. SOMETIMES FRAMES EXCEED THEIR PRACTICAL BOUNDS AND BECOME ART FORMS IN THEIR OWN RIGHT; THEY CAN BE MORE VALUABLE THAN THE MIRROR OR ARTWORK THEY CONTAIN.

# FRAMED *works of art* & MIRRORS

# THE OIL PAINTING

O IL PAINTINGS MAY BE DECORATIVE OBJECTS TO FILL A SPACE ON A WALL, BUT AS FAR AS CARE IS CONCERNED, THEY ARE COMPOSITE STRUCTURES BUILT UP OF DIFFERENT MATERIALS WHICH MAY REACT WITH ONE ANOTHER.

Oil paints consist of colored pigments ground in oil which acts as a medium allowing the pigment to be applied. The paint makes possible a variety of depth, texture, and richness of color, and can be applied in varying degrees of thickness, but the thicker it is, the more likely it is to crack and break off.

*Impasto (left) is applied with thick brushstrokes, or with a palette knife; the paint is thick and rigid, making it vulnerable to being broken off. However, it is much easier to restore than a flat surface with thinner paint, when restoration is more difficult to disguise.*

***Canvas edge:*** *Often partly hidden beneath the frame, this is one of the most vulnerable parts as it is where stress occurs. Sometimes the impression of the stretcher bars may show through to the front; this is disfiguring and hard to rectify.*

***Stretcher keys:*** *These are placed in the corners to provide tension. If they are missing the canvas will be slack, but they can easily be replaced. If they fall between the canvas and bottom stretcher bar they can cause a triangular impression to come through on the front of the canvas.*

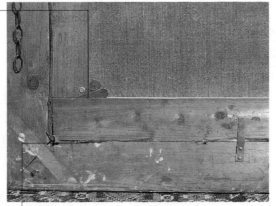

***Stretchers:*** *The wooden frame which pulls the canvas taut, and which must be sound and free of damp or insect infestation. The canvas may come away from the stretchers, or the stretchers may loosen, in which case the canvas will sag. A restorer can retension a canvas, but particularly with a valuable painting, should check for weaknesses before doing so.*

***Verso of the canvas:*** *Look for signs of previous restoration, such as patches, which may be more obvious from the back. If the edges of the canvas where they are tacked to the stretchers are dirty and becoming degraded, the picture might need relining (mounting the canvas on another canvas to give it strength), though this is very expensive, and may devalue.*

**Surface:** *Holes and tears reduce value but can be successfully restored, though at considerable cost. Flaking paint can be easily consolidated but areas of paint loss, though they can be touched in by a restorer, devalue the painting. If a painting has been badly restored in the past you may be able to identify areas of overpainting in a strong or oblique light. Craquelure, caused by breaking down of the paint medium, unless extreme, is generally accepted and does not need retouching.*

18TH-CENTURY PORTRAIT BY JOSEPH WRIGHT, *oil on canvas in original gesso and giltwood frame.*

**Varnish:** *The varnish is a final transparent coat applied to protect the paint and saturate the colors. Usually a natural resin, it yellows and darkens with time, obscuring the painting and changing the colors. Surface dirt and tobacco smoke may add to the discoloration. Old varnish can be removed and replaced, but this needs to be carried out by a professional in keeping with the original varnishes used, and tests are needed to determine solubility.*

*The alla prima technique (left) was favored by the Impressionists in the late 1800s. The final paint surface is achieved by the initial application of paint rather than the traditional method of building up layers of paint.*

## PAINTING TECHNIQUES

Painting in oils was first developed in Flanders around 1400, initially on wooden panels and later on the more transportable canvas. The canvas was primed, and paint and glazes built up in layers, which lasted well. Most early pigments, too, proved to be more resilient than modern equivalents. In the 1900s, many artists no longer handground the pigments, but took them ready-mixed, straight from a tube, and applied them to a variety of potentially unstable surfaces such as paperboard—which are bound to create restoration problems in the future.

## GENERAL CARE

Hang oil paintings in a stable environment away from direct heat and strong light, as temperature and relative humidity variation make the canvas expand and contract, and causing the paint to crack. Have the back of the painting sealed with a board to keep out dust and insects, and if it is on a wall on the outer edge of a house, place corks between the bottom corners of the frame and the wall to protect against cold and dampness. Canvases are taut and easily scratched or torn with the slightest pressure. So if you are taking a group of pictures from a wall, remove the bottom ones first; beware of door handles, and remember that both sides of a canvas are equally vulnerable. Larger pictures will need two people to move them; plan the route you are going to take and make sure it is clear. Ensure that wall fixings are secure and that wall and hanging wires and screws are strong enough to take the weight of the picture.

Because they are usually protected by varnish, oil paintings do not need to be glazed. If a picture is glazed, however, cover the glass with tape before you transport it so that in the event of breakage it will be held in position and not pierce the picture.

If the paint surface is sound, you can surface clean it yourself. Using a soft brush, sweep the dust into the nozzle of a vacuum cleaner on low power—never let the nozzle touch the picture. If the painting is dirty, use a cotton swab moistened with saliva, and wipe it gently over the surface in a circular motion. Test a small area first, perhaps at the edge, do not press hard and check the end of the swab to make sure that only dirt is coming off, not paint or varnish. If the dirt does not shift, repeat the exercise with turpentine, but do spot test first. If the painting appears dull or matte after this procedure, consult a restorer.

If the painting has been exposed to dampness, mold may appear. Leave it to dry gradually—do not heat—and on a dry day take it outside (to prevent the spores from spreading in the house) and brush the mold away with a soft brush.

## THE RESTORER'S BRIEF

Restoration is a matter of striking a balance between doing justice to the work of art as originally executed, and the grace of natural aging. It may save or revitalize a painting which seemed irretrievable, to a spectacular degree that more than justifies the cost. The finely tuned decisions to be made on the level of cleaning and retouching, will vary with each work, or even within different sections of the same work. A painting can be examined under ultraviolet light to assess previous restoration, and so that the restorer can differentiate between the original paint and any subsequent retouching (overpainting blocks the fluorescence of the varnish and appears dark).

Restoring paint loss is highly skilled, very time consuming, and expensive. Ask the restorer to quote, and to explain the priorities and the outcome of each procedure...will removing a discolored varnish expose worse weaknesses beneath, for example? Generally, if paint loss is sensitively touched in, the value of the painting will be maintained.

If a canvas is torn, deformed, or seriously weakened, relining may be necessary, but should be avoided if at all possible to preserve the painting's integrity. It should be done by a specialist reliner in keeping with the original type of canvas.

## THREE ASPECTS OF RESTORATION

*Very yellow nicotine stains and surface dirt have built up. The mildest way of cleaning—and one that can be tried at home—is to gently wipe, in a circular motion, with a cotton swab dampened in saliva, which is warm and slightly alkaline.*

*Retouching a painting is not a permanent process. The retouched area of this painting has discolored with age. It will have to be removed and redone, and the process will have to be repeated when the new retouching discolors.*

*This distinctive circular craquelure is known as a Sigmoid crack, the result of a blow on one point, pushing waves of stress out around it like ripples from an object dropped in water.*

185

# A WATERCOLOR PAINTING

P APER IS A FRAGILE, ORGANIC MATERIAL, BUT THE MEDIA
APPLIED TO IT—SUCH AS INK, WATERCOLOR, PASTEL, AND
CHARCOAL—ALL OF WHICH LIE ON THE SURFACE WITH
VARYING DEGREES OF BONDING—ALSO HAVE A BEARING ON
LONGTERM SURVIVAL

On many artifacts, overall discoloration such as on the featured watercolor
might be regarded as a desirable indication of age, but here it only disfigures
and disguises the original intention of the artist. Watercolor is a delicate
medium, relying for much of its effect, on its translucence and the refraction
of light off the paper. The discoloration is caused by a combination of
circumstances, including bad restoration, such as mounting on poor
quality board.

**Glass:** *Glass protects against atmospheric pollution, humidity,
insects, fire damage, scratches, and tears. In the featured painting
(right), water has splashed over the painting and mount, and there
are black fly specks, neither of which would have occurred if glass
had been present. Broken glass should be replaced immediately.*

**Frame:** *The frame must be
strong and protective enough
for the work of art it is
supporting, with a well-
sealed backboard to reduce
the likelihood of physical
damage and to protect
against insect or atmospheric
damage. Much damage can
be caused where a flimsy
frame has disintegrated while
on a wall, resulting in slivers
of glass becoming embedded
in the paper.*

**Mount:** *Low quality boards and mounts may be very acidic, and will cause discoloration to both mount and picture. A brown line beneath the beveled edges of the cutaway window is indicative of an acidic mount. It is worth having an inferior quality mount changed to an acid-free one.*

LATE 18TH-CENTURY WATERCOLOR ON WOVE PAPER: *It has suffered from virtually everything that can happen to a work on paper with the exception of being set on fire!*

**Surface:** *Dampness causes water stains and cockling—a warped, undulating surface caused by the paper stretching and shrinking, which can be treated. The artwork would have to be removed from its mount, as it may have stretched. Look for black specks and small holes—signs of insect attack. Restoration is possible, but can be expensive, so the value of the painting would have to be taken into account.*

# A DELICATE BALANCE

Paper is a matted web of vegetable matter which has been pulped in water, strained on a sieve-line frame, dried, and pressed into thin sheets; it is one of the most common manufactured substances, and also one of the weakest. It is highly susceptible to dehydrating and curling in light and heat, to stretching and attracting fungal growth in damp conditions, and to attack by insects. Paper gradually degrades because of acids within it—especially in lowgrade paper—and outside pollution. More than any other artifact, therefore, the immediate environment—the mounts, the frames, the albums—in which paper collectibles and works of art are kept is absolutely crucial. Durability has much to do with paper quality, which is highly variable, and the stability and bonding power of the medium applied to it.

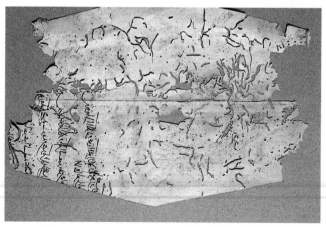

*An extreme case of foxing—a brown fungal infection caused by dampness—begins to eat into the paper (above), and severe insect attack (below). Both are beyond redemption.*

*Colored pastels and chalks fade in light, and red, as in the 16th-century drawing attributed to Annibale Carracci (above), is particularly unstable.*

Paper was first manufactured in the Far East. When it reached Western Europe by the 12th century, the initial source of cellulose was linen obtained from cloth rags. From the 1800s, woodpulp became the prime source, but rag papers are generally higher quality and less acidic.

Early Renaissance drawings and manuscripts were on parchment made from animal skin, using a highly acidic concoction of acetic acid, iron, and oakgall as an ink. Parchment has a greasy surface which the ink etched through, ultimately creating holes. The ink faded to pale brown with exposure to light.

Printing inks, however, are probably the most stable medium used for works of art on paper, and have been developed as such since the 18th and 19th centuries. The inks are normally oil based and once dry are impervious to water with very little fading. Exceptions to the rule include lowgrade and water-soluble inks.

The least stable media are pastels, chalks, and charcoal, used from the 15th century, and common from the 18th century. They bond loosely to paper and continually shed pigment, especially if they are heavily applied. Even the static created by cleaning glass will lift fine particles of pigment from the paper surface onto the glass. Lacquer fixative can be sprayed on to bond the surface of the pigment, but it does not adhere the pigment to the paper. Pastels are also particularly prone to mold growth, especially as they are often on textured paper which provides an easier surface for mold spores to lodge in. This condition is common in 18th-century works.

## GENERAL CARE

Works of art on paper must be kept away from excessive light, either natural or artificial. Even some "purpose-made" picture lamps should not shine directly onto a painting for a prolonged period. Hang on a dry wall—beware of dampness filtering through from the exterior walls of a house.

Frames, mounts, and hanging fixings should be strong enough to support the work. Glazing is essential, and the frame must be deep enough to house backing board, mount, artwork, and glass. Mounting board—which should be museum quality, acid-free board for anything you want to last—should prevent the artwork from coming into contact with the glass, so that friction and wear are avoided, and a thin layer of air is present to deter condensation. The artwork should not touch the backing board either, as this is usually acidic, but it can be sealed with gummed paper tape to minimize intruders such as dust and insects. This also helps hold the artwork firmly within the frame. The inner side can be coated with polyurethane varnish or lined with acid-free tissue to prevent acidity traveling to the artwork.

Check regularly for signs of condensation on the inside of the glass. If it occurs, have the piece removed from the frame immediately, checked by a conservator, dried, and remounted on acid-free board. If one insect is spotted, there are invariably others around; isolate the piece immediately and take it to a conservator. Handle an artwork as little as possible, and wear cotton gloves to prevent finger stains.

Store framed works by covering with a cloth and laying face down. Place unframed works flat, sandwiched between layers of acid-free tissue, and store in a dark place. Never roll or fold as this may cause paint loss. When transporting a glazed piece, apply strips of masking tape over the surface to minimize damage to the artwork should the glass break.

## THE RESTORER'S BRIEF

Ask the conservator the cause of any staining. Tests can be carried out before restoration begins on adhesives or tapes which have been incorrectly used in mounting to see how easily they can be removed, and on pigments to check how water-sensitive they are. A conservator can stabilize the condition of a work of art on paper and reduce disfigurement. Discoloration that is caused by soluble acidity can be removed by washing in a neutral or slightly alkaline water at varying temperatures. Scratched and mold-stained areas can be touched in with materials which are reversible

*Unstable media such as the pastels used by Auguste Renoir in "Portrait de fillette" (below) are extremely vulnerable even when protected by a glazed frame—the space between glass and artwork should be a minimum of 1/2 inch (15 mm).*

and compatible—usually these are the same as the original medium. The level of retouching should be discussed with the conservator so that as much of the original as possible is retained intact. Retouching is normally visible, especially on flat surfaces such as posters, but will maintain the aesthetic value of a work.

Rips or brittle areas should be dealt with immediately, and can be handled in one of two ways: either the whole piece is backed with a conservationally sound paper support, and touched in on the front if necessary, or localized patches can be repaired with fine Japanese paper and starch paste, then consolidated and touched in.

In the 1900s, the quality of much of the surface material and media used declined substantially to the extent that many works of art on paper are auto destructive and the best that a conservator can do is a holding operation rather than a reviving procedure; this can be very expensive for little visual effect.

## STAMPS: A SPECIAL CASE

Mint stamps lose their value completely if they lose their adhesive as a result of being subjected to water. Even though a damaged image can be restored, a stamp so treated would not be considered original, which is the key factor for the serious stamp collector.

Only remove postmarked stamps from an envelope if you are absolutely sure that the postmark itself does not add value. Stamps are particularly thin and fragile paper items, though often on high quality paper, as they are legal tender. Their printed color will fade with prolonged exposure to light, and with changing levels of humidity and temperature they expand, contract, stretch and curl.

### General Care

If you want your stamps to last, they must be mounted in albums or on cards made with acid-free, or chemically-inert, paper available from a specialist dealer. Transparent film sleeves, covers, and page protectors should also be acid-free. Acetate sleeves are fine for display, but do not keep stamps in them permanently, as condensation may form. Store albums on open shelves in a well-ventilated room with stable temperature and humidity, and at least once a month give them an "airing" by flipping slowly through the pages.

Avoid using the adhesive of the stamp itself, or adhesive tape, or gum to attach a stamp to a mount. Use double-gummed, custom-made hinges which peel off easily without marking the stamp in case you need to remove it. This method is not, however, suitable for mint stamps—as their value is sharply reduced by the slightest hint of a hinge on the back—unless you can attach them by the sheet margin if it is still attached. Instead, use special plastic mounting strips, also available in "stock books" with acetate strips which remove the need for any adhesive. With hingeless mounting systems, the stamps are laid on a dark background which is gummed on the

*The album (left) is fitted with pockets to hold the stamps, so that no adhesive is necessary, but the clear plastic or acetate pages must be acid-free.*

*Both the autograph album of 1910-1919 vaudeville (music hall) artists (left), and the Victorian scrapbook (below) have been damaged through careless storage. But to remount and rebind the photographs and memorabilia would destroy the value and character of the albums completely. They should be wrapped in acid-free tissue and kept in a dry, stable environment to ensure survival for the future, but can be brought out for regular airing and checks, and to be enjoyed.*

reverse, and covered with a clear acetate film overlay. The mounts are available in various sizes and can be cut to fit individual specimens.

## BOOKS AND PHOTOGRAPHS

Because of their light-sensitive silver salts content, photographs are particularly susceptible to chemical degradation, including a polluted atmosphere, and are likely to tarnish. Photographs should be mounted in corner mounts in albums with acid-free paper, or, if for display, mounted in closed frames as for a watercolor. Do not let the glass come into contact with the photograph, as it will stick.

If, as in the case with the autograph albums, photographs and other sensitive memorabilia are mounted on poor quality paper, the album should not be reconstructed or broken up, as it would lose its value completely.

The shelf on which books are stored may be made of a highly acidic wood, such as pine, so make sure it is varnished or painted. For extra protection—which provides an insulating barrier as well—line the shelves with acid-free paper. Make sure the shelves are not in direct sunlight as this will fade the spines. If books are enclosed within a cabinet, there should be enough ventilation to prevent formation of

condensation and mildew. Dust books regularly with a soft, fine-bristled brush to avoid buildup of dirt.

Always discuss rebinding an old book with a conservator, as the process is likely to devalue, although spines and board covers can be eased off, repaired and replaced. Always keep any damaged original parts. Book shoes or slipcases can be made to fit individual volumes from acid-free board, with a special support for the text pages.

Solander boxes, protective, acid-free containers, which are designed to isolate objects in a conservation-friendly environment, and obtainable from paper conservators or bookbinders, are well worth investing in for safe storage of any work of art on paper.

# THE GILT-FRAMED MIRROR

MIRRORS DEVELOPED FROM PURELY FUNCTIONAL OBJECTS INTO DECORATIVE FEATURES THAT FOLLOWED THE STYLE OF THE DAY. FRAMES GAVE SOME SUPPORT TO THE FRAGILE PLATE GLASS, BUT ALSO INTRODUCED NEW MATERIALS WITH THEIR OWN WEAKNESSES.

Mirrors were originally designed to be entirely practical; in the 1600s, girandoles—combination candleholders and mirrors—increased illumination by reflecting the light of the candles. The freestanding cheval and dressing-table mirrors, which were increasingly used in the 1700s for private dressingrooms and bedrooms, are generally set in sturdy, plain wood frames. Gradually, however, mirrors with ever more elaborate frames became part of the design scheme in reception rooms and reached their peak in the finely carved scrolls, crestings, and drapery of Rococo style.

## REFLECTIONS OF THE PAST

The Venetians backed glass with tin and mercury foil to create a reflective surface in the 14th century. The size of the plate was restricted by the "broad process" of making glass until the 1600s. This process involved blowing a bubble of glass into a tube, cutting off the ends, slicing down one side, and opening the glass out to form a flat surface. The mirror plates often have a gray, smoky appearance and many imperfections. Authentic pre-1600 mirror plates are exceptionally rare, and should never be replaced.

The technique of casting glass into flat molds was developed by Bernard Perrot in France in 1687 and enabled larger plates to be made. In 1840 the chemical disposition of silver instead of tin and mercury, produced a more even finish, but was thinner and more easily worn.

Most mirror frames are made in carved wood, or a composition of wood ground with molded or carved gesso, or a combination of both, and warp and crack if subjected to an unstable environment. Composition frames can sometimes be identified by right-angle cracks, which is a generally accepted condition, but one that is aggravated by changes in humidity. If composition detail is added to a wood frame, the two different materials react to the environment at different rates, which may loosen the adhesion between them. In 19th-

*Decoration: Elaborate ornament is easily damaged by mishandling. Scratches and loss to carving, gesso, and gilt are common, but as long as they are not too extensive and unsightly, the piece will not be greatly devalued; recent damage to a gesso frame stands out because of the whiteness of the putty. A competent restorer will be able to carve or build up sections in composition plaster, gesso, bole, and gilt, but the process is highly skilled and can be very costly.*

*Bevel: A close look at the beveled edge of the mirror glass may help establish date. Early hand-ground examples tend to be slightly uneven.*

MID 1700s GENOESE MIRROR: *The middle glass plate is probably the largest the manufacturer could manage. These original plates should on no account be replaced.*

**Silvering:** *Speckled or shabby plate is accepted as a sign of age and unless the silvering has disappeared completely, will not detract from overall value and should be left alone. Dampness causes the silvering to flake, and nothing can be done to stabilize this process. Resilvering is rarely recommended since obtaining the correct period hue to the mirror is highly specialized and few companies are capable of doing it.*

**Frame:** *Sometimes the most valuable part of the mirror as a whole. A large crack across a major section of the frame seriously threatens the security of the mirror plate—especially if it is big—and should be repaired. Small cracks are not significant in terms of devaluing a mirror or its frame.*

**Joints:** *The strength of the frame in relation to the glass it is holding is vitally important. On a square frame, check that the mitred joints connecting each of the four sections are sound. Structural repair to such a frame can usually be carried out by a competent wood craftsman.*

**Back:** *Generally paneled, often in soft wood, which is very susceptible to woodworm and/or dampness. It may need to be replaced, and if this is done correctly, it should not detract from value. Structural changes to the back are generally obvious and may indicate that the frame has been reconstructed, cut down to fit, or converted from a picture frame.*

**Mirror plate:** *On early mirrors the plates have more often than not been replaced (see silvering). Hold your thumbnail up to the glass and look at the distance between it and its reflection. Although not a hard and fast rule, earlier mirrors tend to be thinner and the distance will be narrower than with a modern mirror.*

193

*The earliest surviving mirrors from the 1600s onward tend to be set in sturdy frames, like the mirror with candle arm c. 1710-30 (left). This is American, with glass probably imported from Europe; the long narrow shape complemented the paneling of colonial homes.*

*The framed mirror as decorative feature reached its peak in the early 18th century, as in the George III example (right), which is one of a pair, but the more complex the frame, the less secure the mirror. The frame is gilded pine, and like all wood frames is susceptible to woodworm.*

hanging position. Dust the glass with a clean, dry, soft cloth, but take care it does not catch on relief decoration. Do not use commercial glass cleaner, which would be damaging if it seeped between mirror and frame, and may contain solvents that could dissolve gilding, resin, or shellac varnishes. For persistent marks on the glass, use a cotton swab dampened with warm water with a weak solution of mild detergent, or for greasy marks, a very weak solution of mineral spirits.

Water gilding is water soluble, rubs off very easily, and should only be dusted very lightly with a soft-bristled brush; wear cotton gloves if you need to touch the frame. An oil-gilded frame is more resistant and can be very gently wiped with a just-damp cotton swab.

century France, plaster was molded and carved to imitate wood, and the resulting frames are extremely fragile, as the detail chips off easily.

## GENERAL CARE

Mounts, supports, hanging wires and screws, and the wall itself must be strong strong enough to carry the weight of a mirror; it may be necessary to support the base with brackets screwed into the wall.

If necessary, seek assistance when hanging or moving a mirror. Composition frames in particular may crack and splinter with vibration and should be carefully wrapped in acid-free tissue and layers of bubblewrap before transportation. Move all mirrors in an upright position if possible. Wedge folded paper between mirror plate and frame, to stop any movement there. Clean a large mirror in its

## THE RESTORER'S BRIEF

Cracks in mirror plates are virtually impossible to repair invisibly, but they can be consolidated by running resins into the crack. This strengthens the mirror, but makes it even more important to maintain it in an upright position, as any flexing may break the joint. Frames with one, two, or more layers of gilt usually suggest damage to the frame itself and subsequent cover-up jobs. Such overgilding obscures the detail of a finely carved frame, and restorers can spend a great amount of time removing the unnecessary layers to return to the original gilding, which may have a completely different hue from later surface finishes. If a frame is completely stripped and regilded, it will devalue dramatically, so ask a restorer to only rework or retouch damaged areas.

It is possible to fill in missing plaster or wooden details and then retouch with bronze or gold powders, paints, and varnishes, but this is a short cut and may not be appropriate for valuable pieces. The restorer should match the original techniques, materials, and tones as closely as possible. Temporary repairs can be carried out using gold burnishing creams or waxes available in art or craft stores.

## GILDING TECHNIQUES

*Oil and water gilding are the two main processes used for applying gold leaf to a surface. It can be difficult to distinguish between them, but important to do so because of the different vulnerabilities. Water gilding is only suitable for interior work because it is water-soluble. Oil gilding is slightly more matte and is water-resistant. To identify the gilding—which, of course, has a bearing on care—dampen a cotton swab and rub it gently on an inconspicuous spot. If the gold comes off onto the cotton, it is water-based.*

*Keep gilded objects in a constant environment since temperature changes may cause expansion and contraction to the substrate (usually wood), resulting in loss of surface layers through cracking and flaking.*

*Oil gilding*
*The surface is cleaned, cracks filled, and the surface sanded to an ivory-smooth finish. A metal surface, or one that is to be placed outside the surface, is coated with an anticorrosion agent. Two coats of oil primer are applied and left to dry. A slow-drying varnish incorporating linseed oil is applied, and when it is dry but still slightly tacky, the gold leaf is applied in sheets, then smoothed with a fine silk cloth.*

*Water gilding*
*The prepared surface is sealed with diluted animal glue, and up to ten coats of handmade gesso (plaster and slow-drying varnish) are applied, each layer dried thoroughly and sanded to a completely smooth finish. Each layer has to be correctly constructed, and if necessary, carved. The final layer is polished. Up to eight layers of bole are applied, each one left*

*to dry before the next, and applied with opposite brushstrokes. The final layer is polished with steel wool.*

*The surface is flooded with gilding water (the substance that adheres the gilt to the surface), and the gold leaf is applied, left to dry, and then burnished with a "dog's tooth" or agate, then toned, distressed, or antiqued in keeping with the original.*

*Black clay bole, here being smoothed with an agate, forms a receptive surface for the gold leaf, and gives depth and color to the finished gold. Different colored boles are used depending on the period and style of the original gilding.*

*22 carat gold leaf— available in several different tones—is picked up on a gilder's tip and lightly brushed onto the receiving surface.*

STONE AND METAL, THE RAW MATERIALS OF SCULPTURE AND STATUARY, ARE APPARENTLY HARD AND RESISTANT TO DISINTEGRATION AND BREAKAGE. AND INDEED THEY ARE, COMPARED WITH MANY OF THE OTHER MATERIALS IN THIS BOOK. BUT THEY ARE NOT IMMUNE, AND MUCH OF THE ONGOING HEALTH AND GOOD APPEARANCE OF STATUARY WILL HINGE ON WHETHER IT IS SITUATED IN THE HOME OR OUTSIDE, EXPOSED TO EXTREMES OF COLD AND WET AND ATMOSPHERIC POLLUTION, AND ON REGULAR MONITORING. THE INDIVIDUAL PROPERTIES OF DIFFERENT METALS AND STONES ALSO VARY CONSIDERABLY—SO IT IS IMPORTANT TO KNOW WHAT THEY ARE TO BE AWARE OF THEIR VULNERABILITIES. SOMETIMES ORIGINAL CONSTRUCTION METHODS SUCH AS INTERNAL PINNING AND FRAMEWORK ATTEMPTED TO COMPENSATE INTRINSIC WEAKNESSES, BUT ENDED UP CAUSING A HOST OF PROBLEMS OF THEIR OWN.

# SCULPTURE & *statuary*

# OUTSIDE STONE

THE WORD STONE SUGGESTS STRENGTH AND ENDURANCE, YET AS WITH THE NATURAL ROCKS FROM WHICH GARDEN SCULPTURE AND STATUARY IS USUALLY CRAFTED, EVEN THE MOST RESILIENT SUBSTANCES ARE SUBJECT TO EROSION AND DECAY BY WEATHER, THE ENVIRONMENT, AND TIME.

Stone is a nonmetallic, solid mineral ranging from hard, impermeable granite to very soft, easily scratched soapstone. Its texture may be rough and granulated or smooth and dense, but no matter what its makeup, all stone is affected by environmental conditions. It will be eroded by wind and rain, can split and shatter with extremes of heat and cold, and decay with high levels of pollution, or salt in maritime areas. Stone sculpture also suffers from being mishandled, for although it has a good compressive strength, tensile strength is poor, leading to breakage if too much pressure is put on weak points such as legs. The composition of some stone sculpture incorporates incompatible materials such as iron dowels, and these may eat into and stain the surrounding stone.

## ROCKS FOR SCULPTURE

The most common stones used for outside sculpture are marble, limestone, sandstone, and granite. Granite is very durable but lacks versatility; marble is highly versatile as far as sculpting is concerned, but far more vulnerable.

Granite is a very hard, impermeable crystalline rock used since antiquity. It is subject to the problems of all rock and stone, but much more resistant. Granite ranges in color from white-gray to green and almost black, and is usually speckled; its close grained structure means that it can take a high polish—which will dull in a highly polluted environment. Sculpting into shape, however, can be difficult because it is so hard—the Egyptians modeled granite by bashing it with other stones—so the forms granite sculpture tends to take are relatively simple. It has often been used for the bases and mounts of statuary in other materials, especially bronze—which cause corrosion stains.

### Soluble rock

Limestone was often used for garden statuary in the 1800s as a substitute for marble since it is similarly light in color, but readily available, cheaper, softer, and therefore more easily worked. It is, in fact, the uncrystallized form of marble and is highly porous. Most of all, it is susceptible to water erosion, as

**Surface detail:** *Loss of detail to the surface and carving due to weathering is inevitable on outside stonework. The effect on value depends on degree; if facial features are virtually flattened, the loss will be great and there is little a restorer can do. A pitted surface characteristic of weathered marble, which is not disfiguring, does not dramatically devalue or usually warrant restoration.*

**Extremities:** *Slender and protruding parts of statuary are the most likely areas to have been broken off in the past and restored. Check for signs of fillers at breaks or reduced quality in the carving. If the restoration work is well done, value will be maintained; a poor job will detract.*

**Stains:** *A stone conservator will be able to carry out tests on lichen and algae staining before trying to remove it, as the seriousness of the attack depends on the species. Rust staining from iron dowels within the structure may penetrate to the surface, a very serious condition as the dowels expand when they corrode, causing the stone to spall, or break down. Immediate action is necessary. Rust from external brackets and anchoring clamps may streak the surface as rainwater washes the corrosion down.*

LIMESTONE URN AND COVER ON PEDESTAL, 19TH CENTURY, *showing signs of weather erosion at the top.*

**Dowels:** *Check areas (such as arms in statuary), that are joined by dowels, every 6 or 12 months to make sure they are sound; they should be replaced at the first signs of corrosion.*

**Bases and pedestals:** *Make sure that the base is strong enough to take the weight of the sculpture and that the sculpture is securely attached to it. The point where the base meets the ground is vulnerable to water and salt penetration through capillary action and should be waterproofed.*

199

*If an urn like this is used to contain plants, it should be given a lead or glass fiber liner prevent the salts in the earth from reacting with the stone, and emptied in the winter months if temperatures are likely to fall below freezing.*

its constituent, calcium carbonate, dissolves. Airborne moisture laden with chemicals from traffic fumes, the burning of fossil fuels, and other pollutants, forms an acid solution and "acid rain" that dissolves carbonaceous or siliceous rocks such as limestone, sandstone, and marble.

Sandstone, another porous sedimentary rock, is made up of grains of quartz bound together by silica. With its light golden tones, it was very popular in the 18th and 19th centuries for all forms of garden sculpture including sundials and seats. Both rocks develop a surface crust as sulfates leach out to the surface. This "case hardening" feels firm, but conceals a decayed, crumbling interior, identified by a hollow sound if you tap the surface. This is nearly impossible to put right, and hydraulic lime fills (that react with water to produce consituted limestone) or lime putty (a binding medium that reacts with the carbon dioxide in the atmosphere to produce reconstituted limestone), must be pieced in. Though both fills have the same chemical structure as limestone, they are not as strong since they are made quickly without gradual pressure over time. Powdery sandstone can be stabilized, using solutions of chemicals or resins that provide cross links for the molecular structure.

Coade stone, an artificial stone developed in the late 1760s

*The Italian marble urn (right) is more likely to keep free of algae and staining in a mediterranean climate than in a wet, cold, northern one.*

200

in England by Mrs. Eleanor Coade (who kept the ingredients a closely guarded secret) is very durable and can be modeled and cast. Since it is basically a ceramic, it has a protective surface almost like a glaze, which is known as a "fireskin." If this is broken and penetrated by water, Coade stone begins to deteriorate; it is also more easily chipped than natural stone. Coade stone can sometimes be identified by signs of casting on the underside of its base, and a hollow sound if it is tapped.

## GENERAL CARE

The most effective way of halting the decay of outdoor stonework is to remove it from the erosive elements of weather and pollution and bring it indoors. It should be kept it as dry as possible—which includes making sure that water sprinklers are out of range, and away from overhanging foliage that may drip and stain, or a damp, north-facing spot in which lichen and algae may flourish.

The work should be placed on a plinth with an impermeable waterproofing of bitumen or plastic, surrounded by a drainage channel Regularly brush away leaves and other debris from stonework with a soft-bristled brush, as they collect water and create acid solutions that eat into the stone. Keep clear of weeds, and of ivy that clings to the surface by suckers that leave secretions causing irreversible "biological soiling" and etching.

Take valuable, vulnerable statues inside in frost-prone areas during the winter, or cover with a well-ventilated tarpaulin, burlap, or canvas—but never use plastic, which causes condensation. Granite, volcanic rock, and Coade stone should be tough enough to withstand frost.

Moving a heavy item of sculpture may require the help of a fine art moving company with trolleys and specialized lifting apparatus (padded slings rather than chains and ropes), to avoid serious damage not only to the sculpture but to those moving it.

## THE RESTORER'S BRIEF

Weather is a key factor in the conservation of outdoor stonework, and restoration is usually not carried out during cold winter months. Stains that are likely to cause ongoing deterioration or which are disfiguring should be removed from a valuable statue. Experts carry out tests to identify the stain and the most compatible chemicals with which to remove it. This may simply be a solution of mineral spirits and non-ionic detergent (household detergents are not suitable). Poultices also may be used to draw out the stain. Rusting dowels, clamps, and armatures need to be replaced immediately with conservation-grade stainless steel. Depending on the impact on the whole statue, missing sections can be recarved and attached to the original by a specialist stone carver, using hydraulic lime or lime putty. It is also worth asking a stone conservator for advice and help with mounting and siting.

*Lichen or algae not only stain stonework but also eat into the surface; at this stage they are almost impossible to remove and can drastically devalue.*

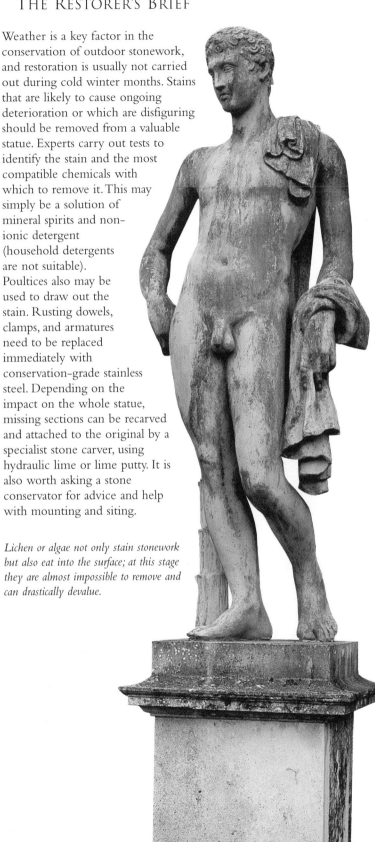

# A MARBLE FIGURE

THE APPARENTLY HARD, SMOOTH, SLIGHTLY TRANSLUCENT, AND OFTEN HIGHLY POLISHED SURFACE OF MARBLE SUGGESTS RESISTANCE AND IMPERMEABILITY, BUT IN FACT IT IS BRITTLE AND EASILY ABSORBS STAINS. HOWEVER, WITH SENSITIVE CARE, IT CAN SURVIVE VERY WELL.

Marble is the crystallized form of limestone. The mineral calcite is recrystallized through heat and pressure, forming an interlocking, granular mosaic of roughly uniform crystals. As a result, it is hard and brittle, and can be worked into a smooth, hard surface able to take a high polish, and its fine-grained structure makes it easy to carve. Add to this its slightly translucent quality, and marble becomes a practical and decorative choice for statuary large and small, architectural features such as fire surrounds, and furniture sections such as tops for washstands and commodes. Because of its range of color and veining, it is often inlaid in conjunction with other marbles or stones as in *pietra dura* (see p. 207).

*Limbs: Judge whether supporting limbs are strong enough to support the design: a carved tree trunk or other form of support is often not a decorative whim, but a crucial extra means of support for slender marble legs. Small areas of damage can usually be repaired and should not affect the value to a great extent as long as the overall structure and appearance of the piece is not affected.*

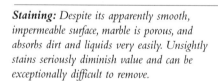

*Staining: Despite its apparently smooth, impermeable surface, marble is porous, and absorbs dirt and liquids very easily. Unsightly stains seriously diminish value and can be exceptionally difficult to remove.*

FLORENCE NIGHTINGALE, 19TH CENTURY *(courtesy Corporation of London), about 3 feet (1 m) high, had her broken fingers replaced and blue paint (applied by vandals) removed from her eyes.*

**Texture:** *The surface texture denotes the overall condition of a piece of marble and gives an indication of the quality of the carving. A pitted, matte surface suggests exposure to weathering. Any friable areas indicate instability and need to be consolidated immediately to avoid further deterioration and dramatic loss of value. Particular places to check are the undersides of overhanging sections. Compare surfaces at these points; they may be black with sulfates which have lodged there.*

**Joins:** *To establish how a piece has been constructed—whether in one or more parts—look very closely for join lines. Separate pieces such as armsmay have been joined onto the main body by dowels or clamps, which are usually apparent only when deterioration has already set in—through corrosive stains. It can be expensive to replace old and deteriorated dowels, but it may be vital for the long-term survival of a piece.*

**Features:** *First areas to show signs of weathering from atmospheric conditions or overcleaning, so check for distinct loss of detail which will affect the value. Fingers and toes are the most likely areas to have been broken off and restored. If resin replacements have been added, these areas may be slightly warmer than the surrounding marble.*

**Base:** *Sometimes the base, or socle (usually a stepped, circular base), is not strong enough to take the weight of the sculpture, in which case a new one that is absolutely secure should be made and the sculpture attached by dry doweling from the base into a hole in the base of the sculpture, or doweled and mortared into place with lime plaster. Plaster of paris is sometimes used but should be replaced as it can transfer corrosive salts to the piece.*

19TH-CENTURY FRENCH MARBLE CHERUB, *18 in (46 cm) had head and arms replaced and rusty iron dowels replaced with stainless steel.*

## A LONG TRADITION

Although surviving only as shards and museum objects, marble has been used for decorative sculpture since the earliest civilizations in Mesopotamia and Egypt. Although there are considerable gaps in production through later centuries, Western style and form stem from the decorative monumental sculpture of Classical Greece, which reached its high point in the Parthenon in Athens c. 430 B.C., and in later Roman copies (the Roman versions had the greatest impact as the Greek originals were not discovered until much later). Eastern style and form is based on a different visual language, but is equally long-established. The fundamental methods of construction, the tools and materials used, and the problems that arise with regard to marble artifacts have remained constant and still apply today. Even after the development of mechanical tools during the Industrial Revolution in the 1800s, and later electric and pneumatic tools, solid sections of marble are chiseled and carved by hand, using chisels and hammers.

It was sometimes easier and cheaper to make the body of a figure—with a raised arm, for example—separately and then attach the arm with a dowel of iron, bronze, or steel. Bronze does not rust, but often lacks the strength required. However, as with any other metal doweling, as it is not causing problems, there is no value in having it replaced. Wrought iron was most common before the second half of the 1800s. Sometimes iron and early steel were encased in lead to help prevent rusting, but the two metals sometimes worked themselves loose from each other. Rusting metals not only cause severe staining but also expand, and cause the surrounding marble to split, which can be difficult and expensive to put right.

From 1913, non corrosive stainless steel was available, but was not common until after the Second World War; now conservation grade stainless steel is used for restoration. However, the problem with this or any other metal doweling is that it is stronger than the surrounding marble and breaks are likely if a piece is knocked where the dowel ends. Marble dowels are compatible, but it is impossible to tell whether they have been used unless a piece is already broken, as they cannot even be picked up on x-ray. Perspex (clear acrylic) can be used for restoring delicate areas, since, if it is subsequently knocked, it should break in the place of the original break. However, because it is not very strong, it is not suitable for loadbearing repairs.

*Even in the protected environment of the London Guildhall, this bust (courtesy Corporation of London) needed a major cleaning after 150 years of being situated above regular dusting level.*

## GENERAL CARE

Marble sculptures should be placed in a clean, stable environment, because temperature changes can cause the stone to crack, and dust and pollution are easily absorbed into the surface. The piece should be firm on its base, and placed on a stable item of furniture.

Always make sure your hands are clean and dry when handling marble, as it stains very easily, even from the use of an inappropriate packing material such as newsprint. In a damp environment, such as around an indoor pool, lichen and algae could form and cause irreversible staining.

If the surface is unstable, do not clean it at all. Dust sound items regularly with a clean, soft artists' or cosmetic brush. Use a cotton swab moistened with saliva to reach into crevices, working with a rotating movement to avoid ingraining the dirt further. Most household detergents and bleaches are chemically inappropriate for cleaning marble; they react with hard water to produce an insoluble scum which grips to the surface. Even water alone, if not wiped off, will stain. To put an attractive and protective finish onto a clean marble surface, apply a light coating of microcrystalline wax with a soft-bristled brush and buff as you go, treating a small area at a time. Pure talc can be lightly dusted onto marble and similar materials such as alabaster or soapstone; this fills the pores and resists build-up of dust.

Wear gloves, preferably with rubber grips, especially if you are handling a highly polished marble statue. Be aware of rings, necklaces, and belt buckles when moving a piece, as they can easily knock against and scratch the surfaces. Remember that marble is dense and heavy: when moving a piece, avoid putting strain on limbs and joints; check how the piece is attached to the base, support from beneath when lifting, and put a figure down gently to avoid damage to it and the surface it is placed upon.

If possible, always transport a statue in its upright position, using plenty of clean padding (not newsprint!), such as tissue and bubble wrap.

## THE RESTORER'S BRIEF

For any cleaning or repair of antique marble, go to a specialist stone conservator who understands its chemical structure. Cleaning, for example, by an unskilled person, could drive a stain deeper into the stone.

If the dowelled sections of a statue have come apart, or are corroded, have them replaced with conservation grade stainless steel for loadbearing areas, or Perspex or marble dowels for delicate areas.

If the piece has an attractive patina, ask the restorer to preserve it, as it could be lost, and value reduced with overcleaning. A restorer will use a combination of poultices which draw the dirt out, and controlled steam cleaning to remove stains and rust, though success is not always guaranteed.

A certain amount of wear and tear on antique marble is inevitable and unless it is is disfiguring, will not greatly affect value. However, missing features, or fingers, though small, are generally worth having repaired. Ask whether it is appropriate for them to be built up with a sympathetic material such as marble itself, or lime plaster. Modern epoxy and polyester resins in various mixes can achieve strong and convincing results, but they do tend to yellow with age, which is particularly unattractive on white marble. They are, however, often quicker, and consequently cheaper, to use. The use of either material will depend on the quality of the object and the purpose of the restoration. If the mount is unstable, it should be made stable as soon as possible.

*The restorer steam cleans a marble statue (right). The nozzle enables treatment of localized surfaces and crevices, and the pressure of the fine jet of steam can be controlled.*

## Marble lookalikes

Alabaster is often confused with marble but is composed largely of gypsum and is soft enough to scratch with a fingernail. Alabaster varies in color from white and yellow to orangey red, and is often streaked. It is easily worked, and less expensive than marble, but because it is so soft, it breaks very easily and needs to be treated with particular delicacy. Alabaster is soluble and should never be placed in damp conditions, or water used to clean it. For more persistent grime use a cotton swab in a solution of mineral spirits, and seek advice for any repairs or further cleaning. Alabaster urns and other objects that have been converted to lamps should only carry a low wattage bulb as prolonged heat can break down the stone.

Scagliola is a marble substitute made from gypsum/plaster, powdered marble chips and fish glue, which has been used since the 18th century for furniture tops and architecture columns and pediments. It takes a high polish and is visually very difficult to differentiate from marble, but is much softer. It chips and scratches easily to reveal a powdery body which can be expensive to repair. Handle and clean as marble and never use paint remover on painted scagliola, as it the surface beneath is likely to

disintegrate.

Steatite or soapstone is a cohesive amalgam of talc which looks very similar to alabaster but is much softer and more easily broken—so should be placed down with extreme care. It is smooth and silky to the touch, and is seen in 18th-century Chinese carved ornaments and Inuit art.

## Bluejohn

A translucent crystalline mineral found exclusively in Derbyshire, England, that has a range of streaked colors ranging from blue and violet to brown and yellow. It is comparatively soft, easily scratched, and when it breaks, it tends to be crumbly, which can be difficult and expensive to repair. Bluejohn was used predominantly in the late 18th and early 19th centuries, particularly in France, to make decorative objects such as urns, and items of jewelry. Larger objects are often made of more than one piece adhered together. Perfect examples should need no more than a light dusting with a soft brush. Handle as for marble, but remember that it not as strong.

*The silver mounts on the casket designed by the Russian jeweler Carl Fabergé may work loose, and can easily be tightened by a restorer before they scratch the highly polished nephrite.*

*The Fabergé hardstone frog (right) on its jade pedestal, only 4¹/₂ inches (11.5 cm) high, would shatter like glass if dropped onto a hard, unresisting surface. Any cracks or chips would be very difficult to repair invisibly.*

## Pietra dura

A mosaic-like technique in which small pieces, or "tesserae," of colored stone, glass, and sometimes semiprecious gemstones, are laid with extreme precision onto a mortar bed to build up a decorative effect. The technique, which literally translates as "hard stone," has been used for tabletops, vases and ewers in combination with ormolu mounts. If tesserae come loose, it is vital to keep them, as some of the harder stones may have taken days to cut to shape. They can be painstakingly put back, but it is expensive to recreate the precision. Replacement pieces can be produced in resins, but this will reduce value.

*The pieces, or "tesserae" that make up a pietra dura table top like the ormolu-mounted Louis-Philippe example (below) are meticulously cut, shaped, and fitted with exquisite precision into an intricate pattern, and the whole surface is highly polished.*

## Jade

Jade refers to both jadeite and nephrite, hard, translucent minerals which can take a high polish. Their color ranges from dark green (which is particularly highly sought), through brown to white (commonly known as "mutton fat jade"). Jade has been extensively used by the Chinese for carving pieces of relatively small decorative sculpture. In the Middle East it has been used for dagger handles, and elsewhere has been widely incorporated in jewelry. It is comparable to glass in its fragility and susceptibility to chipping and shattering if dropped, and should be handled and cleaned in a similar way (see p.85).

## Onyx

Onyx is a variety of agate with alternate color layers, ranging from the most common green, to white or yellow and brown. In the 19th century, it was used for decorative objects such as urns, but later was carved into pedestals, ashtrays, inkstands, and Art Deco figures. It is susceptible to cracks and chips, which can be restored in the same way as for marble.

# A LEAD CHERUB

Lᴇᴀᴅ'ꜱ ꜱᴏꜰᴛ, ᴍᴀʟʟᴇᴀʙʟᴇ ɴᴀᴛᴜʀᴇ ᴀɴᴅ ʟᴏᴡ ᴍᴇʟᴛɪɴɢ POINT MAKE IT EASY TO WORK AND CAST INTO SHAPE, BUT IT REMAINS SOFT AND UNABLE TO SUPPORT ITS OWN WEIGHT, WHICH LEADS TO SERIOUS PROBLEMS.

***Limbs and extremities:*** *Load-bearing and narrow parts of a sculpture are susceptible to damage, and may have been restored in the past. Unsightly joins or oversoldering can be redone, and may boost the value of a piece if well done.*

In the late 17th and 18th centuries, lead was much used for garden sculpture because it was a cheap and fashionable. Many statues were finished with a polychrome paint surface to imitate bronze and stone, but this has since been worn away. Lead is comparatively inert, in that it does not react with many other materials and can withstand most environments—which makes it suitable for outside use. It has also been used in conjunction with other materials such as tin to make low-grade pewter, or bronze to make it more fluid in the casting process.

Although lead is more resistant to atmospheric pollution than bronze, it cannot take such intricate detail. Its softness and weight mean that it gradually "creeps"—flows downward—with the forces of gravity and time. Lead sculptures, therefore, need to be propped up internally with armatures, traditionally of iron, which corrode and cause severe damage.

***Filler:*** *Historically, the approach to restoring lead figures has been to fill them with plaster or cement. But this has proved a temporary remedy with dire consquences, as both substances absorb moisture and expand, especially in freezing temperatures. The outer lead skin then splits. The filler also adds weight which exerts more pressure on weaker areas such as legs, and the lime in cement has a corrosive effect on the lead.*

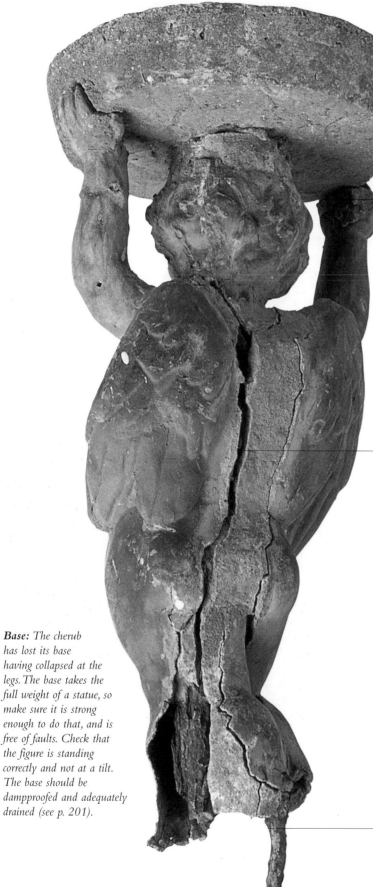

**Surface:** *Powdery crystals on the surface are signs of corrosion. White lead carbonate forms as a large crystalline structure which absorbs moisture and pollutants, setting up a corrosion cycle; it expands and can push the lead out of shape. Red spots are lead oxide, a crystalline structure that emerges onto the surface, causing it to split if not caught in time. Bluish-black corrosion is lead sulfide and has a compact crystalline structure which can act as protective coating. Depending on the structural condition and appearance of the piece, treatment to remove corrosion stains will not detract from the value.*

**Shape:** *Look at the overall shape to identify distortions which have been caused by internal corrosion. Check the narrow areas—neck, ankles, knees—for early signs of collapse: Cure is possible but costly, as armatures need to be replaced and the lead reshaped, but the alternative is a collapsed statue.*

**Base:** *The cherub has lost its base having collapsed at the legs. The base takes the full weight of a statue, so make sure it is strong enough to do that, and is free of faults. Check that the figure is standing correctly and not at a tilt. The base should be dampproofed and adequately drained (see p. 201).*

**Armature:** *Cracks and splits in the surface are signs that the old iron armature has rusted and expanded and is now exerting such pressure on the surface that it is forcing it apart. Lead collapses under its own weight and if the armatures have given way, the whole sculpture will ultimately collapse in on itself.*

209

*It is a good idea to keep lead toys, such as the hollow-cast Royal Artillery set (left) in an enclosed cabinet, but make sure it is not of oak, as this induces lead rot, which cannot be cured. When buying lead soldiers, check the bases, for this is where the first rough, grayish signs of lead rot are likely to appear.*

Keep all outside statuary free of leaves and debris and away from trees; dripping leaves cause staining, and branches scratch. Mount securely on a plinth that is waterproofed and correctly drained, and protect in winter (see p. 201), but make sure air can circulate.

## GENERAL CARE

Avoid placing lead objects in, on, or near acid materials such as oak, cardboard, chipboard, or vinegar, as the vapors from them will act as a catalyst for the lead to react with carbon dioxide and degrade. Because lead is highly toxic, wash your hands thoroughly after handling.

Monitor regularly for signs of corrosion and armature collapse, such as stains on the surface. Clean sound surfaces with a soft-bristled brush, and wipe, if necessary, with cotton wool dampened in a mild detergent solution. Occasional application of one or two coats of microcrystalline wax gently rubbed in with a soft cloth and buffed and dried between coats will offer further protection.

### Outside statuary

If water collects in crevices or trickles constantly down the surface of an outside statue, remove it. Constant water rivulets will remove patina, revealing a fresh layer of metal underneath, and so constantly erode the surface. Outside bronzes are fairly resistant but susceptible to corrosion in highly polluted and coastal areas, and even lead corrodes in high levels of pollution. Line bronze or lead urns or troughs with fiberglass and keep any drainage holes unblocked. If a lead trough is being used for plants place it on wood battens which are not too far apart—or the lead will sag between them.

*Lead was much used for drainage as in the 1780 water butt (above) because it is more resistant than other metals to environmental conditions.*

## THE RESTORER'S BRIEF

A metal conservator should be asked to treat most forms of corrosion and distortion on lead statues immediately. For large areas of damage, welding is necessary and should only be carried out by a trained fine art welder. If armatures have corroded, the statue will have to be taken apart and flushed out with a high pressure jet to remove all traces of corrosion before being replaced with conservation grade stainless steel dowels. These must be electrically insulated where they are attached to the metal, which is usually done with nylon sleeves. Although this highly skilled procedure may well be financially worthwhile on a precious bronze, lead is less valuable, and it is worth asking for a quote and estimate of the value of the piece before having work done.

Ask a conservator for advice on the best mounting materials, and on lifting equipment and companies for transportation.

*The restorer applies solder to the lead skin of the cherub (below) after old materials have been flushed out from the interior.*

## OTHER METALS

### Brass

Brass is an alloy of copper and zinc with a gold appearance, which tarnishes heavily to brown or green-black. It is outwardly strong but bends or snaps under pressure, and compared to ferrous metals, is fairly soft and easily scratched. It is often highly polished, but this is not always desirable on an antique piece, especially, for example, a carriage clock, where a tasteful dullness is preferable, and can be engraved, embossed, or enameled. It should be treated in much the same way as bronze (see p. 212). Regular dusting with a dry cloth should maintain the right level of polish rather than the high gloss produced by commercial brass polishes. Never use an abrasive which will leave scouring marks, or put into contact with salts, lemon juice or vinegar which will stain the surface.

### Ormolu

Gilded bronze or brass ormolu was originally used for furniture mounts, and since the 1700s, for a variety of decorative objects, and has become the generic term for any gilt-colored metal. On true bronze or brass ormolu, the base metal—visible on worn areas— should be golden rather than gray, which would indicate spelter. Often metals are merely dipped and lacquered to give the appearance of ormolu, an effect which is often very difficult to identify. The base metal is often chased and then gilded. The thin layer of gold is particularly prone to wear, so handling should be reduced to a minimum. Wear on ormolu is generally acceptable and as long as it is not

*To preserve their delicate gilt surface, ormolu mounts (left) should be kept away from heat, moisture, and plants.*

completely disfiguring should not detract too much from the value; regilding, however, is almost certain to detract as it is unlikely that the original gilt color can be reproduced exactly.

### Spelter

A cheap bronze substitute for zinc with various additives such as lead, which was used for a whole variety of objects in the second half of the 1800s, even larger outdoor pieces. Spelter is cast in the same way as bronze and was often finished with a coat of electrochemically applied copper and then gilded, patinated, or colored. Spelter is much lighter in weight than bronze, more fragile, and the detail is usually poor by comparison. It should not be placed in direct sunlight or near a heat source—especially if it is painted—or in damp or variable conditions. The cost of restoring spelter is usually high in relation to the low value of the object.

*Spelter statues like this 19th-c example are more thinly cast, softer, and more brittle than the bronze they imitate. Pimples of corrosion appear on the surface, and once this has set in, it is virtually impossible to rectify.*

# A BRONZE FIGURE

**B**RONZE IS A RELATIVELY EASY MEDIUM TO CAST AND WORK WITH, BUT IT DOES CORRODE, AND DESPITE ITS APPARENT STRENGTH, CAN BE EASILY DAMAGED THROUGH MISHANDLING.

*An 18th-century Italian bronze shows how bronze patinates naturally to a highly desirable dark brown.*

Bronze has a fairly low melting point, and when it is molten it flows into complex shapes more easily than other metals, which makes it particularly suitable for casting. It is also relatively strong, can support its own weight, and does not deteriorate as quickly as ferrous metals. Bronze is a manufactured alloy of copper and tin in its purest state, though other ingredients such as zinc and lead are sometimes added, resulting in slightly varying properties. When it is cast, bronze cools to form a crystalline structure that is quite strong but can bend or snap under pressure, especially at weaker narrow sections, and atmospheric pollution can also cause green or even blue corrosion. Bronzes are suitable for outside as well as inside objects and as long as regular monitoring is undertaken will survive very well.

Bronze was produced before 3000 B.C., and during the Shang Dynasty (1600-1027 B.C.), in China. The casting process has undergone only slight variations, although it was mechanized in the 1800s. Other metals, such as lead, may be added to the basic copper/tin alloy, to improve the flow of the molten metal, or extra tin may be added for a paler color. The lost wax method of casting is the most common. A model is made in wax, usually in sections, and coated with plaster. The whole is then heated and the wax model evaporates, leaving room for molten bronze to be poured into the mold. The mold is smashed to reveal the rough-cast bronze model, which can then be tooled or fettled, and finished. Mold lines are removed, holes filled, and the bronze is colored and patinated. You can identify a hollow or solid piece by the sound made by tapping it, although sometimes filler, such as plaster, is left inside, which will mute the hollow ring. Solid or filled figures are heavier than hollow-cast ones, but are less likely to dent or bend.

Since the 1800s, the sections of a bronze statue tended to be soldered or welded together; until then, pinned joints—with the head of the pin flush with the surface—were more usual. Silver or "hard" solder makes a stronger joint than lead, or "soft" solder as it is fired at a higher temperature—and the higher the temperature, the stronger the bond. Welding, in which both sides of the break are melted and then fused together (with any necessary filling done in the same material) is strongest of all and is mainly used on large, outside pieces.

## GENERAL CARE

Bronze statues need regular dusting and display in a dry environment to maintain their health. When handling, wear gloves to prevent salts from causing surface smudges. If a piece is heavily covered with dust, first blow it with a hair dryer set on low, then use a whiskbroom (straw brush), and finally a soft hogshair brush. Never use metal polishes, water, or any solvents, as surface color may be lost. For crevices, use a cotton swab moistened with saliva, and rotate the end along the groove so as not to ingrain the dirt.

Once a year, when the piece is completely dustfree, apply two coats of microcrystalline wax, a very fine, colorless wax, rubbed in gently and evenly, and left to dry between coats.

**Extremities and limbs:** *If missing or broken limbs are replaced by epoxy resin substitutes, this will seriously detract from the value. The replacement limbs feel warmer to the touch than the surrounding metal. Thin ankles and elbows are the weakest points, and if they break can be resoldered; the effect of the repair on value depends on how sensitively this is done.*

## THE RESTORER'S BRIEF

Ask a metal conservator if patination is tipping over into detrimental corrosion. Breakages can be soldered or welded, but make sure he or she can match color in keeping with the original.

Small areas of damage such as missing fingers can be built up with synthetic resins mixed with bronze powder and colored to match, or new sections can be cast and applied.

19TH CENTURY BRONZE FIGURE OF MERCURY: *a delicately balanced statue like this should always be moved in a vertical position; laying it down could put enormous strain on the limbs.*

**Patina:** *Natural, dark brown patination should be cherished; its removal would seriously devalue. Sometimes artificial patination is created on all or part of a bronze; its effect on value is difficult to determine. If done with an unscrupulous intent to deceive, it can devalue, but is virtually impossible to identify. If it is done sympathetically to blend in soldered areas, it will probably raise the value above the damaged state. Often areas that protrude more than others will have greater signs of wear, but unless they are disfiguring, this will not greatly affect the value.*

**Joints and rivets:** *These are likely on older pieces that have been cast in sections and joined. It is almost impossible to cast an object such as the featured statue in one piece, since the molten bronze would cool before reaching the extremities of the mold, so the piece is made in sections. Joints and rivets often become visible, and rivets work loose with time, handling, and wear, but this problem is easily rectified by a restorer and does not greatly affect value. Well-disguised solder lines from previous breaks can sometimes be spotted on the underside of the object.*

**Base:** *Check that the figure is securely attached. Here, as is usually the case, a piece of studding—a length of screw fitting—is used, and will need replacing from time to time. When lifting a statue, always support the weight of the piece from underneath.*

# A POLYCHROME WOOD HORSE

THE TERM "POLYCHROMESCULPTURE" USUALLY APPLIES TO PAINTED WOOD FIGURES (ALTHOUGH IT CAN REFER TO ANY PAINTED SCULPTURE), WHICH, BECAUSE THEY ARE ESSENTIALLY MADE OF ORGANIC MATERIAL, ARE HIGHLY SUSCEPTIBLE TO CHANGES IN TEMPERATURE AND HUMIDITY.

**Wooden carcass:** *Check the texture of the wood; if it is friable, this may be due to breaking down of the cellular structure caused by extreme changes of temperature or humidity, or as a result of insect and fungal infestation. Depending on the extent of the damage, especially on old, valuable items, it is worth having the wood consolidated. Splits are inevitable as part of natural aging and drying out; they can be filled, but this may be neither wise nor necessary.*

**Details:** *The extremities, such as head features, limbs, and additional details, may well have been lost or replaced—look carefully on the surface near them for changes in color and/or texture.*

**Paint layers and gilding:** *Surface coating is highly susceptible to wear and loss; it is preferable to have it stabililized rather than repainted, as paint loss, signs of wear, and even previous overpainting are all part of the history of the object, often contributing interest and charm.*

**Woodworm holes:** *The characteristic holes may not mean ongoing infestation; this is only likely—and a cause of concern—if there are traces of fresh wood dust. Immediate treatment is necessary to protect the piece itself as well as other wooden objects in its vicinity. Extensive insect activity may have left the piece in a fragile condition.*

**Gesso ground:** *Areas of loss and flaking indicate that adhesion between gesso and wood is poor and more will come off with handling. Consolidation can reattach lifting areas to the wood and make the object sound.*

Polychrome wooden figures were made in China during the Han Dynasty (206 B.C.—220 A.D.), for religious purposes in Catholic countries in Europe from the Middle Ages, and from the 1600s in South America. Figures were often carved from a single piece of indigenous wood, though extremities, such as arms, may have been separately carved and doweled into position. The wood surface was usually prepared for paint by the application of a layer of gesso—a mixture of animal glue and chalk (or, in Italy, gypsum). The paint consisted of a pigment held in a film-forming medium such as oil or egg tempera; the surface was sometimes further embellished with gold and silver leaf, and silver was often varnished with a tinted lacquer to mimic gold.

Wood as an organic material responds to environmental changes to a far greater extent than the paint; if temperature and humidity vary in cycles, the wood expands and contracts—movement that may break down the bond between wood and paint and lead to flaking.

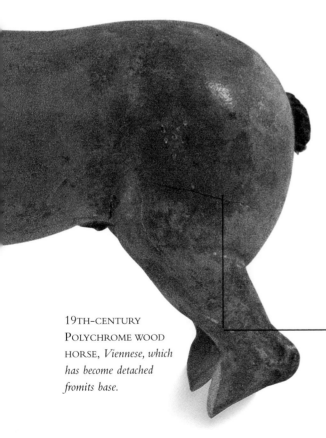

19TH-CENTURY POLYCHROME WOOD HORSE, *Viennese, which has become detached from its base.*

## GENERAL CARE

Because of its extreme vulnerability, wooden statuary must be kept in a stable environment, away from direct heat and at a relative humidity level of 45-55 (monitored by a humidistat). Do not pick the object up by its limbs—always support it from underneath, and handle it as little as possible to minimize paint loss. Dust with a soft-bristled cosmetic or lens brush, rather than a cloth which may catch on rough edges, and concentrate on a small area at a time.

## THE RESTORER'S BRIEF

If a wooden figure has become damp, it should be given to a restorer for controlled drying. Check that any splits are stable; as long as they are, and not completely disfiguring, they should be probably left alone. Flaking, unstable paint surfaces, and paint loss should also be stabilized for a piece to retain its value. Do keep any flakes of paint that fall off; they can be relaid and consolidated by the restorer. If figures have been overpainted well, it may be worth leaving them alone. A restorer can remove paint layers and reveal the original surface, but this is

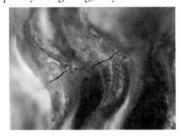

*A restorer can fill a crack (above), but such flaws are inevitable on wood sculpture, and as long they are stable, and do not threaten the piece as a whole, they are better left alone.*

painstaking work and very expensive. Missing sections can be carved and bonded into place to blend in with the original, but whether this is worth doing will depend on the value of the piece and the extent to which it is disfigured.

Even insect prevention or treatment should be done by a conservator, as the wrong substance could cause the decorative finish to blister or craze. Authenticating such figures can be done by carbon dating, but this can be expensive.

**Joints and dowels:** *Test how firmly the limbs are attached by moving them very slightly. Wooden dowels may shrink and expand at a different rate than the substrate, or animal glues may have shrunk, causing the joints to loosen.*

# THE DIRECTORY

The addresses below provide a starting point for information on conservation. Some of the larger institutions, such as museums, are likely to have specialist collections, or a restoration department. If the contacts are not able to deal with your query directly, they may be able to refer you to specialist individuals or companies.

## AUSTRALIA

MUSEUM OF
APPLIED ARTS AND SCIENCES
*Power House Museum*
*PO Box K346*
*Haymarket*
*NSW 2001*

NATIONAL GALLERY OF AUSTRALIA
*PO Box 1150*
*Canberra*
*ACT 2600*

NATIONAL MARITIME MUSEUM
*PO Box 5131*
*Sydney*
*NSW 2001*

UNIVERSITY OF MELBOURNE
CONSERVATION SERVICE
*Ian Potter Art Conservation Centre*
*Parkville*
*Victoria 3052*

## BELGIUM

EUROPEAN CONFEDERATION OF
CONSERVATOR-RESTORERS (ECCO)
*Die Pestraat 18*
*B3061 Leefdaal*
*Belgium*

## CANADA

CANADIAN
CONSERVATION INSTITUTE
*1030 Innes Raod*
*Ottawa*
*Ontario K1A OM5*

CENTRE DE CONSERVATION
DE QUÉBÉC
*1825 Rue Semple*
*Quebéc G1N 4B7*

GENNADY ROUSAKOV
*Leslie & Partner*
*9 Condor Avenue*
*Toronto ONM4 93M5*

## CYPRUS

HAIG G INDJIRDJIAN
*90 Regaena Str*
*PO Box 1506*
*Nicosia*

## DENMARK

KONSERVATORSKOLEN
*Det Kongelige Dankse Kunstakademi*
*Esplanaden 34*
*1263 København K*

## FINLAND

CONSERVATION CENTRE
*Keskikatu 24*
*40700 JYVASKYLA*

## FRANCE

BIBLIOTHÈQUE NATIONALE
DE FRANCE
*Services Restauration*
*58 Rue de Richelieu*
*75084 Paris Cedex 02*

INSTITUTE FRANÇAIS DE
RESTAURATION DES OEUVRES
D'ART (IFROA)
*150 Avenue du President Wilson*
*93120 La Pleine St Denis*

ICOM (INTERNATIONAL COUNCIL
OF MUSEUMS)
*Maison de l'Unesco*
*1 Rue Miollis*
*75015 Paris*

CLAUDE LEBRUN
*'Dujon'*
*Chatreil-Cintrat*
*03140 Chantelle*

ROY STRATTON
*Les Saulles*
*24240 Monbazillac*

## GERMANY

ARBEITSGEMEINSCHAFT DER
RESTAURATOREN (ADR)
*Geschäftstelle HuW Wimmel*
*Fürstenbergstr 7*
*79199 Kirchzarten*

GERMANISCHES NATIONALMUSEUM
*Kartäusergasse 1*
*90402 Nürnberg*

EDWARD GILL
*Kartner Strasse 20*
*48145 Munster*

## HONG KONG

USD CONSERVATION SECTION
*Museum of Art*
*10 Salisbury Road*
*Tsim Sha Tsui*
*Kowloon*

## INDIA

INSTITUTE OF HISTORY OF ART
CONSERVATION AND MUSEOLOGY
*National Museum*
*Janpath*
*New Delhi 110 011*

INTACH CHITRAKALA PARISHATHART
CONSERVATION CENTRE
*Art Complex*
*Murama Krupa Road*
*Bangalore 560 001*

INTACH DELHI ART
CONSERVATION CENTRE
*Bharatiyam*
*Near Humayun Tomb*
*Nizamuddin*
*New Delhi 110 013*

## REPUBLIC OF IRELAND

STEPHEN MCDONNELL
*2 Anglesea Lane*
*Dun Laoghaire*
*Co. Dublin*

## ITALY

ASSOCIAZIONE CONSERVATORI
RESTAURATORI
*Via degli Zingari 24-25*
*00184 Roma*

CIVICI MUSEI VENEZIANI
*S Marco 52*
*30124 Venezia*

INTERNATIONAL CENTRE FOR THE
STUDY OF THE PRESERVATION AND
THE RESTORATION OF CULTURAL
PROPERTY (ICCROM)
*13 via di an Michele*
*1-00153 Roma*

ISTITUTO PER L'ARTE
E IL RESTAURO
*Palazzo Spinelli*
*Borgo Santa Croce 10*
*50121 Firenze*

## NEW ZEALAND

CHARLES RHODES
*65 Butley Drive*
*Pakuranga*
*Aukland*

MUSEUM OF NEW ZEALAND
*Hector Library*
*PO Box 467*
*Wellington*

## NORWAY

BERGEN MUSEUM
*Department of Conservation*
*Årstadveien 22*
*5009 Bergen*

## PORTUGAL

CENTRO DE ESTUDO CONSERVAÇAO
E RESTAURO DOS AÇORES
*Rua de Jesus 119*
*9700 Angra do Heroismo Açores*

## SOUTH AFRICA

DURBAN ART MUSEUM
*PO Box 4085*
*Durban 4000*

KING GEORGE VI ART GALLERY
*1 Park Drive*
*Port Elizabeth 6001*

SOUTH AFRICAN
NATIONAL GALLERY
*PO Box 2420*
*Cape Town 8000*

## SPAIN

CENTRO DE ESTUDIOS DE
RESTAURACIÓN DE OBRAS DE ARTE
C/ Eduardo del Palacio 5
28002 Madrid

CURATOR CONSERVACIÓN
RESTAURACIÓN
Paseo de Extremadura 169
28011 Madrid

DIPUTACIÓN DE CASTELLON
Servicio de Restauración
Complejo Penyeta Roja
12080 Castellon

SERVEI DE CONSERVACIO I
RESTAURACIO DE BENS MOBLES
(Generalitat de Catalunya)
Placa Octavia s/n
Claustres del Monestir
0819 Saint Cugat Del Valles
Barcelona

## SWEDEN

ULF BRUNNE
Head of Furniture Conservation
Carl Malmstens Verkstadsskola
Renstiernas Gata 12
S-116 31 Stockholm

INSTITUTE OF CONSERVATION
University of Goteborg
Bastionsplatsen 2
411 14 Goteborg

NORDISKA MUSEET
Conservation Section
Box 27820
115 93 Stockholm

ANDERS OHLIN
Linnestadens Mobelrenovering
Kastellgatan 20
413 07 Goteborg

## SWITZERLAND

HISTORISCHES MUSEUM BASEL
Steinberg 4
4051 Basel

MUSÉE D'ART ET HISTOIRE
Rue de Morat 12
1700 Fribourg

## THAILAND

CONSERVATION SECTION
Division of National Museums
Fine Arts Department
Bangkok 10200

## TURKEY

BRITISH INSTITUTE
OF ARCHAEOLOGY
Tahran Caddesi 24
Kavaklidere
Ankara 06700

## UNITED KINGDOM

BRITISH ANTIQUE FURNITURE
RESTORERS' ASSOCIATION
The Old Rectory
Warmwell
Dorchester
Dorset DT2 8HQ

CHRISTIE'S
8 King Street,
St James's
London SW1Y 6QT

THE CONSERVATION REGISTER
Museums and Galleries Commisson
16 Queen Anne's Gate
London SW1H 9AA

GLASGOW MUSEUMS
AND ART GALLERIES
Art Gallery and Museum
Kelvingrove
Glasgow G3 8AG

NATIONAL MUSEUM OF WALES
Cathays Park
Cardiff CF1 3NP

NATIONAL MUSEUMS AND
GALLERIES ON MERSYSIDE
The Conservation Centre
Whitechapel
Liverpool L1 6HZ

PLOWDEN & SMITH
190 St Ann's Hill
London
SW18 2RT

SOTHEBY'S RESTORATION
WORKSHOPS
Summers Place
Billingshurst
West Sussex RH14 9AD

TEXTILE CONSERVATION CENTRE
Hampton Court Palace
East Molesey
Surrey KT8 9AU

UNITED KINGDOM INSTITUTE
FOR CONSERVATION
6 Whitehorse Mews
Westminster Bridge Road
London SE1 7QD

UNITED KINGDOM INSTITUTE
FOR CONSERVATION OF HISTORIC
AND ARTISTIC WORKS
109 The Chandlery
50 Westminster Bridge Road
London SE1 7QY

VICTORIA AND ALBERT MUSEUM

Conservation Department
South Kensington
London SW7 2RL

# UNITED STATES OF AMERICA

AMERICAN INSTITUTE
FOR CONSERVATION
1717 K Street NW
Suite 301
Washington DC 20006

AMERICAN INSTITUTE OF
HISTORIC AND ARTISTIC WORKS
(see above)

CHRISTIE'S, NEW YORK
502 Park Avenue at 59th Street
New York
NY 10022

CONSERVATION CENTER FOR
HISTORIC ART AND HISTORIC
ARTEFACTS
264 South 23rd Street
Philadelphia
PA 19103

GETTY CONSERVATION INSTITUTE
1200 Getty Center Drive
Suite 700
Los Angeles
CA 90049-1684

THE J PAUL GETTY MUSEUM
PO Box 2112
Santa Monica
CA 90407

JOHN LAKE
8208 S.W. Brookridge
Portland
OR 97225

METROPOLITAN MUSEUM OF ART
Sherman Fairchild Center for Objects
Conservation
1000 Fifth Avenue
New York
NY 10028

ROCKY MOUNTAIN
CONSERVATION CENTER
University of Denver
2420 S University
Denver
CO 80208

SOTHEBY'S RESTORATION
PO Box 657
33 Maple Avenue
Claverack
NY 12513

SOTHEBY'S RESTORATION
400 East 111th Street
New York
NY 10029

STRAUS CENTER
FOR CONSERVATION
Harvard University Art Museums
32 Quincy street
Cambridge
MA 02138

ROBERT WAITE

# INDEX

# CREDITS

*Every effort has been made to trace and contact all copyright holders. Quarto would like to apologize if any omissions have been made.*

Quarto would like to thank and make acknowedgment to the following for illustrations used in this book:

AKG, London; Trevor Allen, London; American Museum, Bath; Berenger Antiques; British Museum, London; Christie's Images, London; Corning Museum of Glass, United States; e. t. archive, London; FMC/photo: Larry Stein; F. J. Hakimian Inc; Glynn Clarkson Photography; Harvey & Gore, London; Keshishian; Mallett, London; Martin Norris; Phillips Fine Art Auctioneers, London; Queen Victoria, Beauty and the Beasts, London; Derek Roberts Antiques, Tonbridge; The Rocking Horse Gallery, Virginia, United States; B. A. Seaby Ltd; Sotheby's, London; Steinberg & Tolkien, London; Christopher St James, Ritzy, London; André Surmain, Paris/photo: Alfieri, Cannes; Union Centrale des Arts Decoratifs Musée, Paris.

*Quarto would like to thank the following for their help in providing items for photography:*
Plowden & Smith, London (for many items in the process of restoration); Sotheby's Sussex (dolls, bears); Asprey, London (clocks, silverware); Ronald Falloon, Tagore Ltd. (silverware) at Gray's antiques market, London; Beverley R. Forward, Brian and Lynn Holmes, and Charlotte Sayers (precious jewelry) at Grays antiques market; Linda Bee (fashion accessories), at Grays antiques market; Jackie Palmer and Donald Edge (precious jewelry) at Antiquarius antiques market, London; Gilly Cameron Cooper, Paul Davidson, Richard Garnier, Bruce Luckhurst.

*Quarto would especially like to thank all the individual specialists at Plowden & Smith for their expertise and advice.*